Jane
Austen
The
Secret
Radical

An unfinished sketch of Jane Austen by her sister, Cassandra (usually dated to ca. 1810). An amateurish attempt, but the only picture of Jane that we can be reasonably confident was done from life and that shows her face.

Jane Austen The Secret Radical

HELENA KELLY

ICON

This edition published in the UK in 2017
by Icon Books Ltd, Omnibus Business Centre,
39–41 North Road, London N7 9DP
email: info@iconbooks.com
www.iconbooks.com

Previously published in the UK in 2016 by Icon Books Ltd

Sold in the UK, Europe and Asia
by Faber & Faber Ltd, Bloomsbury House,
74–77 Great Russell Street,
London WC1B 3DA or their agents

Distributed in the UK, Europe and Asia
by Grantham Book Services,
Trent Road, Grantham NG31 7XQ

Distributed in Australia and New Zealand
by Allen & Unwin Pty Ltd,
PO Box 8500, 83 Alexander Street,
Crows Nest, NSW 2065

Distributed in South Africa
by Jonathan Ball, Office B4, The District,
41 Sir Lowry Road, Woodstock 7925

Distributed in India by Penguin Books India,
7th Floor, Infinity Tower – C, DLF Cyber City,
Gurgaon 122002, Haryana

ISBN: 978-178578-188-9

Typeset in Dante by Marie Doherty

Printed and bound in the UK by Clays Ltd, St Ives plc

CONTENTS

1. The Authoress   1

2. 'The Anxieties of Common Life' – *Northanger Abbey*   37

3. The Age of Brass – *Sense and Sensibility*   75

4. 'All Our Old Prejudices' – *Pride and Prejudice*   119

5. 'The Chain and the Cross' – *Mansfield Park*   169

6. Gruel – *Emma*   215

7. Decline and Fall – *Persuasion*   259

8. The End   301

   Further Reading   323

   Notes   325

   Index   329

ABOUT THE AUTHOR

Helena Kelly holds degrees in Classics and English from Oxford and King's College London. She is currently teaching at Mansfield College Oxford, and on a programme for American visiting students in Bath. She has taught Austen to hundreds of people, of all ages, nationalities, and backgrounds. *Jane Austen, The Secret Radical* is her first book.

To David and Rory

ACKNOWLEDGEMENTS

Thanks are due to Pamela Hunter, the archivist at Jane Austen's bank, Hoare's, and to the exceptionally helpful David Rymill at the Winchester archives.

I'd also like to thank my agent, Sally Holloway, for doing so much to help me shape my rather incoherent ideas into a book, and my publishers, for being much nicer than Austen's. I'm particularly grateful to Duncan Heath, for his tact and care in editing.

And thank you too to all my students, and to my family.

The Bank of England's concept design for the new
£10 note featuring Jane Austen, released in 2017.
© Bank of England

CHAPTER 1

The Authoress

England in April. Even here, in Southampton, in a town full of soldiers and sailors, in a country at war, April is still April. Sunlight and shadow chase one another across the sea ramparts, while the waves dance, mischievous, sparkling, to welcome in the yearly miracle of an English spring. The sun shines down on the house in Castle Square, and on the garden behind it. It shines on the careful, orderly rows of the shrubbery; on the young leaves; and on a small child in a pinafore, squawking and flapping her arms like wings, then crouching to scoop up a handful of gravel and offer it to her companion, as astonished and enchanted as if she's found jewels. Everything seems new at this time of the year, even in this old-fashioned house. Everything seems possible. A few weeks more, and the lilac will be out, and after the lilac, the long yellow fronds of the laburnum, and then the roses. The buds are still furled tight, but, buffeted by the salt breezes, they're beginning to stir.

The other inhabitants of the house are stirring, too. They have been a dutiful lot in Castle Square, these three years past. The man of the house has spent much of the time at sea, as an officer in His Majesty's navy, leaving all his many womenfolk together – his young wife, his tiny daughter, his widowed mother, his two unmarried sisters, and a family friend who had nowhere else to go. A houseful of women, they have been a comfort to each other during his absences. His brothers have helped to support them, but now, at long last, the richest (newly bereaved, newly generous) is offering help of a more practical kind – a cottage for his mother and sisters, rent-free, on one of his Hampshire estates – and, until that should be made ready, a visit to Godmersham, his grand house in Kent. The captain has done his duty. The Southampton household is to be broken up. They remain for only a few weeks more. The lilac, the laburnum, and the roses will flower here without them.

The child has thrown herself on to the path, legs kicking in fury. Her companion lifts her and, turning towards the house, points up to one of the windows. The little girl exclaims with delight. The woman watching at the window – a brown-haired, brown-eyed woman of 33, caught idling when she ought to be working – waves down at her niece, and mouths an apology to her sister. She turns back to the room, to the neat bed with its dimity cover, the old chair and the small rickety table, which are all that could be spared from downstairs, and to the letter which she hasn't even begun to write.

She's never had any cause to write a letter of business before. At the Abbey school, in Reading, she sat through hours of lessons in French and sewing. A year, did she spend there? It can't have been much more. The garden, the tall trees, are vivid in her memory; so, too, the view to the ruins of the church; the other girls bundled in shawls giggling round the fireplace, dying of laughter, as they used to say. The big girls had lessons, though not, she suspects, very good ones, in all the usual feminine accomplishments, dancing and drawing and music, but if letter-writing was taught at the Abbey, she doesn't recall it. And before that, at Mrs Cawley's ... well, of Mrs Cawley's school, here, in this very town, she remembers little. Only fever-dreams, and her sister Cassandra being sick, too; and their cousin Jane Cooper; and more than anything else the pain that twisted and twisted in her bowels. They nearly died of the typhoid fever.

She was seven, then. More than 25 years have passed, and what has she done, in all that time? She has no husband, no children – unless she counts the ones nestled, sleeping, about her room. Elinor and Marianne tucked up in a tin trunk under the bed, together with all the foolish stories from her childhood; and Susan in the writing box, half-hidden here at the back of the closet, behind a pile of shifts and petticoats, safe from little fingers. She sets the box on the bed, and, kneeling, turns the key in the lock, folds back the lid, opens, looks, touches the faint roughness of the leather on the writing slope. The wood – smooth and cool as satin under her fingers – warms until it almost feels like a living thing. Here are her pens and pencils, her penknife, her inkwell, waiting to be filled. Paper. Wafers of wax to seal her letters. And Susan.

It is about Susan that she is to write. Susan, not the most dear of her children, but nonetheless the only one who has shown any promise to date.

Such a deal of paper, though! The woman – who has not lived for three years in so expensive a town as Southampton without getting to know the price of everything – winces inwardly at the extravagance. To salve her conscience, she leafs through the old correspondence in her writing box, searching for a piece of scrap paper. She finds one sheet which has only a line or two written at the top and, seizing a pencil, scrawls on it the single word 'Gentlemen'.

Well then, to the point.

'In the Spring of the year 1803 a manuscript Novel in 2 volumes entitled *Susan* was sold to you by a Gentleman of the name of—' What was the name again of her brother Henry's lawyer, who had helped to oversee the sale? Seymour. That was it. '—of the name of Seymour, & the purchase money £10 received at the same time. Six years have since passed, & this work of which I avow myself the Authoress—'

She pauses. Why not? Why not avow herself an authoress? After all, she has been writing for nearly all her life.

'—of which I avow myself the Authoress has never to the best of my knowledge, appeared in print, tho' an early publication was stipulated for at the time of Sale.'

She knows little of the publishing trade but is it not queer – extraordinary, even – to purchase a book and never to publish it? How proudly, how happily, she set to the work of copying out her novel for these men, all those years ago; powdering and polishing the pages, tending her pen nib as carefully as ever she could, worrying over the

tiniest smudge of ink. But perhaps publishers, seeing so many manuscripts, don't cherish them as authors and authoresses do. Perhaps
poor Susan is lying forgotten somewhere, nibbled by mice. Maybe
a maidservant has used her to start a fire, thinking that one bundle
of paper would never be missed among so many. Did they think that
the novel was too short, or the title too unexciting? Perhaps it is what
Susan says – but surely there is very little in it that could worry even
the most anxious publisher. And did not this Mr Benjamin Crosby
publish William Godwin's *Things as they Are*? If ever there was a novel
that criticised the world and everything in it—! Only, of course, that
was before the treason trials, and before the publisher Joseph Johnson
was sent to prison for printing a book that did not meet with the
approval of the men in government. Perhaps Mr Crosby has grown
more cautious, since then.

Well, enough of caution. 'I can only account for such an extraordinary circumstance by supposing the manuscript by some carelessness
to have been lost; & if that was the case, am willing to supply You with
another Copy if you are disposed to avail yourselves of it, & will engage
for no farther delay when it comes into your hands.'

But when is she to sit and write out another copy? Not soon. There
is so much to be done. The house to be packed up – all their belongings
– and only she and Cassandra to do it; Frank gone to sea; her sister-in-law
Mary expecting again and complaining; their mother; the visit to her
brother Edward and his motherless children in Kent; a week lost in
travelling there, and another in travelling back again; then setting the
new house in order. She loves her family – truly, she does – but the days
seem to slip through her fingers. There is always some demand on her
time; someone needing to be nursed or entertained, a letter of condolence to be written, paper boats to be sailed on the river, yet another
new niece or nephew to sew caps for. The hours of her life that she has
wasted, feigning deafness while the women of Southampton drink tea
and compare their latest lyings-in; the weeks that have vanished this past
ten years, in moving in and out of rented houses and rented rooms, in

making new acquaintances and taking leave of them again. Sometimes she thinks that, since they left home, she has not remained in the same place for three months together.

That part of her life is over now. No more removals. She will stay in Chawton until she is 70 at least, except for visits. And she means to be more particular about visits. She will go and see Henry in London because she loves him, and because his wife, fashionable, fascinating cousin Eliza, makes her laugh. Besides, London has galleries and theatres and all manner of diversions. And she will go and see her brother Edward because he is rich, and she loves to stay at Godmersham, his great estate in Kent, where the grounds are delightful and the cooking very much superior to her usual fare. She's looking forward to the walks and the dinners she will have soon. Besides, now that Edward's wife is dead, she has a duty to the children; the little ones will soon grow accustomed, but the older ones will not, and poor Fanny, just turned sixteen, is of an age to feel the loss of her mother most acutely.

Chawton is not yet home, but it is no more than fifteen miles from where she grew up. She will have her native skies, her native air and, Cassandra has promised her, time for her writing. It is only a question of being firm, of holding fast, as sailors say, to her purpose.

'—It will not be in my power from particular circumstances to command this Copy before the Month of August, but then, if you accept my proposal, you may depend on receiving it.'

She will sit up at night and copy it out, if need be. She will order working candles every night she is in Kent and then smuggle them to Chawton in her luggage. Writing paper, too. It is not the least of the attractions of Godmersham that there are no quibbles over candles, no complaints about expense. Edward might, perhaps, not even complain about a London publisher addressing letters to her at his house, but he will not care for it. She will instruct the publishers to reply quickly, and to the Southampton post office. It will be easy enough to slip out for half an hour, even in all the bustle of the coming fortnight. But it will have to be soon. They have no idea of time, these people. To hold on to a book for six years and not to publish it! She should have written this letter years ago.

'Be so good as to send me a Line in answer, as soon as possible, as my stay in this place will not exceed a few days. Should no notice be taken of this Address, I shall feel myself at liberty to secure the publication of my work, by applying elsewhere.'

She reads over what she has written, her pencil poised above the page. It is a trifle brusque, perhaps, but this is a letter of business after all, and that last sentence should fetch her a prompt answer, at least. It will do for a first draft. She dashes off her signature: her initial – J – and her surname.

She has always envied her sister Cassandra for having a pretty name. Cassandra is named for their mother, while she is named not for her aunt Philadelphia nor her aunt Leonora – both of whom had names to conjure with – but for her aunt Jane, Jane Cooper's mother, who caught the typhoid fever from them and died. A plain name, and a common one, too. When she was at school she was obliged to share it not only with her cousin Jane but with any number of Janes besides, so that the mistresses, and the other pupils, assigned them all nicknames and nursenames – Jane A., and Jane C., and Janet, and Janice, and Jenny. She had been Jenny – little Jenny, snotty-nosed. Patted on the head, sent away, forgotten.

Has he even read her book? This publisher, this Mr Crosby?

But of course he doesn't yet know it *is* her book. Six years ago, she remained decorously in the background. Henry had thought it necessary. So far as Mr Crosby is concerned, *Susan* is simply a book 'by a lady'. Once she signs her name to this letter, once he knows who she is, will he put it in advertisements? In catalogues? Will it be printed on the book's title page or tooled in gold on a leather binding in the grand libraries of grand houses? It is possible. It's happened to other authoresses. But once it is out it cannot be taken back again. And then, her brothers will be so angry, because after all, the name Austen does not belong only to her—

She pours ink into her inkwell, spilling out the letters of her name in her mind, shuffling them about like the ivory alphabets you play with on a rainy day, when no better entertainment offers. The letters rearrange themselves into a riddle. Who doesn't love a riddle? She can hardly help smiling.

She will create an imaginary husband to give her countenance, and, since he may as well have an elegant name, she will call herself Mrs Ashton Dennis. And she will sign the letter with the initials 'M', 'A', and 'D' – 'I am sirs, your most obedient humble servant, M.A.D.' A joke, to make Mr Crosby take notice of her letter. An acrostic, a word puzzle, to show him that he should read her book more carefully.

A joke, but also a private admission to herself. Ashton is nearly (but not too nearly) her own surname, and Dennis is not so very far from Janice or Jenny. The letter will still be an avowal of sorts – an acknowledgement of her children, a declaration that plain Jane Austen is an authoress, even if no one outside the family ever reads her.

She writes over the pencilled draft in ink, to test out her phrases and to try out her new, imaginary signature, and, though she can hear voices downstairs, duties calling, she selects a sheet of expensive, hot-pressed paper and copies out what she has written, slowly, carefully, stopping every few words to dust the page with powder and rub it dry. The next day she cherishes the perfect polished copy all the way to the post office.

This time the publishers do not keep her waiting long. Mr Richard Crosby's answer reaches her within the week. Torn open with shaking fingers, read in the street, it sends her back to Castle Square as angry as she has ever been in her life, its phrases sounding in her head: '... we purchased of Mʳ Seymour a novel entitled *Susan* and paid him for it the sum of 10£'; that is, it is nothing whatever to do with you, Mrs Ashton Dennis, whoever you may be. The novel is not worth publishing, but it is ours, and ours is a world of stamped receipts and 'full consideration', and threatening 'proceedings to stop the sale' if you try to take the book elsewhere. These matters are, by far, less simple than you imagine, you empty-headed female. And the final insult – you clearly value the novel,

Mrs Ashton Dennis, but because I value it not at all, and because I pity you for your ignorance, you can have it for the £10 that we paid for it.

That night, in the dark, she lies rigid in her narrow bed, cursing herself for her clumsiness, imagining a dozen ways in which she could have managed the business better. Did she think her punning pen name would charm him? Nothing of the sort – he didn't even notice it. How can she avow herself an authoress when she cannot write a simple letter? An authoress, when people don't even bother to read what she's written? Why didn't she speak to Henry, as she should have done? What would a few weeks or months more have mattered, after all this time? Where was the hurry?

The night offers her no answers. Nor does the next day, nor the days after, as she pulls trunks from the box-room, folds clothes, invents games to distract little Mary-Jane, who wanders, cross and bewildered, through the once-familiar rooms. By the time the evenings come she is exhausted, her hands grey with dust. The weather turns chill and damp. Spring, optimism, possibility – all seem far away. It is some consolation to think herself useful, to know that, even if she is a most indifferent kind of authoress, she is a good daughter, a good sister and a good aunt. There is china to be divided between the two households, furniture to be sold or swathed in dustsheets, farewell visits to be made, a last service at the church, a last walk on the sea ramparts.

Her own belongings are packed in haste, on the final evening. She leaves her writing box till the end – she need only empty out the powder pot and the inkwell, and make everything secure so that nothing will rattle about on the journey. She needn't read the letter again – but still she cannot help herself. If only—! But she does not have £10, nor is she likely to, and even if she did, how is such a thing to be managed, without the aid of one of her brothers, drafts on banks, men of business? No. It is not to be thought of any more.

She scrabbles under the bed for the tin trunk and flings its contents on to the bed in brisk handfuls. She had meant only to bury Susan and Mr Crosby's letter at the bottom, under the bundles of paper she has so foolishly treasured all these years, but here too are her notebooks, gifts from long ago, and, reading through them, she grows tender. Here are the absurd plays she wrote, and her tales of legs broken in man-traps and drunkenness and sudden, surprising marriages. A heroine who steals ices from a pastry-cook's shop – how gloriously wicked she and Cassandra had thought it! And *Love and Freindship*, too – she never was a great hand at spelling – the story which made her father cry with laughter. Her *History of England, by a partial, prejudiced and ignorant historian*; Cassandra's pictures of all the kings and queens. Her hand brushes against the story about the clergyman's daughters which she had started but could never finish. Here are other infant novels, begun and abandoned. And some completed, more or less. Wicked Lady Susan is too short, not even a volume. She has never been quite happy with the beginning of *Elinor and Marianne*. *First Impressions*, too. Her father had thought a great deal of her stories, had even written to a publisher about one, though he met with a flat refusal. The whole of her life is here, in ink and paper. She cannot but treasure it.

Little Mary-Jane won't remember the house in Castle Square at all, won't take any memories away.

Jane travels with hers, the tin trunk solid under her feet as they jolt through the streets of Southampton, northwards, towards the common, parallel with the river. She will miss the river, and the sea. She will miss the flowers. By the time the cottage at Chawton is ready for them it will be too late to plant any.

Jane stares out at the pale early morning; the day becoming by degrees brighter, too bright, showing her that the sleeve of her black velvet pelisse is growing sadly rubbed. They will pass through Winchester first, with its ancient cathedral, then on to Alton. Alton to Farnham, Farnham to Bagshot, through Staines, past the charming little villas about Richmond, and so on, to Brentford, and to London. To London, and a night at brother Henry's house. Eliza and the latest fashions await them there, an evening being plied with coffee and plum cake and scandal before they travel on to Godmersham. Jane can imagine it already

– her sister-in-law moving by delicate, insinuating degrees on to family matters.

What luck, Eliza will say, that Edward felt able to promote the scheme of moving to Chawton! And at such a time! How good he is, how truly generous. Have they seen the house? Has it a pleasant aspect? Will they have agreeable neighbours? And Cassandra, with a reproving frown, will reply that Edward is very kind to them.

Cassandra always says what ought to be said, but Jane has very little opinion of Edward's kindness herself. Edward is not the eldest nor the cleverest nor the bravest of her brothers, no, nor the kindest either. He is only the richest. But Edward is bereft, Edward is grieving – this is no time to be thinking about the four years that have passed since their father died, no time for the resentful voice which whispers that a truly generous man would have welcomed his mother and sisters into his own home, either of his homes, rather than housing them in the cottage where his estate manager used to live. Jane sets herself to thinking about the children, about her niece Fanny, and to wondering whether perhaps it had been harder for Edward than she had supposed, to be separated from his family when he was so young – no older than Fanny is now – whether she might love him better if he felt more like a real brother, and she felt less like a poor relation.

The sound of the wheels, the jingling of the harnesses, lull her into restless sleep; thoughts rattle against each other, pictures bloom. Godmersham, Edward's Kentish estate. Sorbet and French wine; chocolate and white rolls for breakfast; the park, walks in the woodland. 'Run mad as often as you chuse …'

Another home left behind; sisters, poor while their brother is rich; a young woman running, tumbling on a hillside; a handsome gentleman with an ugly character; fine houses and cottages; journeys; city streets, London bustle. Sensibility fighting sense. Love and loss, greed and gain.

So long, so long since they have spoken to her, but she thinks – she is almost sure – that the young girl running on the hillside is someone that she knows. An impulsive girl, passionate, grieving for the loss of a father. And a sister, quieter, more serious – rational, controlled, sensible.

Jane's fingers, resting in her lap, twitch. She opens her eyes.

We're going to be seeing a lot more of Jane Austen. 2017 is the bicentenary of her tragically early death at the age of 41. And by way of celebration, the Bank of England is introducing a new £10 note with her face on.

Actually, it's not her face. It's an idealised picture commissioned for a family memoir published 50 years after she died. She looks richer, prettier, and far less grumpy than she does in the amateurish, unfinished sketch it's based on. And there are some other problems with the design for the note.

In the background there's going to be a picture of a big house – Godmersham, where Jane didn't live. Also featured will be an illustration of *Pride and Prejudice*'s Elizabeth Bennet reading some letters and a quotation from the same novel: 'I declare after all there is no enjoyment like reading!' – a line spoken by a character who shortly afterwards yawns and throws her book aside.

The biggest problem, though, it seems to me, is that for most people that's Jane Austen. That's what they recognise – pretty young women, big houses, *Pride and Prejudice* – demure dramas in drawing rooms. Seeing it on a banknote half a dozen times a week is only going to embed it further.

Jane was born five years after the poet William Wordsworth, the year before the American Revolution began. When the French Revolution started, she was thirteen. For almost all of her life, Britain was at war. Two of her brothers were in the navy; one joined the militia. For several years she lived in Southampton, a major naval base. It was a time of clashing armies, and warring ideas, a time of censorship and state surveillance. Enclosures were remaking the landscape; European empire-building was changing the world; science and technology were opening up a whole universe of new possibilities.

We're perfectly willing to accept that writers like Wordsworth were fully engaged with everything that was happening, and to find the references in their work, even when they're veiled or allusive. But we haven't been willing to do it with Jane's work. We know Jane – we know that however delicate her touch, she's essentially writing variations of the same plot, a plot that wouldn't be out of place in any romantic comedy of the last two centuries.

We know wrong.

∞

The indisputable facts of Jane Austen's life are few and simple. She was born in the small Hampshire village of Steventon, on 16th December 1775, the seventh of a clergyman's eight children. Apart from five years spent in Bath between 1801 and 1806 and three years in Southampton, a few months at school, and occasional visits and holidays, she spent all her life in rural Hampshire. She never married. She died in Winchester on 18th July 1817, aged 41, and was buried in Winchester cathedral. In the four years between the end of 1811 and the end of 1815 she published four novels – *Sense and Sensibility*, *Pride and Prejudice*, *Mansfield Park*, and *Emma*. Another two novels – *Northanger Abbey* and *Persuasion* – were published right at the end of 1817, the year she died.*

Two hundred years on, her work is astonishingly popular. It's difficult to think of any other novelist who could be compared to her. Yet Jane herself remains a shadowy, curiously colourless figure; one who seems to have spent the majority of her 41 years being dragged along in the wake of other people's lives.

But what lives the people around Jane had – her father, orphaned in early childhood, who worked his way out of poverty; her mother, who

---

* The novels carry the date of 1818 on their title page, but were published in the final week of 1817.

could claim kinship with a duke but found herself making ends meet in a country vicarage; her aunt Philadelphia, who, with no prospects in England, travelled out to India to find herself a husband; Philadelphia's daughter, Eliza, who lost her French spouse to the guillotine. The eldest of Jane's brothers, James, was raised in the expectation of succeeding to the property owned by his maternal uncle; her second brother George seems to have suffered from some form of disability and lived apart from the rest of the family; her third brother, Edward, was adopted into a life of luxury; Henry, the fourth of the Austen brothers, bounced from career to career – first a soldier in the militia, like that scoundrel George Wickham, then a banker, and then, finally, after his bank went bust, a clergyman. The two youngest brothers, Frank and Charles, born either side of Jane, went into the navy and led lives full of excitement and danger. Even Jane's only sister, Cassandra, had an engagement to her name, a story of her own.

We know what most of these people looked like, we know about their careers, their marriages, their children. We know that one of Jane's aunts was accused of stealing lace from a shop in Bath, and that one of her cousins died in a carriage accident. We know that her sister's fiancé died of yellow fever, and that her great-great-uncle was the Duke of Chandos. All of Jane's modern biographers repeat these facts, just as they reproduce the portraits of her brothers and her aunts and her cousin and the men who may (or, more probably, may not) have wanted to marry her, and the confused, contradictory opinions of people who barely knew her, in the belief that somehow, by combining together every scrap, something will take shape – an outline, a silhouette, a Jane-shaped space. But in spite of all their efforts, Jane remains only a slight figure vanishing into the background, her face turned away – as it is in the only finished portrait we have of her.

The more determined our pursuit, the more elusive Jane becomes. Where should we look for her? Will we find her in modern-day Bath, in the rain-drenched gold-stone buildings that are now flats or dental surgeries, in the park which occupies the place where the Lower Assembly

Rooms once stood, or at the Upper Rooms, which were rebuilt almost entirely after fire damage in the Second World War? Will we find her in the Jane Austen House Museum at Chawton? She did live there, for eight years, and her sister Cassandra for nearly 40. In the middle of the nineteenth century it was divided into separate dwellings; a century later it was turned back into one. Dozens of people have lived there. And if any trace of Jane remains, then the thousands of tourists who trudge through the rooms each year will have driven it away. Visitors are shown a piano 'like' Jane's; a modern reproduction of a bed 'like' the one Jane had when she was twenty; a table at which Jane 'may have' written; the caps that Jane's nieces and nephews wore as babies. The museum's proudest boast is Jane's jewellery – a topaz cross, a bead bracelet, a ring set with a blue stone. These are displayed in a narrow room off the largest bedroom, sitting dumbly in their glass cases, carefully lit but offering no sense of the woman who once wore them.

The rectory at Steventon – the house Jane lived in until she was 25 – is long gone. The church it served survives. It's left open, with a plaque on the wall and flowers, continually replaced, to reassure the pilgrims who make it this far that they really have come to the right place. It's almost possible, closing the church door, brushing past the ancient yew tree, to catch a glimpse of a little girl running ahead of you – but, like all ghosts, this is only a trick of the mind.

We have to look for Jane elsewhere.

In the spring of 1809 the 33-year-old Jane Austen was living, not in the countryside, nor in Bath, but in Southampton, in a house rented by her sea captain brother Francis, usually known as Frank. Southampton is less than twenty miles along the south coast from Portsmouth, where the Price family lives in *Mansfield Park*. A guide book of the period describes Southampton as 'handsomely built' and 'pleasantly situated', with views 'to the water, the New Forest, and the Isle of Wight'. It mentions with approval that the streets are 'well paved and flagged' – a reminder that this was by no means a given for all town centres at this point. What the guide book glosses over is the fact that Southampton was also a naval dockyard. It was heavily fortified and, during the time that Jane was living there, towards the end of the long war with France which dominated her adult life, it was a major port of embarkation for soldiers going to fight Napoleon's armies in Spain and Portugal.

If we associate Jane with an urban space, it's likely to be genteel Bath, not a dock town filled with public drunkenness, street prostitution, and violence. In addition to press-ganging – the state-sanctioned abduction scheme by which the Royal Navy ensured it had enough men to sail its ships – both the army and the navy welcomed into their ranks men who would otherwise have been in prison. Fighting men were, by and large, rough men and Southampton can't have been an altogether pleasant place for a household of women who were usually without a gentleman to protect them. Jane seems to have enjoyed some aspects of her time in Southampton well enough, however. She talks in her letters about walking on the ramparts, and rowing on the River Itchen with her nephews. But – so far as we know – it seems to have been the prospect of leaving Southampton and moving back to the country which reignited Jane's interest in getting her work published.

For some few years before she moved to Southampton at the end of 1806, Jane's life had been unsettled. You'll usually read that Jane lived in Bath from 1801 to 1806, but in fact she was almost continually on the move, and the city was more a base than a home. Together with her sister Cassandra, their mother, and (until his sudden death at the beginning of 1805) their father, she lodged in various parts of Bath – in Sydney Place, Green Park Buildings, Gay Street, and Trim Street – making lengthy visits to family, and for months at a time removing to seaside resorts, among them Dawlish, Sidmouth, Ramsgate (where Wickham trifles with Georgiana Darcy in *Pride and Prejudice*) and Lyme Regis (the setting for some of the pivotal scenes in *Persuasion*). You may also come across the claim that Jane didn't take much interest in her writing while she lived in Bath, but that's not the case. It was during this period, in the spring of 1803, that she first had a novel accepted for publication.

That novel was *Susan*, almost certainly a version of the book we know as *Northanger Abbey*.* We know, too, that Jane had written at least one other full-length novel before she moved to Bath – a book she called *First Impressions*. This may have been an earlier version of *Pride and Prejudice*, and it may or may not be the same book her father offered, unsuccessfully, to the publisher Cadell in 1797. We have a fragment – the beginning of a novel – about a clergyman's numerous family, which is usually known as *The Watsons*, written on some 1803-watermarked paper. A neat copy of *Lady Susan*, a short novella in letters, is written out on paper which bears an 1805 watermark, although it seems probable from the immature style that it was composed earlier. Between 1803 and the spring of 1809, however, we can be certain about virtually nothing connected with Jane's writing, other than that she wrote one poem in December 1808, on her 33rd birthday – a memorial poem to a friend who'd died in a riding accident exactly four years earlier. Maybe she stopped writing prose altogether. Maybe she was working on pre-existing drafts, or on pieces which were later incorporated into the other novels. Maybe she was writing something she later destroyed. We simply don't know.

We do have a list of composition dates for Jane's novels, but it was written by Cassandra, not Jane, and we have no idea when it was drawn up. Writers on Jane have tended to treat this document as if it were completely reliable; they really shouldn't.

One thing we do know for sure is that in April 1809, only a week or two before Jane was due to leave Southampton for a lengthy visit to her brother Edward at Godmersham, she wrote to the publishing firm which had bought *Susan*. We have a draft of Jane's letter, written on a sheet of paper that had originally served as an envelope, with the

---

*   As we'll see in the next chapter, we can be very nearly sure that *Susan* is *Northanger Abbey* and not *Lady Susan*. *Lady Susan* is short – nowhere near two volumes long – and is not at all the sort of work which a publisher would have been likely to accept.

words 'Miss Austen' written on the other side. Jane wrote in pencil initially, inking over the words afterwards, when she also changed the signature from 'J. Austen' to 'M.A.D.' We have Crosby's disobligingly businesslike reply, crammed with quasi-legal terms ('full consideration', 'stamped receipt', 'stipulated', 'bound'), offering to sell her *Susan* for £10, and threatening that he will 'take proceedings' to stop the novel being published anywhere else.

But what effect this letter had on Jane is unclear. We don't find another reference to *Susan/Northanger Abbey* until 1817 and – as we'll see in the next chapter – she continued to view the book very negatively. But she soon had other projects in hand.

Sense and Sensibility was the first of Jane's novels to make it all the way through the publication process. It appeared in October 1811, and must have been completed some time before the end of 1810, as by April 1811 Jane was busy correcting the proofs. Later in her career, when she had a regular publisher, Jane worked on the assumption that a year would intervene between her finishing a novel and that novel appearing. The gap between Jane finishing writing *Sense and Sensibility* and copies being put on sale may well have been longer.

Before Jane could think about sending a novel off, she would have had to copy it out by hand, which would have taken a number of weeks, perhaps a couple of months. Then she had to send the package off, wait for the publisher to read the novel, respond, and negotiate terms. Jane may already have been working on *Sense and Sensibility* before she wrote to Crosby to enquire about *Susan*.

In the summer of 1809 Jane's writing is full of an unaccustomed exuberance, very similar to the bubbling enthusiasm that appears in her letters of 1813 when she receives *Pride and Prejudice* from the printers. Frank's wife Mary had given birth to a boy in the second week of July, and a fortnight later Jane sent her brother a rather lovely piece of writing which can only properly be described as a letter-poem; part congratulation, part affectionate remembrance of their childhood, and part description of her happiness in the house at Chawton. She addresses him warmly as 'My dearest Frank', and expresses the wish that the baby will resemble his father even in his faults – the 'insolence of spirit', and 'saucy words & fiery ways' which the grown-up Frank had worked so hard to correct. 'Ourselves', she assures him, 'are very well', and 'Cassandra's pen' will explain in 'unaffected prose' how much they like their 'Chawton home—'

> —how much we find
> Already in it to our mind,
> And how convinced that when complete,
> It will all other Houses beat,
> That ever have been made or mended,
> With rooms concise or rooms distended.

The poem also offers the rarest of insights into the Austen family nursery, in a charming image of Frank as a naughty little boy with 'curley Locks' poking his head around a door and assuring someone named 'Bet' that 'me be not come to bide'. There's an eagerness and a warmth here which is rare in Jane's other letters to her family, an easy flow to her words which is very different to the rather stiff and formal mourning poem she had written six months earlier, in remembrance of her friend. It's tempting to conclude that something had shifted, that she had started to write again.

Too tempting, perhaps. We don't know what Jane was thinking in the spring and summer of 1809. Having waited for six long years, why write to Crosby then, when she was just about to move? Why the punning initials of the pen name? Why not simply change a few details and publish the novel elsewhere, without alerting him? Why not enlist the help of her brother Henry, who had presumably been involved in selling the manuscript in the first place?

We know so little about Jane's life, and that little is so difficult to interpret accurately, that we can't afford to dismiss what's revealed in her fiction. At least it speaks, and at least it was written by her. As for the rest, there are so many gaps, so many silences, so much that has been left vague, or imprecise, or reported at second or third hand, that the task of filling everything in is very far from being the 'short and easy' one that her brother Henry – the first of her many biographers – claimed in his *Biographical Notice of the Author*.

∽

Of course, if Henry is to be believed, Jane barely thought at all.

On Henry's telling, his sister's books sprang into life fully-formed – painlessly, effortlessly. According to him, Jane's composition was 'rapid and correct', a flow of words which 'cost her nothing', washing through her to appear, as everything she wrote appeared, 'finished from her pen'. We are to imagine no labour, no dedication, no ambition, no intellect or skill, but simply a 'gift', a 'genius', an 'intuitive' power of invention. For modern-day readers, schooled on the image of Jane's near-contemporary, the Romantic poet Samuel Taylor Coleridge, hopped up on vast quantities of opium, writing down his famous poem of Xanadu and Kubla Khan while still in an inspired dream, this is an attractive idea. It allows us to imagine Jane's novels, not as pieces of deliberate, considered art, but instead as whatever we like – a wrestling with her own repressed desires, a rewriting of her own unhappy love affairs, even an accidental tapping into a wellspring of culture and language. Jane's novels have been read in all these ways, and others besides.

The problem with any of these imaginings is that what Henry said was wrong. We don't have very many of Jane's manuscripts, but enough exist to tell us that she worked at her writing. The draft fragment we know as *The Watsons* is dotted with crossings-out, additions, and alterations. We even have an earlier attempt at an ending to *Persuasion* which Jane was dissatisfied with, and rewrote. You can see her, choosing one word over another, checking that the sentence balances, that she's picked the right phrase, and put it in the right place.

Henry's *Biographical Notice of the Author* appeared in the first, joint edition of *Northanger Abbey* and *Persuasion*, which was hurried through the print presses a scant five months after Jane died. The *Notice* is short, but crammed with what might politely be called inconsistencies. Having assured his readers that Jane's novels appeared almost without effort, Henry includes in a postscript Jane's own famous description of her work as akin to miniature painting – a 'little bit (two inches wide) of ivory on which I work with so fine a brush, as produces little effect after much labour'. In the *Notice*, Henry says that Jane never thought of having a book published before *Sense and Sensibility* – even though he was well aware that *Susan / Northanger Abbey* had been accepted for publication in 1803. He claims that Jane never 'trusted herself to comment with unkindness', when it's obvious to even the most uncritical of readers that *Persuasion* contains one exceptionally vicious passage, in which the feelings of a bereaved mother are mocked as 'large fat sighings' simply because the character happens to be 'of a comfortable substantial size'.

A charitable assessment of Henry's comments, noting that he must have begun his biography very soon after Jane died, might call these errors or misreadings, and attribute them to grief. It might be right to do so, if it weren't for the fact that Henry sets out to create an entirely false image of his sister. He does all he can to convince his readers that Jane wasn't a proper author, and never considered herself one. She had, he says, very little opinion of her work, and no thought of obtaining an audience. He tells his readers that, having at last yielded to the persuasions of her family and sent *Sense and Sensibility* to a publisher, she was 'astonished' at its success. This Jane could never have been persuaded to put her name to her novels; indeed, Henry insinuates, they should not be considered as solely her work, since she was 'thankful for praise, open to remark, and submissive to criticism' from her family.

Henry, in short, was lying, and his lies were deliberate ones. In part his aim was to protect himself and his siblings from the damaging idea that their sister may have wanted – or even needed – to write for money. He insists that 'neither the hope of fame nor profit mixed with her early motives'. In his world, gentlewomen didn't work and would never have dreamed of looking for public acclaim. We should bear in mind, too, the context of Henry's remarks – a 'biographical notice' intended to help the sale of two novels, neither of which Jane herself had seen fit to have published.

But then again, his motives may have been fundamentally sound enough. He would have known how very unsympathetically female authors were treated. As a writer called Mary Hays explained in 1801, 'the penalties and discouragements attending the profession of an author fall upon women with a double weight'. They are, she continued, tried in the court of public opinion, 'not merely as writers, but as women, their characters, their conduct' searched into, while 'malignant ingenuity' is 'active and unwearied' in finding out 'their errors and exposing their foibles'.

The reputation of the feminist writer Mary Wollstonecraft had been dragged through the mud after her death in 1797. Rumours circulated that Ann Radcliffe, the author of *The Mysteries of Udolpho* – Catherine Morland's favourite novel in *Northanger Abbey* – had gone insane. Charlotte Smith, whose writing Jane read and enjoyed, anticipated that some people would find the 'political remarks' in her 1792 novel *Desmond* 'displeasing'. And she was right: her forthright defence of the principles of the French Revolution saw the novel rejected by her usual publishers and, we are told, 'lost her some friends'. Even Maria Edgeworth, the most successful novelist of the period, was forced to rewrite her 1801 novel *Belinda* in order to remove a marriage which critics thought 'disgusting' and morally dangerous because one character was white and the other black.

We have to remember, too, that the Austen family lived in a country in which any criticism of the status quo was seen as disloyal and dangerous. Britain and France were at war from 1793 to 1815, with only two brief pauses – in 1802–3, and from summer 1814 to February 1815, when Napoleon was temporarily confined on the island of Elba. From 1812 to 1815, Britain was also at war with America, the colony it had lost in 1776, the year after Jane Austen was born. Revolutionary ideas had travelled from America to France, but the infection had its roots in England, in particular in the writing of Thomas Paine, who'd left his native Norfolk to spread his radical ideas across the globe. In 1792 Paine was convicted in his absence of seditious libel – essentially, of writing down ideas dangerous to the state – but he continued to write, if anything more dangerously than before, questioning the very notion of private property, of organised religion, even.

Saddled with a monarch who was periodically insane, and an heir to the throne who was not only dissolute and expensive to run but had also illegally married a Catholic widow, the British state was under an enormous strain even before the war with France began. The war, for many years, went badly for Britain. French armies marched through Europe, French ships menaced Britain's trade; the fear of invasion was constant. People who criticised the behaviour of the royal family, or complained about corrupt parliamentary elections; who turned away from the Church of England or asked whether those in power should really keep it, were perceived as betraying their country in her hour of need. To question one aspect of the way society worked was to attempt to undermine the whole.

Throughout Jane's late teens and twenties the government built coastal batteries and forts to defend Britain against invasion from France, and it brought in a number of measures designed to protect the country against the spread of danger from within. In the process, Britain began to look more and more like a totalitarian state, with the unpleasant habits that totalitarian states acquire. Habeas corpus – the centuries-old requirement that any detention had to be publicly justified – was suspended. Treason was redefined. It was no longer limited to actively conspiring to overthrow and to kill; it included thinking, writing, printing, reading. Prosecutions were directed not just against avowedly political figures, such as Paine, the radical politician Horne Tooke, or the theologian Gilbert Wakefield, but against their publishers. A schoolmaster was convicted for distributing leaflets. A man was prosecuted for putting up posters. The proprietors of the newspaper *The Morning Chronicle* were brought into court. Booksellers were threatened. Words were dangerous – reciting a piece of doggerel saw one Hampshire carpenter imprisoned for three years. There can hardly have been a thinking person in Britain who didn't understand what was intended – to terrify writers and publishers into policing themselves.

In a letter of 1795 the well-connected Whig politician Charles James Fox pondered 'how any prudent tradesman can venture to publish anything that can in any way be disagreeable to the ministers'. William Wordsworth's brother Richard urged him to 'be cautious in writing or expressing your political opinions', warning him that 'the ministers have great powers'. It was expected that letters would be opened and read by the authorities; it was accepted that publishers would shy away from anything which challenged or questioned societal norms too openly. Conservative writers flourished. The response from writers of a less reactionary frame of mind was to turn to nature and emotion – as the Romantic poets did – or to the relative safety of the past or foreign settings. Sir Walter Scott's *Waverley*, published in 1814, is often described as the first historical novel, but in fact dozens were published in the 1790s and the first decade of the nineteenth century. Almost every Gothic novel is set in the past, usually in the 1400s or 1500s. Writers were wary of writing about the present, and they were right to be. This is the atmosphere that Henry – and Jane – had lived through; this is the context in which Jane Austen wrote.

Of course, Henry's insistence that Jane shouldn't be considered an author, that she hardly intended to publish her work, that she bowed to the superior knowledge of her family – of her brothers, pillars of the establishment, clergymen, naval officers, a landowner – might make us think that he was protesting quite a lot too much. Why, after all, would he be so anxious to assure Jane's readers that she was 'thoroughly religious and devout' and that her opinions 'accorded strictly with those of our Established Church', unless he knew that her novels could easily be read as being critical of the Church of England?

Think of Jane's landowners, of her soldiers, her clergymen, her aristocrats. In *Sense and Sensibility* John Dashwood feels that generosity to his impoverished sisters would demean him; in *Mansfield Park* Henry Crawford elopes with a married woman, the cousin of the very woman he has proposed marriage to. In *Pride and Prejudice*, the militia officers spend their time socialising, flirting, and – on one occasion – cross-dressing, rather than defending the realm. The Reverend Mr Collins is laughable. None of Jane's clergymen characters has a vocation, or even seems to care very much about the well-being – spiritual or physical – of their parishioners.* Does Lady Catherine de Bourgh look like a character designed to justify the aristocracy? Or *Persuasion*'s vain and wasteful Sir Walter Elliot?

Think, too, about the fact that Jane was the only novelist of this period to write novels which were set more or less in the present day, and more or less in the real world – or at any rate a world recognisable to her readers as the one in which they actually lived. Jane doesn't offer us wicked villains and perfect heroines. She doesn't give us storms, or miraculously reappearing heirs. She invents villages and towns (Meryton, Highbury), but locates them within the known landscape – Highbury is in Surrey, exactly sixteen miles from London. Often she has her characters walk along real streets in real places. In *Northanger Abbey* Catherine Morland and Isabella Thorpe saunter together through the streets of Bath. You can follow in their footsteps even now. It's still possible to stand on the harbour wall at Lyme and see where Louisa Musgrove fell in *Persuasion*.

Critics of Jane's own generation praised her for her unparalleled ability to accurately reproduce what she saw around her. 'Her merit consists altogether in her remarkable talent for observation', pronounced Richard Whateley, later the Archbishop of Dublin, in 1821, in a lengthy review of *Northanger Abbey* and *Persuasion*. For Whateley, what made Jane great was her 'accurate and unexaggerated delineation of events and characters'. He was the first to suggest that she was as great as

---

* Captain Wentworth's clergyman brother is a partial exception but we never actually meet him.

Shakespeare, repeatedly comparing the two. Robert Southey, friend to William Wordsworth, brother-in-law to Samuel Taylor Coleridge and one-time revolutionary, was by this point snug in the bosom of the establishment as Poet Laureate, the official poet to royalty. In future years he would strongly discourage Charlotte Brontë from writing, but he admired Jane's novels and thought them 'more true to nature ... than any other of this age'. The American writer Henry Longfellow admitted that Jane's writings were 'a capital picture of real life', but complained that 'she explains and fills out too much'. In 1830 an unsigned essay in the *Edinburgh Review* called Jane 'too natural'. There was clearly an agreement that Jane's novels were realistic, and it was this which made them unique.

With a shift of generation, though, readers began to struggle a little more. Serious literary critics such as Thomas Macaulay and George Henry Lewes (born the year Jane died) repeated and strengthened the comparison to Shakespeare, a comparison which concentrated on Jane's depiction of character to the exclusion of anything else in her novels, and consigned her, not unlike Shakespeare, to the status of genius – inexplicable, mysterious, timeless. Popular opinion echoed, obediently. An early American textbook on literature, published in 1849, claimed that Jane's novels 'may be considered as models of perfection'. An article in an English magazine series on 'Female Novelists' which appeared in 1852 asserted that Jane was the 'perfect mistress of all she touches'.

Few mid-Victorian readers questioned Jane's greatness but often they seemed bemused by her writing. They wondered why Jane should have chosen to depict a society 'which ... presents the fewest salient points of interest and singularity to the novelist'. Charlotte Brontë admitted to finding Jane's novels unengaging, though she thought it was probably 'heresy' to criticise. 'Miss Austen', she announced in a letter to a literary correspondent in 1850, is 'a rather insensible woman'. She may do 'her business of delineating the surface of the lives of genteel English people curiously well', but she 'ruffles her reader by nothing vehement, disturbs him by nothing profound: the Passions are perfectly unknown to her'.

But Charlotte had such a very definite idea of what Jane's writing consists of that, finding it confirmed in the one novel, *Emma*, which she's discussing in this letter, she didn't think it necessary to consider anything else that Jane might have written. As the century went on, increasingly readers appeared to pay more attention to what they already 'knew' about Jane's novels – that is, to what was already said about them – than to the texts themselves. Increasingly, too, there was a hunger not for novels, but for novelists.

Charlotte Brontë died in 1855, and a biography of her appeared two years later. G.H. Lewes, writing about Jane in 1859, complained that so little was known of Jane's life in comparison to Charlotte's. He was, he said, baffled at the spectacle of 'a fine artist whose works are widely known and enjoyed, being all but unknown to the English public, and quite unknown abroad'. This isn't quite true. In 1852 an American fan – the daughter of a former President of Harvard University, no less – had written to Jane's brother Frank, begging for a letter or even a sample of Jane's handwriting. What was still true, though, was that nothing more was known of Jane's life than what Henry had written in 1817.

෴

In the late 1860s, Jane's nephew James-Edward Austen-Leigh – the son of her eldest brother James – started to collect material from his sisters and cousins and published the result in 1869 as *A Memoir of Jane Austen*. Two years later a second edition appeared. Born in 1798, James-Edward had lived through enough of the war period – and absorbed enough of its caution in literary matters – to remain tight-lipped on the subject of his aunt's personal beliefs. He explained that she never wrote about subjects she didn't understand, and paid 'very little' attention to political questions – or only enough to agree with whatever the rest of the family thought. She lived a life 'singularly barren ... of events'. She was 'sweet', 'loving', her personality 'remarkably calm and even'. So entirely devoid of interest is this Jane, in fact, that James-Edward had to pad out his memoir with other material: his own memories of growing up in the rectory at Steventon; some ponderous history lessons on the manners of the late eighteenth century; a letter sent by an aristocratic great-great-grandmother. The second edition of the *Memoir* includes, as well, quite a lot of previously unpublished material by Jane. Notable by its absence – for James-Edward certainly had access to it – is Jane's teenage *History of England*, a hilarious piece of writing which delights in upsetting religious and political sensitivities. At one point the authoress even declares herself 'partial to the roman catholic religion'.

The *Memoir* does, however, succumb to little spurts of Victorian romance. James-Edward gives the reader an improbable story about his uncle Henry and aunt Eliza escaping through wartime France when the brief peace of 1802–3 abruptly ended. He tells us that his aunt Jane had at one point 'declined the addresses of a gentleman who had the rec-ommendations of good character, and connections, and position in life, of everything, in fact, except the subtle power of touching her heart'. He records 'one passage of romance' – an acquaintance with a man at 'some seaside place' who died soon afterwards. Although this tale is so vague as to be scarcely worth the telling – even James-Edward admits that he is 'imperfectly acquainted' with the details, and 'unable to assign name, or date, or place' – he nevertheless assures his readers that 'if Jane ever loved, it was this unnamed gentleman'. His source, at several removes, was apparently Cassandra, whom biographers have tended to view as Jane's confidante and – as James-Edward calls her – a 'sufficient authority'. But in Jane's novels even the closest, the most affectionate of sisters – Marianne and Elinor Dashwood, Jane and Elizabeth Bennet – have secrets from one another.

In fact none of the romantic stories about Jane stands up to scrutiny. The two most frequently repeated ones concern Jane's relationship with a young Irishman called Tom Lefroy, and her 'broken engagement' with a neighbour, Harris Bigg-Wither. The story that Jane was betrothed to Harris for one night, and broke off the engagement in the morning, has been repeated so often that it's viewed as a matter of fact. Biographers even offer a date for the proposal – Thursday 2nd December 1802. This information comes from a letter written in 1870 by James-Edward's sister Caroline. 'I can give, I *believe*', writes Caroline, then aged 65 and so not even alive in 1802, 'the *exact* date of Mr Wither's proposal to my Aunt.' Caroline's source is 'some entries in an old pocket book which make *no* allusion to anything of the sort – but some peculiar comings & goings coinciding exactly with what my Mother more than once told me of *that* affair, leave me in no doubt'. Caroline's mother Mary, whom Jane disliked, had died in 1843. This is family or even neighbourhood gossip, transmitted long after the event; how much can we trust it?

There seems at first to be much more evidence to support the idea that, in her early twenties, Jane had some involvement with Tom Lefroy, the nephew of the vicar in the neighbouring village. He dominates a letter of January 1796 – Tom's birthday, Tom's good looks, Tom's coat, dancing with Tom, sitting out with Tom, Tom being teased about her. In another letter, apparently written around a week later, Jane jokes about giving up her other admirers – 'Mr Heartley', 'C. Powlett', and 'Warren' – because 'I mean to confine myself in future to Mr Tom Lefroy, for whom I donot [*sic*] care sixpence'. Tom is mentioned a second time towards the end of the letter, in a tone which, again, doesn't seem entirely serious, though perhaps the humour is defensive; 'at length the Day is come on which I am to flirt my last with Tom Lefroy, & when you receive this it will all be over – My tears flow as I write, at the melancholy idea.' As late as November 1798 Jane seems still to be emotionally invested in Tom: 'I was too proud to make any enquiries; but on my father's afterwards asking ... I learnt that he was gone back to London in his way to Ireland.' There's been a popular biopic (2007's *Becoming Jane*) based on these letters, and they look very promising – romantic, stirring – until we delve a little deeper.

All three letters are missing. We have no idea where they currently are. Two of them – the first and the last – have never been seen by *anyone* outside the Austen family. Our only authority for what they say – or indeed, for the fact that they existed at all – is the volume of *Letters* published in 1884 by Lord Brabourne (Edward Austen's grandson, and so Jane's great-nephew).

The most recent edition of the complete *Letters*, published in 2011 and edited by Deirdre Le Faye, lists 161 of Jane's letters, notes, and drafts. When it comes to manuscripts of the letters, however – the actual objects themselves, written in Jane's own handwriting – it's a different story. Over twenty are missing altogether. Another 25 are either scraps (some of them tiny) or have been significantly cut about. Of what remains, more than twenty can't really be dated at all, and nearly 30 others only from internal evidence, with varying degrees of confidence.

But biographers need the letters – they need all of them. They need Henry's *Biographical Notice*, even though it's full of lies, and they need James-Edward's *Memoir*, which has so very little to say about Jane. They need Harris Bigg-Wither, and Tom Lefroy, and they're not prepared to let the absence of proof that anything happened between Jane and either of these two men stand in their way.

There is a story to be told, though. We don't need to doubt everything. We can use quite a number of the letters, with caution – certainly the ones written in Jane's own hand, and which can be dated confidently. And even if we accept that we'll never know whether Jane really wrote on a small table in the dining room at Chawton, or whether there was a huge hiatus in her writing life, we do still have the writing itself – in particular, the novels of her maturity, balanced, considered, artful.

We can't discount the possibility that her novels underwent some degree of external editing. In a letter written in January 1813, Jane, brimming with happiness at the publication of *Pride and Prejudice*, cheerfully mentions some 'typical errors' (that is, typographical errors made in the setting of the book), and talks about having 'lop't and crop't' it at some point. We have no way of knowing whether this shortening was the result of Jane's own artistic judgement or was suggested by the publisher.

Even edited, even shortened, it's the novels as they were printed that bring us as close to Jane as we're ever going to get, closer than any memoir or biography could – closer not necessarily to what she might have done or felt, but to what she thought. It's impossible for anyone to write thousands upon thousands of words and reveal nothing of how they think or what they believe. And, contrary to popular opinion, Jane *did* reveal her beliefs, not just about domestic life and relationships, but about the wider political and social issues of the day.

She did so warily – and with good reason, as we have seen. But when she was writing, she was anticipating that her readers would understand how to read between the lines, how to mine her books for meaning, just as readers in Communist states learned how to read what writers had to learn how to write. Jane's novels were produced in a state which was, essentially, totalitarian. She had to write with that in mind. The trick was never to be too explicit, too obvious, never to have a sentence or a paragraph to which someone could point, and say – Look, there – it's there you criticise the state, it's there you say that marriage traps women, that the Church is crammed with hypocrites, that you promote breaking society's rules. Jane did fail, once, to err on the side of caution. *Mansfield Park*, alone of all her books, wasn't reviewed on publication. This, as I will show, is because it was an inescapably political novel, from the title onwards – a 'fanatical novel' which continually forced its readers to confront the Church of England's complicity in slavery.

Jane talks in one letter about wanting readers who have 'a great deal of ingenuity', who will read her carefully. In wartime, in a totalitarian regime, and in a culture which took the written word far more seriously than we do, she could have expected to find them. Jane expected to be read slowly – perhaps aloud, in the evenings, or over a period of weeks as each volume was borrowed in turn from the circulating library. She expected that her readers would think about what she wrote, would even discuss it with each other.

She never expected to be read the way we read her, gulped down as escapist historical fiction, fodder for romantic fantasies. Yes, she wanted to be enjoyed; she wanted people to feel as strongly about her characters as she did herself. But for Jane a story about love and marriage wasn't ever a light and frothy confection. Generally speaking, we view sex as an enjoyable recreational activity; we have access to reliable contraception; we have very low rates of maternal and infant mortality. None of these things was true for the society in which Jane lived. The four of her brothers who became fathers produced, between them, 33 children. Three of those brothers lost a wife to complications of pregnancy and childbirth. Another of Jane's sisters-in-law collapsed and died suddenly at the age of 36; it sounds very much as if the cause might have been the rupturing of an ectopic pregnancy, which was, then, impossible to treat. Marriage as Jane knew it involved a woman giving up everything to her husband – her money, her body, her very existence as a legal adult. Husbands could beat their wives, rape them, imprison them, take their children away, all within the bounds of the law. Avowedly feminist writers such as Mary Wollstonecraft and the novelist Charlotte Smith were beginning to explore these injustices during Jane's lifetime. Understand what a serious subject marriage was then, how important it was, and all of a sudden courtship plots start to seem like a more suitable vehicle for discussing other serious things.

No more than a handful of the marriages Jane depicts in her novels are happy ones. And, with the possible exception of *Pride and Prejudice*, even the relationships between Jane's central characters are less than ideal – certainly not love's young dream. Marriage mattered because it was the defining action of a woman's life; to accept or refuse a proposal was almost the only decision that a woman could make for herself, the only sort of control she could exert in a world which must very often have seemed as if it was spiralling into turmoil. Jane's novels aren't romantic. But it's become increasingly difficult for readers to see this.

For a reader today, opening one of Jane's novels, there's an enormous amount standing between them and the text. There's the passage of 200 years, for a start, and then there's everything else – biographies and biopics, the lies and half-truths of the family memoirs, the adaptations and sequels, rewritings and re-imaginings.

When it comes to Jane, so many images have been danced before us; so rich, so vivid, so prettily presented. They've been seared onto our retinas in the sweaty darkness of a cinema, and the after-effect remains, a shadow on top of everything we look at subsequently.

It's hard; it requires an effort for most readers to blink those images away, to be able to see Edward Ferrars cutting up a scissor case (a scene which arguably carries a strong suggestion of sexual violence) rather than Hugh Grant nervously rearranging the china ornaments on the mantelpiece. By the time you've seen Darcy poised to dive into a lake 50 times, it's made a synaptic pathway in your brain. Indeed, I'd question whether we can get away from that, certainly how we do.

And this ought to concern us, because a lot of the images – like the images on the banknote – are simplistic, and some of them are plain wrong. Pemberley *isn't* on the scale of Chatsworth; Captain Wentworth *doesn't* buy Kellynch Hall for Anne as a wedding present at the end of *Persuasion*; the environs of Highbury, the setting for *Emma*, aren't a golden pastoral idyll. We have, really, very little reason to believe that Jane was in love with Tom Lefroy. But each image colours our understanding in some way or another, from Henry Austen's careful portrait of his sister as an accidental author to Lily James delivering roundhouse kicks in the recent film of *Pride and Prejudice and Zombies*.

The effect of all of them together is to make us read novels that aren't actually there.

In the run-up to the invasion of Iraq, the then Secretary of Defense, Donald Rumsfeld, famously suggested that there were three classes of knowledge. There were known knowns – things you know you know. There were known unknowns – things you know you don't know. And there were unknown unknowns – things you don't know you don't know.

I would suggest that, when dealing with someone like Jane Austen we could add another, and more dangerous, class of knowledge; what might be termed the unknown knowns – things we don't actually know, but think we do.

If we want to be the best readers of Jane's novels that we can be, the readers that she hoped for, then we have to take her seriously. We can't make the mistake that Crosby made, and let our eyes slide over what doesn't seem to be important. We can't shrug off apparent contradictions, or look only for confirmation of what we think we already know. We have to read and we have to read carefully, because Jane had to write carefully, because she was a woman, and because she was living through a time when ideas both scared and excited people.

And once we read like this, we start to see her novels in an entirely new light. Not an undifferentiated procession of witty, ironical stories about romance and drawing rooms, but books in which an authoress reflects back to her readers their world as it really is – complicated, messy, filled with error and injustice. This is a world in which parents and guardians can be stupid, and selfish; in which the Church ignores the needs of the faithful; in which landowners and magistrates are eager to enrich themselves even when that means driving the poorest into criminality. Jane's novels, in truth, are as revolutionary, at their heart, as anything that Wollstonecraft or Tom Paine wrote. But, by and large, they're so cleverly crafted that unless readers are looking in the right places – reading them in the right way – they simply won't understand.

Jane wasn't a genius – inspired, unthinking; she was an artist. She compared herself to a miniature painter; in her work every stroke of the brush, every word, every character name and every line of poetry quoted, every location, matters.

It's here, in the novels, that we find Jane – what there is of her to find, after all these years, after all her family's efforts at concealment. It's here we find a clever woman, clear-sighted, a woman 'of information', who knew what was going on in the world and what she thought about it. An authoress who knew that the novel, until then widely seen as mindless 'trash', could be a great art form and who did a lot – perhaps more than any other writer – to make it into one.

We've grown too accustomed to the other Janes – to Henry's perfect sister and James-Edward's maiden aunt; to the romantic, reckless girl in *Becoming Jane* and the woman on the banknote. I'll try hard to shake these Janes off. In what follows, I offer flashes of an imaginary Jane Austen, sometimes in ordinary life, sometimes in the places she revisited in her books, but always primarily as a writer. They're intended as glimpses of what the authoress might have been thinking, of how real events and locations, and people, might have made their way into her novels. I don't claim these as biography; even though they stay close to Jane's manuscript correspondence, and to her own writing, they're fiction.

Jane wouldn't, I think, have disapproved of this approach. *Northanger Abbey* contains a lengthy passage about history, about its blend of fact and fiction. The naive heroine Catherine Morland states an undoubted truth, that 'a great deal' of history is made up – 'the speeches that are put into the heroes' mouths, their thoughts and designs – the chief of all this must be invention'. The older and more intelligent Eleanor Tilney, who reads history chiefly for pleasure, expresses herself 'very well contented to take the false with the true'. For Jane herself, though, fiction isn't simply an enjoyable embellishment. It can offer deeper truths than fact. It's in fiction, Jane says, that we should look for 'the most thorough knowledge of human nature, the happiest delineation of its varieties'.

The 'truthful fictions' in *Jane Austen, The Secret Radical*, the glimpses of an unfamiliar woman, should help to prepare readers for novels which will also become suddenly unfamiliar. Each chapter is devoted to one book and suggests how, by forgetting what we think we know, and focusing instead on the historical background, and on the texts themselves, we can make an attempt at reading as Jane intended us to. Tackling them in the order in which they were made ready for publication, we'll move from *Northanger Abbey* to *Sense and Sensibility* and *Pride and Prejudice* and then on to *Mansfield Park*, *Emma*, and *Persuasion*. But these won't be the novels you know and love. These novels deal with slavery, with sexual abuse, with land enclosure, evolution, and women's rights. They poke fun at the monarchy, and question religion. I'll also shed new light on characters – on their behaviours and motivations – and the results won't always make for easy reading.

If you want to stay with the novels and the Jane Austen you already know, then you should stop reading now. If you want to read Jane as she wanted to be read – if you want to know her – then read on.

A copperplate illustration from the 1803 edition of Radcliffe's *Mysteries of Udolpho*.
At the beginning of volume 3 the heroine, Emily, attempts to gain access to
her imprisoned aunt and is horrified to discover what appears to be a corpse.
© Courtesy of the British Library

CHAPTER 2

'The Anxieties of Common Life'

Northanger Abbey

*Summer 1799, the pleasure gardens at Bath.**

Trumpets sound. Fireworks explode against the night sky.

One gentleman, who has been squinting frowningly at the crowd, reaches a decision. He thrusts the watch away and looks about him for his sister. She is standing with a group of their Bath acquaintance, smiling and laughing, and it takes some little time to extricate her.

Would Jane be so obliging as to come with him to find his wife? He wouldn't ask, only Elizabeth has been gone these twenty minutes or more. He is concerned that she might have been taken ill.

Jane takes her brother Edward's arm and allows him to escort her along the avenue, between high hedges hung about with lanterns. They pass a couple murmuring and sighing in the shadows as the drifting light of a rocket reveals a bosom barer than even the most outlandish fashion is ever likely to approve.

Edward mutters something under his breath and hurries Jane on. She starts to giggle, and is still giggling as she skips up the steps and into the ladies' retiring room. She stops only when she sees Elizabeth. Elizabeth is sitting on a chair, a basin on her lap, her face green. Jane, who has been drinking rack punch all the evening, feels her own stomach turn.

---

* Based on Jane Austen's letters to Cassandra Austen (11th June and 19th June 1799).

Is it something Elizabeth has eaten? Jane asks. Or a bilious attack? Jane knows all about bilious attacks; half her family suffers from them.

No, replies Elizabeth, with what seems unwarranted ill-temper, not something that she's eaten, and she would have thought Jane knew enough of the world by now – she jerks forward and retches painfully into the bowl.

Jane, sobering, demands a cloth from one of the attendants and hesitantly – for she has never been close to her sister-in-law – sets about helping her.

And all she can think, all the while, is that William, the baby, is scarce nine months old, and that women aren't even sick straight away, and how could Edward—

☙❧

Let's begin with *Northanger Abbey*, though I'm not altogether sure it's what Jane would have wanted.

The novel wasn't published until after her death in 1817, when it appeared together with *Persuasion*, but it belongs much earlier, to the beginning of her career as an 'authoress'. We've almost certainly had a glimpse of it already. Unless exactly the same fate befell two of her books independently, we can be confident that it's a version of *Susan*, the two-volume novel sold to the publisher Crosby in 1803. And unless yet another manuscript has gone missing altogether, we can also be fairly confident in identifying *Susan/Northanger Abbey* with the novel which, in one of her letters, Jane calls 'Miss Catherine'.*

---

* The issue is complicated by the survival among Jane's papers of a (very) short novel-in-letters focusing on the shockingly immoral behaviour of a character named Lady Susan Vernon and usually referred to as *Lady Susan*, though the title isn't Jane's. This survives copied onto paper which bears an 1805 watermark. There's also a short fragment of writing about a young girl called Catherine. The first isn't long enough to fill even half a volume, let alone two, while the second

But, whatever you want to call it, it wasn't a work which Jane could be confident about. It had been her first taste of success as a writer – £10, all of her own, her novel advertised in the press – but that success had turned into humiliating, inexplicable failure. For years the novel had sat on a shelf or in a drawer in Crosby's publishing house, tantalisingly out of her reach, utterly beyond her control.

Aside from its pre-publication history, and the fact that it's the shortest of Jane's six novels – even shorter than *Persuasion* – there's not, on the surface, much that's remarkable about *Northanger Abbey*. Few people ever name it as their favourite Jane Austen novel. Few people hate the book, either; it tends not to evoke particularly strong feelings from readers. And you can see why.

The main male character, Henry Tilney, definitely belongs to the second tier of heroes; he's not a Darcy, or a Wentworth. He is 'rather tall', has 'a pleasing countenance' and 'a very intelligent and lively eye', but he is 'not quite handsome'. Firmly under the paternal thumb for most of the novel, he dominates where he can, lecturing the women in his life about anything and everything. At times this is teasing, it can even be flirtatious; over time, one suspects, it would grow wearisome. We're told that Henry's love for Catherine, the heroine, 'originated in nothing better than gratitude', that 'a persuasion of her partiality for him had been the only cause of giving her a serious thought'. It's hardly a romance to echo down the ages.

Catherine has none of Lizzy Bennet's impatient intelligence, none of Fanny Price's panicky fastidiousness. She isn't self-consciously

---

is not much more than a very tentative first sketch of an opening. Unless we start inventing manuscripts from nowhere, then, the safest hypothesis is that *Susan*, 'Miss Catherine' and *Northanger Abbey* are essentially one and the same text. As we'll see, nearly all the incidental detail in *Northanger Abbey* points to it having been written in the late 1790s or the first couple of years of the nineteenth century, strengthening the supposition that it is *Susan*. The identification remains hypothesis, however, rather than fact.

unconventional like Marianne, or complacent like Emma. Comparing her to Anne Elliot, the heroine of *Persuasion*, published alongside *Northanger Abbey* and, like *Northanger*, set partly in Bath, shows how far Jane matured as a novelist between her twenties and her early forties. Anne is clever, she is good, but she's also fully psychologically real.

Catherine is … well, nothing very much. She's neither intelligent nor dim; 'often inattentive and occasionally stupid', she nevertheless learns to recite 'the fable of "The Hare and Many Friends" as quickly as any girl in England'. On her best days, in the first flush of her youthful bloom, she is 'almost pretty'. Even her virtues are vague, weak, described by *not* being faults: 'she had neither a bad heart nor a bad temper, was seldom stubborn, scarcely ever quarrelsome, and very kind to the little ones, with few interruptions of tyranny.'

What she is, is malleable, impressible. As a child with three older brothers she's 'fond of all boy's plays' – 'cricket, base ball, riding on horseback and running about the country'. With the onset of puberty, she adapts herself with great docility to the business of becoming a young woman. She begins to 'curl her hair and long for balls'. She develops 'an inclination for finery'. In matters of gender conformity, of fashion, of flirtation, in her own conception of herself, Catherine is easily swayed. She retains a tendency to run rather than walk, and she has moments of resistance and independent thought, but they're few and far between, and readers of a pessimistic disposition may worry that marriage to Henry will do very little to encourage her to think for herself.

Catherine isn't much of a heroine. It's the point that Jane makes over and over again. She's a heroine whom 'no one' would imagine 'born to be a heroine'. Everything is against her; 'her situation in life, the character of her father and mother, her own person and disposition'. Her mind is 'unpropitious for heroism'. Even her artistic skills fall 'miserably short of the true heroic height'. She has 'by nature nothing heroic about her'. It's something she has to work at, to be 'in training for'.

Her training takes the form of reading. 'From fifteen to seventeen', Catherine ploughs through 'all such works as heroines must read'. The reading itself isn't a new pastime for her; it's only the 'works', the texts, which have changed. Reading is the sole pleasure which survives from Catherine's childhood, the only occupation she's been allowed to pursue throughout her life. The horse-riding, the cricket, the 'rolling down the green slope at the back of the house', she's had to abandon all of these. Even as a tomboyish child, though, she liked to read, 'she never objected to books at all'.

But she does it wrong, doesn't she? Everyone knows that's what *Northanger Abbey* is about – Catherine's inability to read properly, her inability to interpret texts correctly, to separate fiction and reality. Excited, and rapidly obsessed by Gothic novels, she convinces herself that they present an accurate picture of the world around her. When the modern appearance of Northanger Abbey disappoints her fevered expectations, she invents a Gothic plot for herself – a secret chamber, a wife murdered or imprisoned by her husband. Henry discovers her suspicions, shows her how absurd they are, and she obligingly abandons the 'alarms of romance' for 'the anxieties of common life'. That's what happens; that's the point, the moral. Silly girls shouldn't read silly novels.

Are we sure, though, that *we're* reading properly?

Northanger Abbey, after all, is the book which includes a lengthy passage defending the novel, as a genre, against its critics. 'I will not', Jane begins, 'adopt that ungenerous and impolitic custom so common with novel-writers, of degrading by their contemptuous censure the very performances, to the number of which they are themselves adding.' She's addressing (ostensibly at least) not her readers, but other novelists. 'Let us not desert one another,' she pleads, 'we are an injured body.' Novelists shouldn't join in with the 'threadbare' complaints of 'the reviewers', Jane says. Rather than censuring or abusing novels, Jane praises them – and in grandiose terms. 'Our productions have afforded more extensive and unaffected pleasure than those of any other literary corporation in the world', she declares. Novels have 'genius, wit, and taste'; they display the 'greatest powers of the mind'. In them, 'the most thorough knowledge of human nature, the happiest delineation of its varieties, the liveliest effusions of wit and humour, are conveyed to the world in the best-chosen language'. The novels she mentions by name – *Cecilia, Camilla, Belinda* – aren't just named for women, they're written by them too.

It wouldn't make all that much sense for Jane to go from celebrating women's novels to openly deriding a particular subset of novels – Gothic ones – which were also largely female-authored. In fact, the first reference to Gothic novels comes immediately after this impassioned defence of novels and novelists. It's true that Jane invites us to sneer at the 'literary taste' which Catherine and her new friend, the vapid Isabella Thorpe display, their desire for 'horrid' novels. A little later, though, she tells us that both Henry Tilney and his altogether admirable sister Eleanor enjoy Gothic authors.

We're missing something.

And this – it seems – was precisely what Jane worried about.

∽

As we've seen, the publishing firm Crosby, having bought *Susan* in 1803, did nothing with it. Shortly before she moved from Southampton to Chawton, Jane wrote to them, in an attempt to force their hand. The attempt failed. We have no really reliable record of how and when she regained the rights,* but around 1816 or the beginning of 1817 she seems to have devoted some time to looking over the manuscript, and to thinking about finally publishing it. In the eight years that had passed since her run-in with Crosby in 1809 Jane had published four novels, had seen favourable reviews – some very favourable – and had been invited to dedicate one of her books to the Prince Regent. None of this had

---

* The story recounted in the family memoirs that Henry bought it back before taunting the publisher with the fact that the author had also written *Pride and Prejudice* seems terribly neat; possibly too neat to be true.

done away with her resentment. She composed a short, acidic 'advertisement', apparently intended as some sort of foreword to the book, and explaining what had happened to it. Most of the advertisement is a complaint about Crosby, though the firm is never named. It indicates how bruising the encounter had been, how sore a point the refusal to publish still was for her.

And perhaps her feelings were justified, because so far as Jane was concerned the delay in publication created endless – perhaps insurmountable – issues for her readers. The thirteen years that had passed since Crosby had accepted the book, the 'many more years' before then that she had worked on it, had, as she explains in the advertisement, made 'parts of the work ... comparatively obsolete'. Not only 'places', but 'manners, books, and opinions have undergone considerable changes'.

If we believe Jane – and who else should we believe? – this tells us that we should be looking for the beginnings of the novel to a period 'many' years before 1803 – that is, to Jane's early twenties, somewhere in the mid-to-late 1790s.

We have a few of Jane's letters from this period. Several describe a visit to Bath in 1799 with her mother, her brother Edward and his wife Elizabeth. Edward rented a house in Queen Square, an area which, in *Persuasion*, the Musgrove sisters think undesirable, but which Jane liked, even if the house was number 13. It was 'chearful', and the view from the drawing room window was 'rather picturesque'. She enjoyed travelling with her rich brother – the 'comfortable rooms' at the inn in Devizes, the 'asparagus, & lobster' and 'cheesecakes' they had for dinner.[1] She enjoyed the Bath shops – so much so that at times an underlying kinship with *Northanger Abbey*'s fashion-obsessed chaperone Mrs Allen becomes apparent, with Jane sketching the pattern of some lace in the margin of a letter and announcing that, 'I saw some Gauzes in a shop in Bath Street yesterday at only 4s a yard, but they were not so good or so pretty as mine'.[2]

Like Catherine Morland, Jane was caught up in the social whirl of Bath. She saw an evening concert and fireworks display in the pleasure gardens; 'the Fire-works ... were really beautiful, & surpassing my expectation; – the illuminations too were very pretty', she writes. Like Catherine, she attended a ball at the Assembly Rooms, promenaded in the Pump Room, and arranged to go to the theatre, which we know was showing *The Birthday* and *Blue Beard*.[3]

The Birthday, or *The Reconciliation*, is a sentimental comedy adapted from a German original by August von Kotzebue. Kotzebue also wrote the original German version of *Lovers' Vows*, which Jane has her characters plan to perform in *Mansfield Park*.

The Birthday features a lovely young woman – seventeen, like Catherine Morland – softening an unpleasant, bullying older man. It's preoccupied with novels. 'O dear! You must not read novels', says the heroine's sick father, 'I scarcely know three or four of them that I would put into your hands'. A man with a romantic interest in the heroine tries to seduce her with novels and, when his attempts at seduction fail, blackens her character. But the hero of *The Birthday* (in as far as there is one) is a doctor who actually writes novels. In addition, there's a dead mother and a locked chest.

Blue Beard was a comic operetta, a hugely popular Orientalised version of the fairy tale we're familiar with, in which a young woman, encouraged to wander freely around the house of an older, tyrannical man, is forbidden access to only one room – which she immediately becomes obsessed with getting into.

There are several other flashes in the letters from this visit which illuminate *Northanger Abbey*.

Driving into Bath, the Austens pass two acquaintances on the street, suggesting that the constant coincidental meetings in *Northanger* and *Persuasion* are a reflection of reality and not novelistic contrivance. Edward renews his friendship with a Mr Evelyn, a 'Yahoo', according to Jane, who 'has all his life thought more of Horses than of anything else'. Jane encounters a Mr Gould, who 'walked home with me after Tea; — he is a very Young Man, just entered of Oxford, wears Spectacles, & has heard that Evelina was written by Dr Johnson'. If we want to, we can find something of these two gentlemen in John Thorpe. He too is obsessed with horses, and he too is an Oxford student with absurd views about novels. Mr Gould thinks that Fanny Burney's novel *Evelina* must have been written by a man; John Thorpe doesn't express an opinion on *Evelina*, but he dismisses Burney's *Camilla* as a 'stupid book', 'the horridest nonsense you can imagine', adding a touch of mindless racism about the author's marriage to 'a French emigrant' for good measure.

The references to Burney in *Northanger Abbey* date to the late 1790s or very early 1800s, certainly no later than 1802 or 1803, since in 1802 Burney travelled to France to assist her French husband in some family business, taking advantage of the short-lived cessation of hostilities between France and Britain. When the war resumed in 1803, she was trapped on the wrong side of the Channel, remaining there for the next ten years. She didn't return to England until shortly before the publication of her final novel, *The Wanderer*, in 1814 – a novel which sold poorly. For a reader of 1816 or 1817, Burney's name would have had a very different meaning to the one it had held a decade or more earlier.

One of the books which had 'undergone considerable changes' between 1803 and 1816 was Maria Edgeworth's *Belinda*. In the original version of the novel a reader would have found reference to an interracial marriage. They would also have found a heroine who gives serious consideration to marrying a 'Creole' character. The term is a notoriously slippery one. At the end of the eighteenth century it denoted – usually – someone born in the West Indies, though whether of European parentage, or African, or of mixed racial heritage, wasn't ever entirely clear. Edgeworth's description of her 'Creole' character (Mr Vincent) is no more fixed. His 'aquiline nose' suggests European ancestry, but he has 'large dark eyes' and a 'manly sunburnt complexion'. Purely European? Well, just like the first Mrs Rochester in *Jane Eyre*, maybe not. The 1810 edition of the novel, though, excises every suggestion of interracial or possibly interracial relationships.

It's the first version of *Belinda* which Jane holds up as an example of the greatness of the novel, not the second, censored version. Her literary references had taken on a different meaning; they no longer read as she'd originally intended. There was, in the late 1790s, something of a fashion for locked boxes in literature, and not just in Gothic novels. As mentioned above, they appear in Kotzebue's play *The Birthday*, in the novel *Caleb Williams* (written by Mary Shelley's father, the anarchist philosopher and conservative hate figure William Godwin), and in the play clearly based on *Caleb Williams*, *The Iron Chest*. These are the texts which Catherine's adventures at the abbey ought to be calling to mind.

The delay in publication separated *Northanger Abbey* for ever from the readership it had been designed for.

Did Jane decide that, after all, the delay had been too long, that the book couldn't be read as she had meant it to be? A letter to her niece Fanny suggests that the manuscript came to profoundly dissatisfy her, certainly that she didn't any longer consider it fit to be published as it stood: 'Miss Catherine is put upon the Shelve for the present, and I do not know that she will ever come out.' This letter can be dated, from the postmark, to March 1817. Jane was taken very ill in April and continued that way for five or six weeks. In May she moved to Winchester for medical treatment. By the middle of July she was dead. There's not really much time for her to have revised the book. If 'Miss Catherine' is *Northanger Abbey* – and there's no other obvious candidate – then the text that Jane was so dissatisfied with, the text that she'd decided to put back on the shelf, perhaps to leave there permanently, must be almost exactly, word-for-word, the text that we're reading.

❧

When we open *Northanger Abbey*, when we leaf through its pages, we're venturing somewhere that Jane wasn't really willing to let us go.

We're trespassing.

In a way it's quite fitting. Catherine, the heroine of *Northanger Abbey*, is constantly making her way into places where she has no business being; pushing past a servant at a front door; opening chests and cabinets; sneaking into a bedroom she knows she isn't meant to enter.

Jane herself – like so many people at a time when families of ten children were common, and families of twenty not unheard of – didn't ever have that much privacy.* But in her novels, bedrooms – unless they're also sick rooms – are clearly considered private spaces. The rule even applies to guest rooms. While staying with her friend Charlotte in Kent, Lizzy Bennet retreats to the 'solitude of her chamber' to think, or to read letters from her sister. No one disturbs her there. When, in *Sense and Sensibility*, the Dashwood sisters are staying in London with the well-meaning but vulgar Mrs Jennings, Jane sees fit to remark that the lady of the house doesn't always wait for her knock to be answered before coming into their room – it's a breach, not of etiquette precisely, but of a more profound social rule. It's viewed as invasive.

And it's seldom that we, as readers, are allowed into bedrooms – Jane takes us there far less often than the film and television adaptations would lead you to believe. Take *Mansfield Park*, for example; there are times when Sir Thomas Bertram's interest in his niece Fanny Price drifts a little too far from the purely avuncular, but he never pursues her into her bedroom to berate her, as happens in the 1999 film version. Fanny's cousin Edmund never sits on her bed to chat. She has a sitting room of her own. You'll look in vain in *Pride and Prejudice* for the scene where Mrs Bennet, a heap of trembling lace propped up in bed, wails to her daughters and her brother about the runaway Lydia; we're told specifically that she's in her 'dressing-room'.

It can be difficult to recognise the taboos of your own culture until you're somewhere that doesn't observe them. There's a taboo, in modern British culture at least, against going into the bedroom of a married couple, a taboo which becomes far stronger when neither half of that couple is a member of your blood family. I hadn't appreciated quite how

---

* The best-selling author of the day, Maria Edgeworth (who we'll encounter briefly in the chapter on *Emma*), had 21 siblings and half-siblings. The Duchess of Leinster, mother of the Irish rebel leader Lord Edward Fitzgerald, gave birth 22 times.

strong it was until a few years ago, when I was in India for a friend's wedding. We were visiting her fiancé's house, and were ushered up into his parents' bedroom, where they were lying on the bed. They were fully dressed; there was a table of tea things. It's a normal way to socialise, apparently, in middle-class Delhi circles. But I had to force myself over the threshold of their bedroom. It felt profoundly unnatural to me. And this taboo – or one very similar to it – also seems to be operating in Jane's novels.

Jane makes a particular point of not taking us into the bedrooms of married women. She ventures in there on only two occasions. One is the brief scene in *Persuasion* when the unconscious Louisa Musgrove is carried to the bed of Captain and Mrs Harville, which doesn't really count, because Louisa is ill. The other occasion – the one which stands out – is in *Northanger Abbey*, when Catherine becomes obsessed with the idea of getting into the bedroom which belonged to the dead Mrs Tilney.

In fact *Northanger Abbey* is very much the exception when it comes to bedrooms. In it Jane offers us no fewer than three bedroom scenes, all of them lengthy, and all of them featuring the heroine Catherine.

In each scene we see Catherine working herself into a frenzy of excitement before opening or entering something. In one scene we're invited to visualise her half-dressed, her clothes falling off her ('having slipped one arm into her gown'). In another she's in her nightie. The sexual element is unmistakable.

Jane was a spinster, yes, but she wasn't prudish. The birds and the bees weren't a mystery to her. She grew up in the country, for one thing; in addition to his duties as a clergyman, and his tutoring, her father farmed. During her lifetime, her brothers produced 23 nieces and nephews for her. She often comments on pregnant women and childbirth in her letters. A sister-in-law 'is to be confined in the middle of April'.[4] A neighbour, a Mrs Warren, 'has got rid of some part of her child, & danced away with great activity, looking by no means very large'.[5] 'Dame Tilbury's daughter has lain in', Jane tells Cassandra, noting a few lines later that another neighbour has been 'brought to bed of a dead child'.[6] She boasts about picking a scandalous woman out of a crowd – 'I have a very good eye at an Adultress'.[7] Her novels feature sex outside marriage, illegitimate children, adultery.

But English culture in the late eighteenth and early nineteenth centuries wasn't all that prudish either. It was sexist and morally judgemental, absolutely, but in other respects it was far more relaxed about bodies than we are. You find adverts for nipple cream in early nineteenth-century newspapers.* I've never seen a commercial on television or in the national press for that kind of product. An advertisement for 'Balm of Gilead' – again, in a newspaper – has no hesitation in announcing that it 'assists wonderfully in recovering the tone of the urinary and genital organs'. The advertisement refers openly to 'bad lyings-in', 'immoderate courses of the menses', 'repeated and difficult labours'. The only moments of bashfulness come when discussing masturbation and sexually transmitted disease, and even then the euphemisms are pretty transparent – 'those unhappy youths, who have been deluded at an early age into a secret and destructive vice'; 'where the fountain is polluted, the streams that flow from it cannot be pure'.[8]

There's a matter-of-factness here about sex and its dangers, and about the physical toll that childbirth takes on the female body, an awareness, a respect, almost, that in some ways we've lost. It was generally accepted that pregnancy and giving birth weren't unalloyed pleasures for women; in fact the eighteenth century saw quite a lot of research and development into surgical devices designed specifically to correct anal and vaginal prolapse. All of this perhaps goes some way towards explaining why, for the first two-thirds of Jane's life, abortion was perfectly legal. Up until 'quickening', that is, when it becomes possible to feel foetal movement, which usually happens closer to five months' gestation than four, women could take whatever measures they chose

---

* For example, in June 1799, when Jane was in Bath, the *Bath Chronicle and Weekly Gazette* was running adverts for 'nipple liniment'.

to restore their 'natural courses' – their periods. In fact, before the passing of The Malicious Shooting or Stabbing Act (also known as Lord Ellenborough's Act) in 1803, the law wasn't altogether clear that even late abortion, after quickening, was a crime.*

Throughout the eighteenth century 'female pills' were freely advertised and sold alongside toothpaste, cough mixture, and face cream. It was claimed that they would correct 'blocked' or 'suppressed' periods. The adverts often mention something called chlorosis, or green-sickness, an illness unique to women who were past puberty but still virgins, and which was thought to be caused by a blockage of menstrual blood. There was, then, a 'genuine' medical need for such products, unrelated to abortion. But it's difficult to believe that suppliers didn't intend to suggest that their pills could 'correct' an unwanted pregnancy as well. We know the composition of some of these pills, either from *materia medica* (chemists' recipe books) or because adverts list the ingredients. Many contained recognised abortifacients – myrrh, aloes, senna, savin oil. They might not have worked, but they weren't difficult to come by. Even after 1803 the advertisements continued unabated. You could purchase by mail-order, at chemists, at booksellers and – a point to bear in mind – in circulating libraries.†

The culture Jane had grown up in didn't require women to be always joyously accepting of pregnancy.

Childbirth, after all, was dangerous. The figures are difficult to get to grips with, because cause of death was seldom recorded, and even where it was, accuracy can be an issue. Historians of the subject generally agree, though, that maternal mortality fell quite substantially between the mid-seventeenth century and the mid-nineteenth century.

---

* Lord Ellenborough's Act also altered the law on infanticide, which previously automatically assumed that the mother of an illegitimate newborn baby found dead had murdered it.

† Britain's largest chain of chemists, Boots, ran lending libraries in many of their stores until the middle of the twentieth century.

The fall doesn't coincide either with the move towards 'man-midwives' or the introduction of forceps. Of course, England was in the throes of a bloody civil war during the middle of the seventeenth century. There would have been an increase in levels of stress and in the incidence of sexually transmitted diseases, and a decrease in the quality of nutrition – all of which can affect pregnancy outcomes, often for more than one generation – so part of the fall may be a return to more 'normal' levels.

But those levels are still, for us, unimaginably high.

It's estimated that during the Regency period, two women died for every hundred babies that were born, so a 1 in 50 risk. That compares to modern maternal death rates in the UK of about 1 in 12,000 live births, and of about 1 in 7,000 live births in the US, according to the most recent figures from the World Health Organization. Still, 1 in 50 doesn't sound all that bad, does it, for the olden days? But these figures aren't the lifetime risk for a woman. That is higher, and it depends – now, as then – on how many children she gives birth to: nowadays, in developed countries with access to contraception, rarely more than two or three, but during Jane's lifetime perhaps as many as eight (as in her own family), or ten, or a dozen or more.

Not every labour is dangerous, but having lots is. Even now, first labours are statistically riskier, with the risk then decreasing before rising again sharply on the rare occasions that pregnancies get towards double figures. Independently of the number of pregnancies a woman has had, she runs a greater risk the older she is. Very young women are also in greater danger. But the fact remains that during the eighteenth and early nineteenth centuries the lifetime risk of a woman dying while giving birth or from complications of labour was substantial. Post-partum haemorrhage, sepsis; they were very likely to kill you. And there were complications of pregnancy to be considered as well. Ectopic pregnancy was inevitably fatal. In 1855, the novelist Charlotte Brontë died from what was very probably hyperemesis – the violent, unrelenting nausea and vomiting which the current Duchess of Cambridge has suffered from in both her pregnancies. The only treatment for eclampsia was to deliver the baby (this remained the sole treatment until 1957). Caesarean section was very rarely used; surgeons weren't skilled in it. In the pre-hygiene era, it amounted to a death sentence for the mother anyway.

Almost every family had a tale of maternal death to tell, though of course they might not always have told it. One of Jane's own grandmothers, Rebecca Austen, seems to have died giving birth. Class and wealth didn't make much difference. At the end of 1817, Princess Charlotte, the second in line to the throne, laboured for two days to give birth to a still-born son, before dying herself.

And even when childbirth didn't prove fatal, even when there weren't life-altering birth injuries, frequent and repeated pregnancies took a physical toll. This is very much the view that Jane expresses in her letters. Consoling her niece Fanny on a disappointed love affair, she points out that, 'by not beginning the business of Mothering quite so early in life, you will be young in Constitution, spirits, figure & countenance, while Mʳˢ Wᵐ Hammond [one of Fanny's friends] is growing old by confinements & nursing'. Later in the letter, she glumly informs Fanny that another niece, Anna, seems to be pregnant again; 'Anna has had a bad cold, looks pale, & we fear something else. — She has just weaned Julia.'

After Anna's pregnancy had been confirmed, Jane wrote to Fanny again, a letter which fairly reverberates with rage about the endless child-bearing she saw all around her. 'Poor Animal', she says of Anna, 'she will be worn out before she is thirty. — I am very sorry for her. — Mʳˢ Clement too is in that way again. I am quite tired of so many Children. — Mʳˢ Benn has a 13ᵗʰ —.'[9]

This negative attitude towards pregnancy and childbirth, the sense of how relentless reproduction could be, isn't really expressed in the novels. A number of Jane's married female characters are childless – more than one would expect. The Crofts, in *Persuasion*, have no children, nor do the Allens in *Northanger Abbey*. Lady Russell, Mrs Smith, Mrs Norris – all were married for years and none, so far as we know, has ever had a child.

With the possible exception of Mary Musgrove, in *Persuasion*, the characters who are mothers take pregnancy in their stride.* The two children to be born in the main action of the novels – and it is only two, since we don't learn about one of the births in *Sense and Sensibility* until afterwards – make their appearance very unproblematically. Mrs Palmer is pregnant for most of *Sense and Sensibility*, giving birth about two-thirds of the way through; there's no indication that anyone ever worries about her at all. In *Emma*, when the heroine's friend and former governess Mrs Weston gives birth, we're told that her 'friends all rejoiced in her safety', indicating an undercurrent of suppressed anxiety. But this is the only place in the text that anything approaching concern for her condition is mentioned – even by the health-obsessed Mr Woodhouse.

True, in *Mansfield Park*, the heroine's mother, married, we're told, eleven years and already 'preparing for her ninth lying-in', is described – unsurprisingly – as 'bewailing the circumstance'. The pregnancy is unwanted – surely resented. But the problem appears to be money. There is 'such a superfluity of children, and such a want of almost everything else'. Other large families in the novels – the Lucases in *Pride and Prejudice*; the Morlands in *Northanger Abbey*; the Musgroves in *Persuasion* – are generally pretty cheerful. The mothers, in each case, are hale and hearty.

It's odd. We know that this isn't how Jane saw the matter, and that it isn't an accurate representation of childbirth at the time. And it's particularly odd in fiction. Novels of the period almost always made their heroes and heroines orphans, or apparently orphans. Tragic deaths in childbirth happened all the time in books.

Jane even jokes about it, at the very beginning of *Northanger Abbey*, saying how 'remarkable' it is that her heroine's mother should possess

---

* It seems probable that Mary Musgrove is pregnant during the main action of *Persuasion*. She likes to coddle herself, but the younger of her two sons is two years old, a very usual age-gap, and we're told that she is 'indisposed' and expects 'that she should not have a day's health all the autumn'.

such a 'good constitution', how unexpected that, rather than dying having Catherine, Mrs Morland has 'lived on to have six children more' and 'see them growing up around her'. It's part of the fun Jane has in the opening chapters, skewering every novelistic convention she can think of.

But when Jane re-read the novel in 1816 or 1817, with a view to possibly publishing, did she wince at this passage? In 1814, after all, her sister-in-law Frances died giving birth to a fourth child. Edward's wife Elizabeth had given birth to ten children without turning a hair – just like Mrs Morland. In 1808, an eleventh child killed her.

What is clear is that Jane was aware that, in the absence of any information to the contrary, her readers would assume that it was complications of labour which had killed characters of child-bearing age. She quite often makes a point of explaining that a death wasn't related to childbirth. A 'lingering illness' does for one character. Anne Elliot's mother, it appears, has also been ill for some time – she anticipates her own demise. Two characters die of consumption – or so we're told: Jane Fairfax's mother in *Emma*, and Colonel Brandon's first love Eliza in *Sense and Sensibility*.*

Just as we, hearing of the sudden death of a young or youngish woman, default to ideas of a car crash or cancer, so Jane's readers would guess at childbirth as a cause of death before anything else, for married women at least. So even if Jane herself had a less negative view of the risks of reproduction at the time she wrote *Northanger Abbey*, before her sisters-in-law started to die in childbed, she knew that for her readers the prospect of dying giving birth wasn't distant. The real risk was substantial; the fear must have haunted every pregnant woman. It wouldn't have been amusing – it was deathly serious.

∞

---

* Consumption was a leading cause of death, but as we'll see later, there could be reasons to mistrust some of the assertions made about these two deaths.

But most critics agree that *Northanger Abbey* shouldn't be taken too seriously. It's comic – ridiculous, light-hearted, Jane's 'funniest novel'.[10] They all agree that Catherine's view of the world, her expectations of what she'll find at Northanger, are completely – and hilariously – warped by the Gothic novels she's read.

As we've seen, though, Jane surely hoped – she surely intended, when she wrote it – for her readers to find something different and altogether more complicated in the novel. Jane assumed, when she was writing the book, that her readers would know certain novels and plays, would read certain references into the text. This is what she's talking about, in the advertisement. She expected, originally, readers who were familiar enough with Gothic novels to realise what's passed nearly every modern reader by – the fact that Catherine Morland, probably the best-known Gothic novel reader in the world, reads only one Gothic novel, and doesn't even seem to finish it.

We're told that the Gothic is a new sub-genre for Catherine, told, indeed, that she hasn't read very many novels, certainly not as many as the other characters she encounters. 'New books', she explains, 'do not fall in our way.' The only 'new book' she does read, or begin to read, is *The Mysteries of Udolpho*, by Ann Radcliffe. Radcliffe was the most famous Gothic novelist of the 1790s. She wrote six novels and a book of travel writing, and made quite a lot of money by doing so. She received £800 for one of her works, a considerable sum for the rights to a novel. *The Mysteries of Udolpho*, published in 1794, is Radcliffe's fourth novel. It's a big book – getting towards 700 pages in the modern Oxford World's Classics edition, four volumes in the original. It's set during the sixteenth century and tells the story of a French girl, Emily St Aubert, beautiful, virtuous, and unlucky. Her mother dies at the end of the first chapter, her father in Chapter 7. Taken in by an unfeeling aunt, she shortly acquires a new uncle in the form of the villainous Italian Montoni, and is carted off to Italy – first to Venice and then to the mysterious, crumbling Castle of Udolpho.

Udolpho, as the novel's title suggests, is full of mysteries, and of threats – unwanted suitors, brigands, the unspeakable horror that lurks behind a picture covered with a 'black veil'. The most tangible threat, though, is Montoni himself, who wants to gain control of his wife's money and estates. Once his wife dies in suspicious circumstances, Montoni turns the pressure onto Emily, who is her aunt's heiress. Emily eventually escapes, returns to France, is rescued from a shipwreck, and takes refuge with the Count de Villefort and his children, Henri and Blanche. Mysteries continue, however; haunting music plays, strange sounds are heard, characters inexplicably resemble the dead, or vanish from a locked room. Mad nuns mutter. But the truth, when it emerges, is all resolutely natural. There are no ghosts; everything is explained. There has been murder, though. One of Emily's uncles has indeed murdered his wife, but a different uncle, not Montoni. Montoni has only ever been interested in money. Emily eventually marries Valancourt, her anaemic love interest, and returns to her family estates in France.

Catherine Morland, or so we gather, is introduced to *The Mysteries of Udolpho* by her friend Isabella Thorpe. Isabella, who is four years older than Catherine, and 'at least four years better informed' in matters of society and fashion, has a course of 'horrid' novel reading planned; 'when you have finished Udolpho', she tells Catherine, 'we will read the Italian together; and I have made out a list of ten or twelve more of the same kind for you'. The list, in fact, contains only seven titles – 'Castle of Wolfenbach, Clermont, Mysterious Warnings, Necromancer of the Black Forest, Midnight Bell, Orphan of the Rhine, and Horrid Mysteries'. These are all real novels; they're a handful of the rash of second-rate imitations that emerged as the Gothic became successful. Jane probably wouldn't have ever anticipated that her audience would know them really well.

Isabella, it's clear, hasn't read any of these novels herself; she's going on the recommendation of her 'particular friend' Miss Andrews who has 'read every one of them'. *Not* reading is quite a theme in this most self-consciously bookish of Jane's novels.

How much of *Udolpho* Isabella has read is unclear. Catherine announces that 'I am got to the black veil', that is, early in Volume 2, where Emily becomes intrigued by a veiled picture frame hung in a 'dark corner' of one of the castle's many unoccupied chambers. Isabella's response is to exclaim, 'Are you indeed? How delightful! Oh! I would not tell you what is behind the black veil for the world! Are not you wild to know?', which suggests that she has at least glanced at the final pages of the last volume. There's no indication she's read more, though. Elsewhere in *Northanger*, Jane takes the time to indicate exactly how familiar a character is with a particular novel. Henry Tilney demonstrates that he has indeed read *Udolpho*; he comes close, at one point, to quoting sections of it from memory. It's made just as clear that Isabella's brother John tends to skim-read the novels he does bother to open. Isabella, fickle and impatient, may well have developed similar reading habits. So too, it turns out, may Catherine.

At the time Jane tells us she was writing *Northanger*, though, most readers *would* have read *Udolpho*. Jane could have expected them to recognise that, if Catherine has only got as far as the 'black veil', she has another two and a half volumes of *Udolpho* to go, over 400 pages in modern money. And she has no time to read them.

In fact, from the very point that we're told how far Catherine has got in the text, everything conspires to interrupt her reading.

In the next chapter, her brother James and Isabella's brother John, who are university friends, arrive in Bath.* Catherine reads a little more during that afternoon, and a little the next morning, but later that day drives out to Claverton Down. The evening is spent at a theatre, the morning after at the Pump Room. All that afternoon, and the next day (a Thursday), her 'chief concern' is 'what gown and what head-dress she should wear' at the ball on Thursday evening. On the Friday morning, Catherine doesn't read but instead divides her attention between the

---

*   Incidentally, since it's February and term-time, they're breaking the University of Oxford's strict residence requirements.

window and 'the clock', anxious that her planned walk with Eleanor Tilney will have to be put off because of the weather. She drives out in the afternoon – tricked into it by John Thorpe, who claims that he has seen the Tilneys setting off without her. The evening is spent with the Thorpes. On Saturday, Catherine can think of little else but her fear that she has offended the Tilneys; in the evening she sees them at the theatre and is happy to discover that the situation is repairable. No reading here.

The day after, as Jane makes a point of reminding us, is Sunday and Catherine, clergyman's daughter that she is, surely doesn't read novels on a Sunday. On Monday she goes for a walk to Beechen Cliff with Eleanor and Henry Tilney, and then goes shopping 'for some indispensible yard of ribbon'. She may perhaps read a little, but we're not told that she does. On Tuesday the news of Isabella and James's engagement is revealed. Catherine spends most of this day, and the next, with Isabella, 'in schemes of sisterly happiness'; later that day she dines with the Tilneys. The next day she visits Isabella, and the evening is spent at a ball – there is no mention of reading.

At the beginning of Chapter 17 we learn that Catherine has been in Bath for five weeks. There's a week or ten days which passed before Catherine made any acquaintances. She then met Henry one day, and the Thorpes the next. 'Eight or nine days' later, James and John arrive. Call that three weeks or thereabouts. Almost all of the next two weeks are detailed above. It's also in Chapter 17 that Eleanor Tilney invites Catherine to come for a visit when they leave Bath at the end of the week. That week, for Catherine, passes away in dreams of Northanger, and in growing suspicions of Isabella's devotion to James, but not, it seems, in reading.

Henry Tilney is highly educated, highly literate, a self-confessed lover of novels ('I have read hundreds and hundreds'). He's an expert reader. He boasts that he finished *Udolpho* 'in two days', that's two full days of uninterrupted reading. Catherine never manages to carve out anything approaching this kind of reading time. And she isn't a terribly experienced novel reader – she hasn't, for example, read Burney's

Camilla, which was a hugely successful, popular book. As we saw above, it's clear that she's read the first volume of *Udolpho*, and that she's started the second.

But it's also strongly suggested that, even though Catherine at one point seems to mention a scene which takes place in the fourth volume, she *hasn't* read any of the rest of the second half of the novel, or if she has, she's been flicking through in an effort to find all the really exciting bits. On the journey to Northanger, Henry starts to tease her about what she might find at the abbey:

> 'But you must be aware that when a young lady is (by whatever means) introduced into a dwelling of this kind, she is always lodged apart from the rest of the family. While they snugly repair to their own end of the house, she is formally conducted by Dorothy, the ancient housekeeper, up a different staircase, and along many gloomy passages, into an apartment never used since some cousin or kin died in it about twenty years before. Can you stand such a ceremony as this? Will not your mind misgive you when you find yourself in this gloomy chamber—too lofty and extensive for you, with only the feeble rays of a single lamp to take in its size—its walls hung with tapestry exhibiting figures as large as life, and the bed, of dark green stuff or purple velvet, presenting even a funereal appearance? Will not your heart sink within you? [...] Dorothy, meanwhile, no less struck by your appearance, gazes on you in great agitation, and drops a few unintelligible hints.'

Catherine is naively entranced. 'Oh! Mr Tilney, how frightful! This is just like a book!' It's like lots of books – Henry's patching together scenes and descriptions from Gothic novels and adding his own exaggerations. He takes the bedchamber without a lock from the second volume of *Udolpho*, but what the whole passage most resembles is the third and fourth volumes of the novel, in particular the chapters when the family of the Count de Villefort arrive at Chateau-le-Blanc and, shortly afterwards, help to rescue Emily from shipwreck, and the chapters which concentrate on the apparently haunted bedchamber in which the former mistress of the chateau died.

The housekeeper at the Chateau-le-Blanc is called Dorothée. On the first night that Blanche, the daughter of the Count de Villefort, spends at the chateau, she has to pass 'through a long oak gallery' to reach her bed-chamber, a room with 'spacious and lofty walls' and 'high anti-quated casements'. It has a 'gloomy air' and is in 'a remote situation', away from the rest of the family. The chamber is 'hung' with 'faded tap-estry'. Blanche's canopied bed is draped with 'blue damask'. Dorothée later remarks on Emily's similarity to her late mistress (unsurprisingly, since Emily is that lady's niece). A little later in his story Henry men-tions a fluttering tapestry which conceals a secret entrance; that, too, is a scene which takes place at the Chateau-le-Blanc.

Catherine doesn't seem to register any of these quite obvious sim-ilarities. 'I am sure your housekeeper is not really Dorothy', she says, half-doubtingly – surely if she'd actually read these chapters, she would have recognised not just the name but this part of the story, straight away, would realise that Henry is teasing her. She would get the joke, as Henry means for her to do. But it seems to sail over her head. Concerns about ghosts, madness, or secret entrances – all of which are prominent towards the end of *Udolpho* – never occur to her. Nor does she seem to realise that there's a character named 'Henri' in the novel – and that the name of Henri's sister Blanche, like the name Eleanor, is a French name, associated with European royalty.* Wouldn't the coincidence have caught her interest?

When Catherine finds the chest in her bedroom at the abbey, she's completely perplexed by the monogram; 'She could not, in whatever direction she took it, believe the last letter to be a T; and yet that it should be anything else in that house was a circumstance to raise no common degree of astonishment.' Why is she so astonished? The chest has presumably come from one of the women who married into the

---

*   One of the granddaughters of Eleanor of Aquitaine was named Blanche.

Tilney family. If Catherine has read the second half of *Udolpho*, she's encountered numerous examples of female characters inheriting property from other women.

Well, actually, all of this points to the same conclusion as her continued fascination with the character of Montoni: she hasn't read the second half of the novel. The characters of Henri and Blanche aren't introduced until the middle of the third volume; what Henry's Gothic story does, as well as igniting Catherine's imagination, is to indicate that, just as we ought to be suspecting from how little time she's spent reading, Catherine hasn't reached that point in the book yet. Thinking of Gothic buildings, she doesn't think about the Chateau-le-Blanc, the building which dominates the last third of *Udolpho*. She talks about buildings being 'uninhabited and left deserted for years, and then the family come back to it unawares, without giving any notice, as generally happens' – that's what happens with Udolpho, but in the case of the Chateau, servants are sent ahead from Paris to prepare the house.

Catherine, we're told, has brought both her writing desk and her netting box with her to Northanger; she hasn't brought *Udolpho*. We don't know where her copy of the novel – probably the property of a circulating library – even is at this point. She has no opportunity to return to the text. Catherine is, from the first, enthralled by *Udolpho* – 'I should like to spend my whole life in reading it', she says – and it seems that we're meant to understand that, in essence, this is what happens. She's destined never to complete the novel, to spend her whole life in the state of reading it, its mysteries remaining forever mysterious to her.

What Jane's trying to do here, it seems to me, is to keep Catherine trapped in a state of suspense which her own readers never have to share. Jane's readers, if they've read *Udolpho* properly, to the end, ought to be able to pick out all the references and in-jokes that pass Catherine by so completely. Jane's readers ought to be able to pat themselves on the back for recognising that the names Henry and Eleanor deliberately echo Henri and Blanche. They should know Catherine's suspicions about General Tilney are absurd precisely because she compares him to Montoni, and they're already aware, not only that Montoni hasn't murdered his wife, but that, in the second half of the novel, he doesn't pose any threat. Reading the second volume of *Northanger Abbey*, we ought to be continually coming across passages which we recognise already, anticipating scenes and settings and actions before they occur.

Any reader familiar with *Udolpho* ought to have been waiting for Catherine to find her way into Mrs Tilney's room – just as Emily St Aubert makes her way into the rooms of the dead Marchioness. Alerted by the close resemblance between Henry's story and the Chateau-le-Blanc chapters of *Udolpho*, they would have found echo after echo. Catherine shares her distaste for the new with Blanche, who prefers the 'antient' to 'the modern ... gay and elegant'. Like Blanche, she explores the building. The position of the late Mrs Tilney's room – in a 'gallery', close by a 'winding staircase' – seems intended to recall Blanche's discovery of the rooms of the Marchioness, that other dead mistress of a house ('she found herself in another gallery, one end of which was terminated by a back stair-case'). When Henry comes up the staircase, and finds Catherine loitering outside his mother's room, her reaction ('How came you here?' she demands, her voice one 'of more than common astonishment') corresponds to the aged Dorothée's surprise at unexpectedly finding Blanche: 'How could you find your way hither?' she asks, her 'countenance' marked with 'terror and surprise'.

All of this leads us to the rather odd conclusion that Catherine, at Northanger, is acting out parts of *Udolpho*, slipping from one role to another, but – apparently – without being aware of what she's doing.

It's only fair to mention that there is one point where Catherine does seem to refer consciously to a scene in the second half of *Udolpho* ('Would the veil in which Mrs Tilney had last walked, or the volume in which she had last read, remain to tell what nothing else was allowed to whisper?'), but this is one solitary, fleeting reference to weigh against every other indication in the text. She's ignorant of everything else.

It's not even entirely clear that we're in Catherine's mind at this point – the voice of the narrator is more intrusive in *Northanger* than it is in Jane's later novels, and far less deftly deployed. Then, too, there was, by 1803, a copper-plate illustration of precisely this scene in *Udolpho* – when Emily and Dorothée venture into the rooms of the dead Marchioness, untouched since her death years before.* Perhaps Jane means to indicate that Catherine has done no more than glance at the illustration in the fourth volume while Isabella Thorpe was reading it.

Catherine finds nothing Gothic in Mrs Tilney's room – no veils cracked with age, no prayer books, no discarded gloves. She's disappointed, and profoundly ashamed of herself. Henry's discovery of her compounds her feelings; he all but forces Catherine into naming her hazy suspicions about General Tilney, and then scolds her for doing so. In spite of the fact that he was the one to excite her expectations of Northanger when he might just as easily have calmed them, Henry appears genuinely appalled; 'What have you been judging from?' he demands, 'Dearest Miss Morland, what ideas have you been admitting?'

Poor Catherine scuttles off to her own room. Once there, she's quick to locate all the blame at the feet of 'Mrs Radcliffe'. There's no breath of criticism of Henry's foolish story-telling (that 'dearest' has perhaps had its effect). Catherine doesn't even really blame herself very much. She blames Gothic novels: 'She saw that the infatuation had been created, the mischief settled, long before her quitting Bath, and it seemed as if the whole might be traced to the influence of that sort of reading which she had there indulged.'

Critics have tended to agree with Catherine, but, as I think the reader must have been intended to recognise, this is grossly unfair. Jane has gone to quite a lot of trouble to suggest that Catherine either hasn't read more than half a Gothic novel, or, if she has, has read it with such a breathtaking lack of attention that she might as well not have bothered. If Catherine had read *Udolpho* properly, read it to the end, she

---

*   In a French edition of the novel from 1803.

would have discovered, in the final pages, one of Radcliffe's clearest messages: 'when the mind has once begun to yield [...] trifles impress it with the force of conviction'. Even as early as the first volume of *Udolpho*, Radcliffe remarks how 'lamentable' it is, that Emily's 'excellent understanding should have yielded, even for a moment, to the reveries of superstition, or rather to those starts of imagination, which deceive the senses'. If Catherine had taken that on board, her experiences at Northanger might have been very different.

What Jane is trying to show with Catherine, I would suggest, is a reader who doesn't read properly, who brings her own preconceptions and expectations to the text, who blames the author for the ideas she's gained from an incomplete, inattentive reading. Jane doesn't intend to 'desert' her sister-authoress Radcliffe, to expose her to ridicule. She's attempting to do the opposite.

∽

Jane indicates what Catherine hasn't read. But she also tells us what she has.

In the first chapter she names two of the texts which Catherine learned by heart as a child. We're told that Catherine has read Samuel Richardson's 1750s novel *Sir Charles Grandison* at home (or that she has heard it read aloud); it's a novel her mother likes. We know that she's read 'poetry and plays, and things of that sort' and does not 'dislike travels'. We know that she's read some history, though she doesn't care for it: 'it tells me nothing that does not either vex or weary me. The quarrels of popes and kings, with wars or pestilences, in every page; the men all so good for nothing, and hardly any women at all—it is very tiresome.'

Among Catherine's earliest introductions to reading were *The Beggar's Petition* and *The Hare and Many Friends*, a version of one of Aesop's fables. *The Hare and Many Friends*, with its combination of anthropomorphism and danger, and its suggestion of moral failings in the older generation, seems to have appealed quite strongly to Catherine who, we're told, learned it 'as quickly as any girl in England'. *The Beggar's Petition*, though, is, to the modern mind, a very odd choice of reading (and of learning by heart) for a small child. It deals with uncomfortable subjects: war, enclosure, abuse of power, the kind of subjects which – wrongly – we consider distant from Jane's novels.

Sir Charles Grandison features a young heiress kidnapped by the villainous (and extravagantly-named) Sir Hargrave Pollexfen. She's eventually rescued by the heroic Sir Charles Grandison, dully virtuous except in the small matter of his engagement to a mentally unstable Italian Catholic. Catherine's history reading seems to have been concentrated largely in the middle ages, perhaps stretching as far as the Tudors. We can't be certain which plays and poems she's read, but we're told specifically which ones she can quote (or misquote) from: *Elegy to the Memory of an Unfortunate Lady*, by Alexander Pope; Thomas Gray's *Elegy in a Country Churchyard*; James Thomson's *The Seasons*; and three Shakespeare plays – *Othello*, *Measure for Measure*, and *Twelfth Night*.

It's just as much these texts that Catherine is 'judging from' as her incomplete, uncomprehending reading of *Udolpho*. The wider literary climate, the texts which are accepted reading, do as much to influence Catherine's ideas as Mrs Radcliffe does.

When Catherine is first beginning to give way to her extravagant suspicions of General Tilney, she compares him to Montoni, but also to the people she's read about in history books: 'many instances of beings equally hardened in guilt might [...] be produced. She could remember dozens who had persevered in every possible vice, murdering whomsoever they chose, without any feeling of humanity or remorse; till a violent death, or a religious retirement closed their black career.' *Elegy to the Memory of an Unfortunate Lady*, with its 'ghost' and corpse left unburied, practically qualifies as Gothic. We're informed that Catherine has 'read too much not to be perfectly aware of the ease with which a waxen figure might be introduced, and a suppositious funeral carried on'. If she ever ventured further in her Shakespeare, she would have encountered plenty of 'suppositious funerals', plenty of characters whose deaths are faked – Juliet, Hero in *Much Ado About Nothing*, Helena in *All's Well That Ends Well*, Imogen in *Cymbeline*, Hermione in *A Winter's Tale*, who, towards the end of the play, appears disguised as a statue of herself. Catherine may have read Lewis Theobald's *The Fatal Secret*, an eighteenth-century reworking of Webster's *The Duchess of Malfi* with a happy ending in which the Duchess is hidden safely away, and her would-be murderous brother deceived by 'a waxen image'. Both history and drama will have furnished her with husbands who succeed in murdering their wives – Othello, Iago, Henry VIII.

There are plenty of cultural sources for Catherine's wilder imaginings besides Gothic novels.

And actually, Archbishop Whateley, an early reviewer of *Northanger Abbey*, makes almost exactly this point in his review of the book, that it's foolish for parents to ban novels while allowing uncontrolled access to other forms of literature:

> [...] we are acquainted with a careful mother whose daughters, while they never in their lives read a novel of any kind, are permitted to peruse, without reserve, any plays that happen to fall in their way; and with another, from whom no lessons, however excellent, of wisdom and piety, contained in a prose-fiction, can obtain quarter; but who, on the other hand, is no less indiscriminately indulgent to her children in the article of tales in verse, of whatever character [...]

Catherine's 'indulgence' in *Udolpho* is only the match to a pile of literary and cultural fuel; what burns, what drives her behaviour, are half-remembered episodes from English history, Shakespeare's plays, anti-Catholicism. The chest and cabinet she nerves herself to throw open, searching for secrets, glance towards the novel in which William Godwin – perhaps the most radical of the 1790s radicals – laid bare the state of 'things as they are'. There are stronger, more deeply-rooted forces drawing Catherine towards Mrs Tilney's bedroom than a few pages of a novel, or a copper-plate illustration.

We've been skirting round these bedroom scenes for quite long enough; it's time to get to grips with them.

⬥

One of the central characters in David Lodge's series of campus novels is an American academic, Morris Zapp. Zapp works on Jane Austen. He aims to produce a completely exhaustive study of Jane's novels. His teaching is supposedly 'designed to shock … students out of a sloppily reverent attitude to literature'. But it becomes clear that he in fact just likes to shock. In one tutorial he reads aloud to his students 'the moment in *Persuasion* when Captain Wentworth lifted the little brat Walter off Anne Elliot's shoulders', dwelling on all the vaguely suggestive words before demanding, 'If that isn't an *orgasm*, what is it?'

The students are 'flabbergasted', and so is the reader. The more complicated bit of the joke is that this isn't total nonsense. As we've seen, Jane isn't a prude; nor were her contemporaries, the people she expected to read her work. But Zapp's picked the wrong book. Of all Jane's novels it's not *Persuasion* but *Northanger Abbey* which comes closest to sexual explicitness.

Despite what the film adaptations would have you believe, we don't often see Jane's heroines in their nightgowns or their underwear. In *Northanger Abbey*, we do. Its three bedroom scenes are charged – entirely deliberately – with an erotic thrill. You don't have to be Morris Zapp to find them sexy.

In the first, the half-dressed Catherine flings open the lid of a chest to find 'a white cotton counterpane, properly folded'. A counterpane is a bed-cover – usually embroidered, often with quilt-work. It's removed when the bed is in use. Jane invites us, here, to see the bed behind Catherine, ready for her to slip into, that night.

In the second scene, it *is* night. Catherine, we are to assume, has changed into nightwear. She is 'beginning to think of stepping into bed, when, on giving a parting glance round the room, she was struck by the appearance of a high, old-fashioned black cabinet'. What she finds in the cabinet is a far cry from the 'diamonds' which Henry laughingly promised: petty accounts, a bill for treating a horse, and laundry lists, for a man, a list of a man's clothes – 'shirts, stockings, cravats, and waistcoats' – a list which conjures up the image of a naked male body.

And the passage which describes how she comes to find it is probably the sexiest thing you'll read in Jane's novels:

> [...] she applied herself to the key, and after moving it in every possible way for some instants with the determined celerity of hope's last effort, the door suddenly yielded to her hand: her heart leaped with exultation at such a victory, and having thrown open each folding door [...] a double range of small drawers appeared in view, with some larger drawers above and below them; and in the centre, a small door, closed also with a lock and key, secured in all probability a cavity of importance.
>
> Catherine's heart beat quick, but her courage did not fail her. With a cheek flushed by hope, and an eye straining with curiosity, her fingers grasped the handle of a drawer and drew it forth. [...] The place in the middle alone remained now unexplored [...] It was some time however before she could unfasten the door, the same difficulty occurring in the management of this inner lock as of the outer; but at length it did open; and not vain, as hitherto, was her search; her quick eyes directly fell on a roll of paper pushed back into the further part of the cavity, apparently for concealment, and her feelings at that moment were indescribable. Her heart fluttered, her knees trembled, and her cheeks grew pale. She seized, with an unsteady hand, the precious manuscript [...]

Let's not mince words here. With all those folds and cavities, the key, the fingers, the fluttering and trembling, this looks a lot like a thinly veiled description of female masturbation.

And that's not so extraordinary. Jane's society viewed it as common knowledge that girls, as well as boys, indulged in the 'secret and destructive vice'. Youthful female self-pleasuring was something to be worried about. A series of newspaper advertisements for Balm of Gilead, that late-eighteenth-century panacea for everything to do with your bits, mentions that the youth 'of both sexes' engaged in the practice.

The third bedroom scene is about sex too.

Catherine dreams of one day, perhaps, becoming 'Mrs Tilney'. Part of her motivation for wanting to see Mrs Tilney's room must be to imagine herself into the role of a married woman, to try out what it's like to venture across that threshold. Indeed, Eleanor Tilney's eagerness to show her mother's room to Catherine hints at a not-unrelated desire to bring her prospective sister-in-law into proximity with the 'mother' she will never have a chance to know.

The first object to strike Catherine's eye, when she finally does enter the room, is the bed. It's 'arranged as unoccupied', with a counterpane (and perhaps bed-hangings) of 'dimity' – white cotton, with a pattern worked into the weave. The counterpane is similar, perhaps even identical, to the 'white cotton counterpane' which was removed from the bed in Catherine's room and placed into the chest. Mrs Tilney's room is flooded with daylight, the modern 'Bath stove' is 'bright'. The wardrobes are made from 'mahogany', a wood which wasn't much used in furniture-making until the eighteenth century; the chairs are 'neatly painted'. The bed, too, one imagines, is modern. It's not without history, though. This is the bed – one presumes – in which Mrs Tilney gave birth, and 'lay in' with her babies, perhaps where she breast-fed them. This is the bed in which she conceived her children. The counterpane hasn't always lain smooth and flat. The bed-linen hasn't always been white and unsullied.

Is country-bred Catherine, the fourth of ten children, ignorant of how babies come into the world? Surely not. She must have seen her own mother lying in, a new brother or sister in her arms, squashed and shrieking, the bloodied sheets being bundled downstairs. The Morlands' country vicarage may be far less Gothic than an abbey, but it's had its own, temporary torture chamber at times, and Catherine will have heard the screams.

For those who wonder, endlessly, why Jane never married, there's a reason right here. Mrs Tilney's room – the only marital bedroom Jane ever shows us in detail – is associated, indelibly, with death. Not only is this the room in which, as we're told, Mrs Tilney died, it's a room haunted by the ghosts of literature, by the dead Marchioness' suite at the Chateau-le-Blanc; by Blue Beard's chamber, filled with the corpses of his dead wives.

It's haunted not just by dead women, but by women who've been murdered by their husbands.

Catherine, shamed at being caught outside Mrs Tilney's room, humiliated by the scolding she receives from Henry, disowns her suspicions of General Tilney. As we've seen, she blames Gothic novels alone for sending her imagination haywire, and not any of the more enduring cultural patterns and ideas she has been exposed to:

> Charming as were all Mrs Radcliffe's works, and charming even as were the works of her imitators, it was not in them perhaps that human nature, at least in the midland counties of England, was to be looked for. Of the Alps and Pyrenees, with their pine forests and their vices, they might give a faithful delineation; and Italy, Switzerland, and the South of France, might be as fruitful in horrors as they were there represented. But in the central part of England there was surely some security for the existence even of a wife not beloved, in the laws of the land, and the manners of the age. Murder was not tolerated, servants were not slaves, and neither poison nor sleeping potions to be procured, like rhubarb, from every druggist.

What Catherine's surely forgetting here is that a husband doesn't need sleeping potions to effectively immobilise his wife, and nor does he necessarily require poison to kill her. Rhubarb was used as a purgative and, in high enough doses, could affect a pregnancy. Pregnant women are still warned against drinking herbal teas containing rhubarb leaves. Is it coincidence that, of all the products a 'druggist' might sell, Jane chooses to mention rhubarb, that she reminds us of pregnancy, and the possibility that it might be unwanted, in this sentence, in the context of husbands killing their wives?

Henry asserts that his mother died from what he calls 'bilious fever', a 'malady ... from which she had often suffered ... its cause therefore constitutional'. It's a catch-all term; used to cover everything from cholera and yellow fever to common-or-garden stomach upsets. Jane's mother and several of her brothers suffered periodically from bilious complaints. An acquaintance, a young woman called Marianne Mapleton, died of her bilious fever.

But 'bilious' symptoms are vomiting, abdominal pain, constipation and diarrhoea; these are also signs of pregnancy, and of the early stages of labour or of miscarriage. Mrs Tilney, at the time of her death, would still have been of child-bearing age. The 'physician' who first attends her is 'one in whom she had always placed great confidence' – one who helped her in her earlier confinements, perhaps. Two others are called in; to do what? Mrs Tilney clearly isn't suffering from cholera or yellow fever, because her sons are permitted to see her. The treatment for the less dramatic bilious fevers was to bleed the patient and wait. But in cases of pregnancy and labour there were different approaches and treatments to try. We ought to consider the possibility that Jane's first readers might well have considered – that what Henry is unwittingly describing here is a miscarriage or disastrously mismanaged early labour, that Mrs Tilney's 'constitutional' tendency to biliousness is in fact a series of pregnancies and miscarriages.

Why, after all, does General Tilney 'not love' his wife's 'favourite walk'? Why is he unwilling to allow his daughter to show Catherine into his wife's room? Does he have a guilty conscience? Well, yes, perhaps.

This, in the end, is the mystery, the terrifying secret at the heart of *Northanger Abbey*. If we laughed at the hilarious notion of Catherine's mother dying during one of her ten pregnancies and labours, then this is where we should stop laughing; sex can kill you. All of Jane's heroines – all of the women in her novels who marry – are taking a terrifying risk. They're placing their lives, potentially, in the hands of their husbands.

Catherine, Jane tells us, abandons the 'alarms of romance' for the 'anxieties of common life'. It's probably going to be a while before she'll be able to enjoy the 'alarms of romance' again, but we can only hope that she carries on reading novels, that she keeps up a library subscription. There may come a time when the anxieties of common life – pregnancy, childbirth – begin to seem far more threatening than the nightmares conjured up by Mrs Radcliffe. Catherine might learn to value a library more for the medicines it sells – the Balm of Gilead, the 'female pills' that promise to 'restore' the menstrual cycle – than for mere novels.

William Dent, William Moore, *The Wise Man of the East* (1788). The greed, luxury, and rapaciousness of the East India Company are here depicted at the very heart of Britain itself, in the person of the king, George III. The man in the turban is identified as Warren Hastings, who was personally known to the Austen family.

CHAPTER 3

The Age of Brass

Sense and Sensibility

Steventon, January 1801. *

Jane, standing just inside the church porch, looks out on a gloomy prospect. The bare branches of the trees, the low cloud, the rain, sharp and freezing, like tiny pins run in under the skin. The yew tree close by the door drips, and against its dark needles the red berries glow.

That's a baleful tree, young Jenny, that is. Bide here by me, little maid, and never touch it.

Later, when she was a little older, and had come to think it a silly country superstition, she had laughed, superior. But it was true enough. Her father had said so, had found the passage in – Caesar? Tacitus? – and translated it for her, word for word, as she leaned against his shoulder. A long summer evening, long ago.

The tenor of the rain changes, it becomes sleet, hail, drumming down on the roof, jumping and bouncing on the grass. The weather has set in, for the present. She places her basket on the floor and, bending down, works at the fastenings of her pattens. They are caked in mud. Her ankles ache from the effort of staying upright, of sliding and slithering along the lanes. Madness to go out in such weather. She wipes her feet, very thoroughly, and then lifts the latch and slips into the church. It had seemed so large when she was a little girl. How many times has

---

* Based on Jane Austen's letters to Cassandra Austen (3rd–5th January 1801 and 8th–9th January 1801).

she done this? A thousand, three thousand? There are not many times left to her.

Scarcely a day passes without visitors coming to the house, now that everyone in the neighbourhood knows they are to leave it. And each visitor has a cousin or an uncle or an acquaintance, who got quite stout at Bath, though the medical men had despaired of them entirely, who found the waters of no benefit at all, and preferred Harrogate or the Hot-Wells at Bristol, who married a post-captain with a fortune in prize-money and now live in a great way in London.

This morning James's wife arrived with a party of friends. Mary looks on the house as quite her own, already, it appears. The house and every stick of furniture in it. No, Jane was quite forgetting. They are to take the beds with them to Bath. But the tables, the sideboards, the chests of drawers, the pictures, her piano, the books—

Naturally – naturally – they cannot take all the furniture with them. Of course they cannot. She realises that. And who is she to disagree, if her father and her mother approve the plan? Only it seems hard, when James is set to inherit from their uncle, that he should be given all this as well.

And so sudden a decision, too, for her parents to throw off everything they have known for 40 years as if it has become, all at once, a burden too great for them to bear, as if they cannot be rid of it – the farms, the bailiffs, the house and everything in it, this church – too quickly for their liking.

Jane, walking slowly up the aisle, has arrived in front of the altar. She turns, and traces a stone in the floor with the toe of one boot. Jane Leigh. Her grandmother, dead before she was born. Jane's own mother has hardly ever spoken of her.

It is the way of the world, is it not? Women hardly matter. They pass from one family to another, and are never truly part of either.

The rain has ceased. She ought to go back. She cannot stay here.

Jane never knew any of her grandparents. They all died before she was born. Her father was an orphan by the time he was seven. Cast out of their home by a wicked stepmother, he and his sisters were thrown on the charity of aunts and uncles. Thomas Leigh – Jane's mother's father – was a clergyman and fellow of All Souls College Oxford. He died shortly before Jane's parents got married; the timing suggests, indeed, that he may have opposed the relationship.

The only grandparent whose life really came close to touching Jane's was her maternal grandmother, her namesake Jane Leigh, *née* Walker. As well as the blunt genealogical details – that she was born, that she was related to families of Walkers and Perrots, that she married, had six children, and was widowed – we know that she lived with her daughter and son-in-law in the vicarage at Steventon for a time before she died. She's buried in the churchyard there. Inside the church, a small square stone, so plain as to be almost entirely pointless, is set slantwise into the floor by the altar. It doesn't even mention her maiden name.

Few of the characters in Jane's novels are grandparents, except to the youngest of grandchildren; and none of her central heroes or heroines has a single grandparent living.* A reader might imagine that no one survived much beyond 50 in the early nineteenth century, though in fact, if you adjust for the far higher rates of infant and maternal mortality, life expectancy wasn't so very much lower than it is today.

In their secret hearts, though, there were those who might have wished that it was.

In Britain, in the early nineteenth century, land was everything. If you wanted to sit on a jury, to serve as a magistrate, to vote in elections, to hunt, it was the ownership of land over a certain value which qualified you to do it. Without land, you were nothing, certainly not a fully-functioning member of society. Add a desire to mimic the behaviour of the aristocracy, and, on top of that, the fact that

---

* Jane Fairfax, in *Emma*, has a living grandmother, but Mrs Bates is very much an exception to the general rule.

a woman's property automatically became her husband's when she married, unless complex legal documents were drawn up first, and it starts to become apparent why family estates were almost always left to eldest sons. Where land was power and influence, only a fool would choose to squander that influence or to see it pass into another family altogether.

If you were to die tomorrow intestate – that is, without leaving a testament, a will – modern English law would hand your property, up to a certain amount, to your spouse.* If you were worth more, a portion would be set aside for your children. If you had neither children nor spouse, then your property would track back up your family tree – parents, siblings, nieces and nephews, grandparents, aunts and uncles, cousins, and so on. The division is based, essentially, on the degree of their biological relationship to you; it's mathematically exact, scrupulously equal. People who have been legally adopted into your family are included; so too, in most cases, are family members born outside marriage.

Two hundred years ago, intestacy worked very differently.

In the absence of any other financial arrangements, a widow was entitled to 'jointure' – that is, she could use a third of her late husband's property until she died, when it would be reabsorbed into his estate. But if, say, a man died unmarried leaving two sons, three daughters, and no will, all his land – every square inch of it – would be handed straight to the oldest son. Intestacy law wouldn't hand full legal ownership of land to a wife. It would hand it to a daughter, or daughters, only when there were no sons. And in that case, in a return to what feels more like natural fairness, the sisters would all inherit equally. But illegitimate children weren't included at all.

There are countries where it's impossible to disinherit any of your children. In eighteenth-century England, the state was waiting to do it

---

* It is possible in certain circumstances for children to make a claim on this first amount.

for you. Primogeniture amounted almost to a fetish and first-born sons were very nearly sacred.

Jane's extended family included aristocrats, and money, too.* There was an estate – Stoneleigh Abbey, in Warwickshire – shimmering mirage-like in the distance. But the life Jane's parents lived wasn't aristocratic or monied or propertied. If Grandfather Leigh really had been loth to acquire Mr Austen as a son-in-law, he had a point. George Austen wasn't that much of a catch. He had no fortune or property; he had hardly any family behind him – no financial resources, no network of support. His only asset was the distant relationship to the Knights – the couple who essentially gave him the job at Steventon and ended up adopting his son Edward. It's easy to laugh at Mary Crawford, when in *Mansfield Park* she asserts that 'there is generally an uncle or a grandfather to leave a fortune to the second son'. It's wishful thinking, a sign of how privileged – and spoiled – she is, but younger children couldn't live on air, and the fewer relations they had, the less chance there was of anyone leaving them anything.

The Austen parents had inherited only very small sums of money themselves; they had eight children. They'd always known that whenever the Reverend George Austen died, the rectory at Steventon would be needed for the new vicar and his family.

Their behaviour as parents indicates a certain amount of hard-headed practicality in the face of this knowledge. They gave up one son to the rich relatives who lacked an heir of their own. The two youngest sons – Frank and Charles – were sent off to the navy as children. Joining the army, even as a junior officer, cost a substantial amount of money; joining the navy didn't.

But, in spite of the fact that they had so little to leave, and so many children, in spite of the fact that Mr Austen knew for himself what it

---

* The family were apparently very proud of their connection to the Dukes of Chandos – Jane's nephew James-Edward Austen-Leigh devotes several pages of his memoir to explaining the connection, though it wasn't particularly close.

was like to be disinherited, they couldn't shake off the cultural prejudice in favour of oldest sons.

At the end of 1800 Jane's father decided to hand his parish over to his eldest son James and retire to Bath. Mr Austen could easily have done what most other vicars did when they felt that the demands of the job were getting too much: he could have employed a curate (a junior clergyman), reserving most of the parish income for himself, or, indeed, saving it to leave among his children. Instead, he gave the lion's share of his income, the family home, and almost everything in it to James.

James had a daughter, Anna, by his first marriage. In 1798, his second wife Mary had given birth to a son. This son – the James-Edward who would later become Jane's second biographer – wasn't the first Austen grandson, but he was the first who was at all likely to carry on the family name. Edward's children were nominally Austens, but it was already apparent that Edward would probably have to change his surname to that of his adoptive parents. Frank and Charles weren't, in 1800, in a position to think of marrying. George junior (subject to mysterious fits, seldom mentioned) would never do so. Henry, whose wife was nearing 40, appeared unlikely to produce children of his own.

In James, and his son, lay the future of the Austen line, as far as Mr Austen was concerned. Even so, abandoning his job, his position, his house, as he did, was a very unusual decision to take.

In 1805, announcing the news of their father's death to her brother Frank, Jane called him an 'excellent' parent, full of 'tenderness'.[1] But however indulgent he might otherwise have been – buying Jane notebooks, encouraging her in her writing, perhaps even teaching her a smattering of Latin – he did very little for her, in terms of securing her future.* He clearly believed that sons, especially eldest sons, were of greater importance than daughters. It was irrelevant that James was

---

* Jane certainly knew a little Latin. One of the notebooks in which her youthful writing is preserved is inscribed, in Latin, 'ex doni mei patris' ('Given to me by my father'), and she includes Latin phrases in her letters on more than one occasion.

already able to support himself and his family, and had expectations of inheriting from a rich uncle – his comfort and security, his pride, mattered more than that of his sisters. Mr and Mrs Austen, in fact, hardly seem to have considered their daughters. Perhaps they imagined that Edward, adopted into luxury, would always keep a roof over their heads. No effort was made to provide the Austen girls with even the smallest of independent dowries. Cassandra inherited a little money on the death of her fiancé, enough that she would always be just about able to support herself. She'd been lucky to find a man who was willing to marry her, when she had nothing to bring to the table.

Jane was penniless. Her father may have loved her, but at his death he left her nothing at all, and even before he died, he'd made her homeless.

∞

Nowhere in her surviving letters is Jane openly critical of her father, or of her brothers. But in both *Sense and Sensibility* and *Pride and Prejudice* she permits herself to write about the carelessness, and thoughtlessness, of men who do nothing to provide for their female dependants, and to touch on female financial anxiety, and the psychological pressures of being beholden to more fortunate relations.

Readers influenced by the screen adaptations of *Pride and Prejudice* may see Mr Bennet as an affable, mildly eccentric, delightfully humorous father. Jane makes it clear, though, that he is dangerously lax – ineffectual, incompetent. According to Lizzy, her father has 'talents', but they have not been 'rightly used' – a damning indictment in a church-going culture still steeped in the language and stories of the Bible.* He has

---

* The sentence structure here looks like a fairly explicit reference to the parable of the talents in Matthew 25:14–30 which, on a literal reading at least, praises investment and financial savviness over laziness, or even caution. The parable concludes with the warning that the rich do inherit the earth: 'For unto every one that hath shall be given, and he shall have abundance: but from him that hath not shall be taken away even that which he hath.'

not 'done his duty' – his financial duty. When Mr Bennet was first married, 'economy was held to be perfectly useless'. When, later, he began to wish that 'instead of spending his whole income, he had laid by an annual sum for the better provision of his children, and of his wife, if she survived him', he only wished it, and failed to actually do anything, persuading himself that 'it was too late to begin saving'.

Elinor and Marianne's father, in *Sense and Sensibility*, is another financial incompetent, far happier to live off other people than to take the trouble of husbanding his own fortune, or of earning money for himself. We're given ample information to enable us to work out his financial situation and to judge of the common sense – or otherwise – shown by his behaviour over the years. Though his own independent fortune is small, his first wife was an heiress (her fortune 'had been large'), and until he himself dies he enjoys half the income from her money. When he was first invited to live with his uncle, the financially prudent course would have been to rent out his own property at Stanhill, rather than to sell it. If he'd done that, then there would have been twelve years of rental income to put aside for his second family and – crucially – they would still have owned the house itself.

Can we trace these fictional examples of financial mismanagement back into Jane's own life? Perhaps. It's difficult to pin down the composition of either novel to a particular point in time. There was, by 1799, a manuscript known as *First Impressions*.* Whether or not this is the manuscript which Jane's father sent to the high-profile publisher Thomas Cadell in 1797 we simply don't know; nor can we be sure that *First Impressions* became *Pride and Prejudice* – plenty of character reassessment goes on in *Sense and Sensibility*, after all, and indeed in all of Jane's novels. The family tradition that there was an earlier version of *Sense and Sensibility* entitled *Elinor and Marianne* is just that, family tradition, possibly true, possibly complete fiction, just like the often-repeated

---

* 'I do not wonder at your wanting to read first impressions [*sic*] again', writes Jane in a letter to her sister (8th–9th January 1799).

assertion that either or both of the books were originally written in the form of letters between the characters.

But it's certainly conceivable that *Sense and Sensibility* was first written, in some form, during the 1790s. A reference to 'a needle book made by some emigrant', given as a gift, indicates a setting during the period when London was full of refugees from the French Revolution, many of them impoverished and reliant on charity. The term was fairly common during that decade (a 1793 poem by the popular writer Charlotte Smith is entitled *The Emigrants*) but was falling out of use by the time of publication in 1811, at least in England: its presence is likely to have made the novel seem either a little dated or historical to its first readers.

A sister of Colonel Brandon's – referred to only once, in passing – is, somewhat unexpectedly, in Avignon in the south of France, for her health. This suggests a very much more restricted time setting: 1802–3, during the Peace of Amiens, the only period between 1794 and 1814 when travel to France was possible. Marianne admires the poetry of William Cowper – a poet we'll encounter again – and of Walter Scott. Cowper's work was popular throughout the 1790s and the first decades of the nineteenth century and so doesn't give us any indication as to time.

Nowadays Scott is best known for his novels (*Ivanhoe*, *Rob Roy*) but from 1805 he found fame as a poet. There were earlier books of his poetry – a collection of translated German ballads, published in 1796, and *The Minstrelsy of the Scottish Border*, which appeared at the beginning of the following decade. But Scott wasn't anything like as widely known in the 1790s as he became a few years later. Mentioning his name would, though, have been an easy way to update the novel in 1811.

There are one or two other elements in *Sense and Sensibility* which may perhaps point to revision taking place after 1805, and even as late as 1809–10. As we saw in Chapter 1, it was in the summer of 1809 that Jane, her sister Cassandra, their mother, and their old friend Martha Lloyd set up home together in the village of Chawton in Hampshire, in a cottage made available to them by Edward Austen. Edward owned a large house and estate at Chawton in addition to his Kentish property.

Chawton Cottage resembles, in almost every particular, even name, Barton Cottage, the small house to which the Dashwood women – all four of them – are obliged to remove:

> As a house, Barton Cottage, though small, was comfortable and compact; but as a cottage it was defective, for the building was regular, the roof was tiled, the window shutters were not painted green, nor were the walls covered with honeysuckles. A narrow passage led directly through the house into the garden behind. On each side of the entrance was a sitting room, about sixteen feet square; and beyond them were the offices and the stairs. Four bed-rooms and two garrets formed the rest of the house.

This could almost be a description of Chawton Cottage, which is now open to visitors as the Jane Austen House Museum.* Both the real and the fictional cottages are part of the estate of a rich male relation.

Edward's generosity was welcome, but it was a trifle tardy. The Reverend Austen had died in January 1805, meaning that it took Edward four and a half years to get around to providing his widowed mother and his sisters with a home, four and a half years in which the Austen women had moved from Green Park Buildings to other sets of rooms in Bath, first on Gay Street, then on Trim Street; had paid lengthy visits to Kent, to Bristol, to Gloucestershire, to Staffordshire, before moving to Southampton, to the house in Castle Square where we encountered Jane at the beginning of Chapter 1. So far as we can tell, the offer of the cottage at Chawton arose almost immediately after the death of Edward's wife Elizabeth – an intriguing coincidence, though one about which we can do no more than speculate.

---

* After the death of Jane's sister, Cassandra, Chawton Cottage was divided and used as homes for estate workers. The current floorplan is an approximation of what it would have been when Jane lived there.

This isn't the only apparent autobiographical echo in *Sense and Sensibility*. The annual income of the Dashwood women, after Mr Dashwood has died, is £500. The Austen women had around £450 per annum to keep themselves on, plus Martha Lloyd's contribution. Readers who leap to disliking Lucy Steele should perhaps bear in mind that there exists a degree of similarity between Lucy, who becomes engaged to a young man who's been educated by her uncle, and Jane's own sister, Cassandra, whose fiancé had been a pupil at the school the Reverend Austen ran at Steventon. The Steele sisters, who are very often away from home, and who pay for their board and lodging in the houses of various relations and acquaintances by entertaining any children, are not so very different to Jane and Cassandra. It's clear from Jane's letters that the two went on frequent visits, and were expected to take on quite a substantial amount of childcare when they did.

Whether it was intended or not, the most painful echo surely lies in the opening pages of *Sense and Sensibility*, where the security of the Dashwood girls, and their mother, is sacrificed to the future of a toddling little boy; where a home, and almost everything in it, is lost, taken over by a sister-in-law who is seen as a usurper. This – as we know from Jane's letters of January 1801 – is very much what happened, what she felt had happened, in her own family. The family home given up; financial possibilities sacrificed, and all for a small boy who was unlikely to want for much, all for a dream of carrying on the family name, of shoring up the family legacy. Was James Austen's wife Mary, who brought friends to look around the Steventon vicarage while her in-laws were still living there, a real-life version of *Sense and Sensibility*'s acquisitive Fanny Dashwood, with her eye for 'china' and 'any handsome article of furniture'? Well, perhaps. It's tempting to believe so. At any rate, Jane specifically states that the Dashwood women take both the 'books' and Marianne's 'handsome pianoforte' away with them, which is more than she had been allowed to do herself.

❦

The novel begins with the words, 'The family of Dashwood had been long settled in Sussex'. But 'family', it soon becomes clear, can expand or shrink at will. There's little that is truly settled about the Dashwoods.

The 'old gentleman' who we meet so briefly in the first paragraph, and whose last will and testament precipitates the plot, is the only survivor of his generation – an oldest son, who had 'a sister' (either unmarried or widowed, since she lived with him until her death) and, clearly, a younger brother. We know the last fact because the old gentleman has a nephew who shares his surname and is 'the legal inheritor' of the estate, that is, the person who would inherit it under intestacy laws. This is the first instance of a sibling pattern that we see repeated over and over again in the novel – a pattern of two brothers and a sister. It's so neat a way of examining the question of inheritance that it looks very much as if it must be design.

Other examples of the pattern are the Ferrars – Edward, the oldest, Robert, the second son, and Fanny, who marries into the Dashwood family – and the Brandons – Colonel Brandon had an older brother who is now dead, and he has, we know, a sister. It also appears in the family of Sir John Middleton, where, though we're once told that there are four children, only three are particularised – John, 'the second boy' William, and 'sweet little Annamaria', small cousins of the Dashwood sisters.

An early and generally very favourable review of the novel in the conservative, Church of England-affiliated *British Critic* announced that 'there is a little perplexity in the genealogy of the first chapter, and the reader is somewhat bewildered among half-sisters, cousins, and so forth'.[2] The bewilderment is deliberate, or so it seems to me. What Jane describes in the opening is the setting up of an entail – the same legal device for controlling inheritance which menaces the future well-being of the Bennet sisters in Jane's next novel, *Pride and Prejudice*, and the Crawley family in the recent long-running television series *Downton Abbey*.

Entails were only ever able to exist because English law assumes that something can be owned in two different ways by different people simultaneously.* Say I own a pen – it's my pen, I bought it with money I earned myself. Legally and morally that pen is mine, there's no question. I can do whatever I like with it: throw it away, give it away, sell it, leave it to a cats' home in my will. But say I was left a watch by my grandfather and that his will also stated I should leave the watch to my eldest daughter. From the moment I inherit it with that instruction attached, she part-owns it too, the two of us own it together. I can wear it or keep it in a drawer, just as I like, but I can't sell it, I can't leave it to my nephew, and I can't give it away. It has to go to her after my death, because she has a kind of ownership of it already – equitable ownership – and that ownership is enforceable through the courts.

What the old gentleman does in his will – and what some ancestor of the Bennet family must have done too – is a more complicated version of this. In simple terms, he leaves Norland Park, the Dashwood family estate, to three individuals at the same time: his nephew, his great-nephew, and his great-great-nephew. His nephew owns it, but not outright; John Dashwood, and his son, little Harry, have ownership too, though they don't have the right to use Norland until it's their 'turn', so to speak. This doesn't just control inheritance, it means that Elinor and Marianne's father is hugely restricted as to what he can do with the property: 'it was secured, in such a way, as to leave [...] no power of providing for those who were most dear to him, and who most needed a provision by any charge on the estate, or by any sale of its valuable woods.' He can't raise a mortgage, because the land isn't his to mortgage. He can't sell the timber, because that counts as 'waste' – defrauding the other owners. But when John Dashwood takes over Norland, he can't do those things either. And depending on the exact legal phrasing, this is a state of affairs that could continue

---

* The Law of Property Act 1925 banned the setting up of new entails, but a number are still running, though the courts have become slightly more sympathetic to the idea of forcibly breaking them.

indefinitely, with no one owner ever actually being able to deal freely with the property.*

An entail basically forces adherence to primogeniture on a family – it makes explicit the superiority and greater importance of oldest sons.[†] No one else matters – not siblings, not widows, not younger sons, and certainly not daughters. Given that the term 'family tree' already existed before Jane was born, it isn't such a stretch to wonder whether the name Dashwood was chosen deliberately. What she's sketching out for her readers in the opening of the novel is, after all, a family tree in which all the extraneous branches and twigs are broken off, and cast aside.

The opening chapter is bewildering because the concept it describes is. Jane is making explicit a deeply held (and deeply inconsistent) cultural belief – that women, the very people who are supposed to spend their life at home, in the bosom of their families, don't really belong there. Whatever the domestic contribution of the Dashwood women – the 'solid comfort' and 'cheerfulness' they have provided, the 'attention' they have given – it's worth nothing at all, its 'value' can easily

---

* It was possible to break an entail if the individual (or individuals) lower down the 'chain' of inheritance were agreeable. Some form of financial arrangement would be agreed or, if all the individuals were within the nuclear family, emotional pressure could be brought to bear. Three-generation entails, though, usually couldn't be broken unless everyone with rights was over the age of 21 so this couldn't happen with the Dashwoods anyway.

† It was equally feasible, in theory, to leave property to a line of, say, second-born daughters, but, for the reasons I outlined above, oldest sons was the norm. It may well be, though, that the original Bennet entail in *Pride and Prejudice* stipulated inheritance by eldest son, eldest grandson, great-grandson, etc., with a provision that if that male line failed, inheritance should flip to the male line descended from a daughter. This would explain why Mr Collins and Mr Bennet have different surnames, though it's also possible that either side of the family may have changed surnames in order to marry an heiress, or to inherit from another relative, both of which happened sufficiently often during the eighteenth century that the circumstance wasn't thought of as remarkable. There are two examples of it in Jane's own close family, in addition to her brother Edward's adoption.

be outweighed, ignored, dismissed. Behind Elinor and Marianne and Margaret and their mother are a whole imaginary army of others, generations of them, a disinherited multitude of Dashwoods both male and female.

Jane wasn't alone in questioning the fundamental fairness of primogeniture. The feminist writer Mary Wollstonecraft did it too, in her 1792 book *A Vindication of the Rights of Woman*, asserting that 'children of the same parents' have 'an equal right'. The passage in which she makes this claim is worth looking at more closely.

Wollstonecraft begins by talking about the common opposition between male 'reason' and female 'sensibility', before moving on to discuss how women are persuaded – or coerced – into devoting themselves to 'the duties of a mother and the mistress of a family'. Next Wollstonecraft touches on inherited wealth, on its tendency to promote selfishness and vice, a state of affairs which she suggests will persist 'till hereditary possessions are spread abroad [i.e. more widely]'. Then she goes back to talking about sensibility, about how women's 'power' is 'sensibility' and how 'men not aware of the consequence, do all they can to make this power swallow up every other'. For Wollstonecraft, 'female sensibility' becomes akin to sexual responsiveness; society being what it is, women are prepared and educated for only one thing – attracting a marriage partner. If they fail to do so, their sensibility is no use to them at all, because it's no use to anyone else.

Girls, who have been thus weakly educated [she continues], are often cruelly left by their parents without any provision; and, of course, are dependent on, not only the reason, but the bounty of their brothers. These brothers are, to view the fairest side of the question, good sort of men, and give as a favour, what children of the same parents had an equal right to. In this equivocal humiliating situation, a docile female may remain some time, with a tolerable degree of comfort. But, when the brother marries, a probable circumstance, from being considered as the mistress of the family, she is viewed with averted looks as an intruder, an unnecessary burden on the benevolence of the master of the house, and his new partner.

Who can recount the misery, which many unfortunate beings, whose minds and bodies are equally weak, suffer in such situations—unable to work and ashamed to beg? The wife, a cold-hearted, narrow-minded woman, and this is not an unfair supposition; for the present mode of education does not tend to enlarge the heart any more than the understanding, is jealous of the little kindness which her husband shows to his relations; and her sensibility not rising to humanity, she is displeased at seeing the property of *her* children lavished on an helpless sister.

This is a longer chunk of text than I usually quote, but the reason, I imagine, becomes clear very quickly – here, in a nutshell, are the first few chapters of *Sense and Sensibility*, the relationships and resentments that develop between the various Dashwoods, and all of it tied up with a discussion of sensibility, inheritance, and the damaging effects of both.

For Wollstonecraft, it's clear that the current system of inheritance erodes instincts of fairness and generosity, that it warps the very idea of family and natural affection. In a society like this, even sensibility, fine feeling, a sense of connection to others, can only ever operate bluntly, selfishly, and with an eye to the main chance. And the sexual responsiveness that (most) men are looking for in women? Well that becomes something to be exchanged, too.

The idea that Jane is drawing from *A Vindication of the Rights of Woman* in *Sense and Sensibility* isn't a new one. If you put this passage in front of a roomful of students nearly all of them will pick out the parallels. It's really quite obvious. But is it obvious enough for us to conclude that Jane meant her novel to be read as a Wollstonecraftian critique of women's position in society? That rather depends, of course, on when she first came up with the story. As I pointed out in the first chapter, Wollstonecraft was subjected to a vicious character assassination after her death in 1797. Even before her death, her illicit relationship with the anarchist philosopher William Godwin had put her firmly in the sights of conservative thinkers. If *Sense and Sensibility* is a work of the 1790s or early 1800s then it looks like it was written as a deliberately and self-consciously feminist one. By 1811, of course, that effect would have been muted for a fair portion of readers who were less familiar with Wollstonecraft.

What we can say is that *Sense and Sensibility*, even in 1811, would have been read as a novel about property, and inheritance – about greed and need, and the terrible, selfish things that families do to each other for the sake of money.

In his poem *Letter to Lord Byron*, first published in the late 1930s, W.H. Auden talks about how profoundly unsettling he finds Jane's novels:

> You could not shock her more than she shocks me;
>   Besides her Joyce seems innocent as grass.
> It makes me most uncomfortable to see
>   An English spinster of the middle class
>   Describe the amorous effects of 'brass',
> Reveal so frankly and with such sobriety
> The economic basis of society.

Of all Jane's novels it's this one, the first to be published, that pays the most sustained attention to 'the economic basis of society' and to 'brass'.

∞

'Brass' has been slang for money since the middle ages; so too have 'gold' and 'silver'. In the early nineteenth century 'tin' and 'pewter' came into use as well. In a letter to her niece Fanny, Jane complains that people aren't buying *Mansfield Park*, borrowing the phrasing of one of her nephews: 'tho' I like praise as well as anybody', she admits, 'I like what Edward calls Pewter too.'[3]

Sense and Sensibility is preoccupied with metal, particularly with metal as a means of exchange, as payment, or as a way of transferring wealth. John Dashwood and his wife obsess over the 'plate' which is taken away to Barton Cottage. 'Plate' is the massive silver dinner services, generally worth hundreds if not thousands of pounds – a secure way of storing money, with the added advantage of being readily sellable and reasonably portable. When Willoughby dismisses Colonel Brandon's experiences in the East Indies, he mockingly mentions such stereotypically eighteenth-century Indian things as 'nabobs, gold mohrs, and palanquins'. A mohr (often spelt 'moher' or 'mohur') was a unit of Indian currency, made of gold and worth, according to the 1801 *Encyclopaedia Britannica*, 'about 33 shillings', so a touch less than twice the value of an English pound.

There's much more reference to jewellery in *Sense and Sensibility* than is common in Jane's novels, and to jewellery being bought or sold. While in London Elinor has business at a jeweller, a real-life one, Gray's – 'a negotiation for the exchange of a few old-fashioned jewels of her mother', we're told. She's selling or pawning them: either way, converting them into cash. At the same shop, she encounters Robert Ferrars, Edward's brother, who is 'giving orders for a toothpick-case', to be ornamented with 'ivory', 'gold', and 'pearls'. She also bumps into her brother John, who's ordering 'a seal' for his wife – to impress on the wax used to secure letters. In their next conversation together, John Dashwood complains about the many calls on his purse; his aim, Jane explains, is 'to do away the necessity of buying a pair of ear-rings for each of his sisters' when he returns to the jeweller to pick up his order. Characters make baskets of filigree, delicate work done in gold and silver thread or wire, or metallic paper. Lucy Steele gives her betrothed, Edward, a ring set with her hair.*

Then, too, an astonishing proportion of the surnames in *Sense and Sensibility* are metallic ones. We have the Steele sisters. We have the

---

* Hair jewellery, though it seems peculiar to us, was commonplace during the eighteenth and nineteenth centuries, both for mourning and as a love token.

Ferrars family (that is, ferrous, containing iron). Willoughby's rich cousin is called Mrs Smith – a common name, true, and one which Jane uses in three separate novels, but nevertheless, a smith is a worker of metal.* Willoughby marries an heiress called Miss Grey, recalling the jeweller Grays – the sharing of names is something we'll return to. Coincidentally (or perhaps not) a 'gray' or 'grey' is also a spot of discoloration which marks the flaw in a metal, particularly in a gun, and when we first encounter Willoughby, he's carrying a gun.†

Guns, and knives, and scissors, and needles, and pins crop up fairly frequently in Jane's novels. But it's only here, in *Sense and Sensibility*, that they're all mentioned, and it's only here that they do damage.‡ Little Annamaria Middleton, the Dashwoods' cousin, is injured (though trivially) by 'a pin in her ladyship's head dress slightly scratching the child's neck'. Willoughby cuts off a lock of Marianne's hair as a love token. When Edward Ferrars, released from his engagement to Lucy Steele, comes to Barton Cottage to explain his behaviour to the Dashwoods, he expresses his pent-up feelings by taking up 'a pair of scissors that lay there, and [...] spoiling both them and their sheath by cutting the latter to pieces as he spoke'. Lucy Steele – later Ferrars and so doubly metallic – is thrice described as 'sharp'. Characters 'cut' their acquaintance, refuse to acknowledge that they are acquainted, a word which doesn't appear in this context in Jane's other novels.

The world of *Sense and Sensibility* is a sharp and glittering one, one in which an embrace can draw blood, in which metal is both bribe

---

* There are two Mrs Smiths, one in *Sense and Sensibility* and one in *Persuasion*, and Harriet Smith, in *Emma*.

† Willoughby shares his surname with the deeply unpleasant Sir Clement Willoughby, in Fanny Burney's *Evelina* (1778), and with the hero of Charlotte Smith's *Celestina* (1791), whose cruel behaviour to the heroine turns out to have been caused by an unfortunate misunderstanding.

‡ Mr Elton apparently cuts his finger in *Emma* – Harriet Smith cherishes a part of the plaster he's given – but it's not a scene we're shown. The injuries in *Persuasion* are connected to falls.

and weapon, reward and threat. The novel features the richest of Jane's heiresses, Miss Sophia Grey, who according to Mrs Jennings is worth £50,000. This figure is likely to be an accurate one. Mrs Jennings may be vulgar, she may love to leap to conclusions, but she is shrewd and she knows Miss Grey's family ('I remember her aunt very well, Biddy Henshawe; she married a very wealthy man. But the family are all rich together'). Besides, this was the kind of information which tended to be common knowledge; it was perfectly normal, during Jane's lifetime, for the fortune a woman brought to a marriage to be included at the end of the wedding announcement printed in the newspapers.

Is Miss Grey's £50,000 safe from Willoughby? She is, apparently, 'of age and may choose for herself'; that is, she is over 21 and needs no one's permission to marry. Presumably then, her money is also entirely at her own disposal. One hopes, though, that her one-time guardians, the Ellisons, will help her with drawing up a watertight marriage settlement, especially with so expensive a husband as Willoughby on the cards. Marriage settlements generally made a point of balancing the financial interests of the husband and the wife; they put money or property in trust for the woman and, often, for her children if she should die before her husband. Married women, remember, didn't exist legally, and couldn't own money or property themselves. But single women, including widows, could and did.

Under a marriage settlement, a woman owned her property in the same way that little Harry Dashwood owns Norland; the ownership came into effect – and was legally enforceable – only in certain circumstances, namely, when she was widowed. The balance struck by each marriage settlement was different; it was dependent on who wanted the marriage more, on what each party was gaining, and on who occupied the stronger position. Usually parents or other relatives were involved. John Dashwood's mother clearly had a decent settlement drawn up when she married, since we're told that half her fortune passes to her son 'on his coming of age', while the other half is 'secured' to him when his father dies. Settlements are the reason men tried to elope with heiresses; they're the reason it was, in some circumstances, a specific crime to do so – at the moment of marriage a woman became what was known as a *feme covert*, a 'covered' or 'protected' woman. She was legally merged with her husband and everything she possessed or came to possess during the marriage was his, to do with as he pleased.* Running away with an heiress was, effectively, stealing her inheritance. From what we see of her, Miss Grey seems, thankfully, to be made of stern stuff. Willoughby is marrying her for her money, but quite how much of it he will succeed in getting isn't clear.

Sense and Sensibility features a large number of financially independent single women. Mrs Jennings has a jointure – she owns her house and her income but only for life, and after she dies it will go to her daughters, or, depending on the precise terms of their marriage settlements, to their husbands. But there is Mrs Dashwood, who may not be particularly financially competent, but who controls her £7,000 fortune. Willoughby's cousin Mrs Smith, it appears, owns Allenham outright, since Willoughby takes her threats to disinherit him seriously. Fanny Dashwood – a Ferrars by birth – mentions that the money left by her father 'would have been entirely at my mother's disposal, without any restriction whatever' were it not for the matter of three annuities to servants.

It's worth pointing out how unusual this situation was for women, both in Jane's novels and in the real-life society in which she lived. Despite what many readers believe, Rosings Park, in *Pride and Prejudice*, belongs not to the fearsome Lady Catherine de Bourgh, but to her daughter, Anne ('the heiress of Rosings, and of very extensive property').† For a

---

* Under a statute dating from the reign of Henry VII, a man who ran off with a woman who had any substantial property of her own (or was likely to in the future) committed a crime if at any point in the process she was not completely willing.

† Anne de Bourgh is, presumably, still under-age.

man to leave his property totally at the disposal of his widow was hugely risky at a time when remarriage could see everything immediately pass away from any children of the marriage to a second husband. It required a high degree of trust in a wife's intelligence and financial acumen.

One reason for doing it, of course, would be to leave a wife the means of controlling the behaviour and life-choices of any children. As William Blackstone, the great eighteenth-century legal commentator explains, though fathers had legal rights over their children as minors – to physically chastise them, to benefit from their labour, and to refuse them permission to marry – 'a mother, as such, is entitled to no power, but only to reverence and respect'.[4] A mother who holds the purse strings, though, is in a position to discourage her sons from pursuing ill-thought-out careers or pastimes (such as gambling or horse-racing), and to steer all of her offspring towards prudent marriages, and she remains in that position even when her children are adult. It's mercenary to wish one's children to marry well, it's perhaps power-hungry to be ambitious for one's eldest son, but this is really as far as Mrs Ferrars' sins stretch.

Nevertheless, our instinct as readers is to dislike her, to scoff disbelievingly when her son-in-law John Dashwood insists that she is 'a most excellent mother'. It's true that she is rather rude to Elinor, but it's equally true that from early on in the novel, long before she's given any real justification, Elinor is determined to dislike *her*.* 'What his mother really is we cannot know', she admits to her sister, 'but [...] we have never been disposed to think her amiable.' For Elinor and, to a lesser degree, for her mother and Marianne, Mrs Ferrars is a very

---

* We shouldn't be surprised that Mrs Ferrars and Elinor haven't met, even though Mrs Ferrars' daughter is married to Elinor's brother. Weddings were very much smaller, lower-key affairs during Jane's lifetime than they are now, and it was perfectly usual for even quite close family members not to attend. None of Edward Ferrars' family attend his wedding to Elinor, though they do pay formal visits to the newly-married couple afterwards.

convenient scapegoat. Everything inexplicable or confusing in Edward's behaviour towards them is blamed on his mother. 'Elinor placed all that was astonishing in this way of acting to his mother's account', we're told, consoling herself with the idea that it is only Edward's 'dependent situation' which prevents 'the indulgence of his affection' for her. As Jane drily notes: 'it was happy for her that he had a mother whose character was so imperfectly known to her, as to be the general excuse for every thing strange on the part of her son.' The truth is far less palatable.

Mrs Ferrars is undoubtedly a generous mother – very generous, provided that her children do as she wishes. Fanny's marriage to John Dashwood clearly met with maternal approval; Fanny brought money to her marriage and while in London receives 'bank-notes' from her mother 'to the amount of two hundred pounds' to help defray the expenses of making a good appearance in society. Remember, this is nearly half the annual income of the Devonshire Dashwoods, a vast sum to be giving away.

And both Edward and his brother Robert must be receiving large allowances from their mother. Edward has only 'a trifling sum' himself, but he can afford to travel about the country more or less as he pleases. Robert dresses 'in the first style of fashion' and buys such fripperies as jewelled toothpick-cases; he can't be kept short of money.

Nevertheless, Mrs Ferrars subscribes to the popular notion that the most important of her children is her eldest son. From what we can gather she spends a good deal of time fretting about Edward's career prospects: 'His mother wished to interest him in political concerns, to get him into parliament, or to see him connected with some of the great men of the day.' She wants to obtain power and influence for her family, in other words – it's simply unfortunate that it is Edward who is the eldest son. As Mrs Dashwood remarks, indulgently dismissive, Edward has 'no inclination for expense, no affection for strangers, no profession, and no assurance'. He will never make 'a great orator'.

'I have no wish to be distinguished', explains Edward at one point in the novel. No wish to be, and no chance of being. Nor is Robert, with his 'natural, sterling insignificance', well suited to public life. The only member of the Ferrars family with the gift of persuasive speech is Fanny, who we see talk her husband round in the first chapter of the novel. But women have no way of taking part in public life directly; they have to sublimate their ambition, and focus their energies on their menfolk.

Disappointed of her political ambitions for Edward, Mrs Ferrars goes to the trouble of attempting to arrange a prosperous marriage for him instead, 'a most eligible connection', with Miss Morton, 'the daughter of Lord Morton' and heiress to £30,000. Her rage when she discovers that he has for years been secretly engaged to marry Lucy Steele – penniless, badly connected, and wholly ineligible – is understandable.

Less understandable is her decision to not merely reject Edward, but to settle on his younger brother Robert the family estate in Norfolk, which produces an income of £1,000 a year. When one son has shown himself to be ungrateful and disobedient, it seems reckless to make the other son financially independent of her. Mrs Jennings is made to remark on it; 'Everybody has a way of their own. But I don't think mine would be, to make one son independent, because another had plagued me.'

Jane is less interested in psychological plausibility here, I think, than in resolving the plot – Robert's sudden acquisition of wealth and independence wins him the affections of practical-minded Lucy Steele, freeing Edward to marry Elinor. But it also shows how arbitrary and absurd it is to concentrate resources on any one child to the disadvantage of the others, how unnatural. Nearly every character in the novel is taken aback at Mrs Ferrars' decision to make Robert 'to all intents and purposes [...] the eldest', at 'so unfair a division of his mother's love and liberality'; there's much talk of how unfortunate Edward is, of how unkind his family are being to him. This, though, is exactly what primogeniture always did – it's a zero-sum game.

As Jane shows us repeatedly in *Sense and Sensibility*, one person's gain is always another's loss.

This is a novel in which Willoughby admits that he has run up debts for years, built himself a financial prison from which he fully expects other people to rescue him, no matter what it costs them. 'The death of my old cousin, Mrs Smith, was to set me free', he says, blithely, but 'that event being uncertain, and possibly far distant', he intended 'to re-establish my circumstances by marrying a woman of fortune'. He's been living on his expectations, borrowing money, getting credit on the basis that he's going to inherit. He treats Mrs Smith's house as if it's already his own when he shows Marianne around it; he treats Mrs Smith's money as if it's already his own. His long-standing intention is to marry a 'woman of fortune', his aim to get his hands on as much of that fortune as is practicable.

Given Willoughby's highly acquisitive nature, it makes sense for Mrs Smith to attempt to control him through money. And her controlling impulses have the saving grace of moral uprightness behind them. When it comes to her attention that Willoughby has seduced and abandoned Colonel Brandon's ward Eliza, leaving her pregnant and alone, Mrs Smith takes him to task. The result, we're told, is 'a total breach'. She insists that he atone for his sin by marrying the girl; when Willoughby refuses ('That could not be'), he is 'formally dismissed' from Mrs Smith's 'favour and her house'.

Willoughby calls his cousin a 'good woman', but it's clear he has little time for goodness when it interferes with his own advancement: 'The purity of her life, the formality of her notions, her ignorance of the world—every thing was against me', he complains. Moreover, he insinuates that Mrs Smith was 'discontented with the very little attention, the very little portion of my time that I had bestowed on her'. For Willoughby, even morality has to be secretly motivated by selfishness. As for Eliza, the teenage girl he seduced and left, she is, in Willoughby's mind, as much to blame as he is. He talks of 'the violence of her passions, the weakness of her understanding'; suggests that 'common sense' could have told her how to find him. His wife, the rich wife he schemed to get? 'Do not talk to me of my wife', he sighs to Elinor, 'She does not deserve your compassion. — She knew I had no regard for her when we married.' He's even able to fantasise about his wife's death – a 'blessed chance' which would set him 'at liberty again', at liberty and with a large chunk of someone else's money in his pocket.

Willoughby is happy to take things from women – money, a lock of hair, virginity and respectability. We, as readers, shouldn't make the mistake of giving him our sympathy too. His explanation may excite 'a degree of commiseration' in Elinor, 'a tenderness, a regret, rather in proportion, as she soon acknowledged within herself—to his wishes than to his merits', but once the charm of his presence is removed, she comes to a more reasoned conclusion, that 'The whole of his behaviour […] has been grounded on selfishness'.

Jane doesn't come up with any excuse for what Willoughby's done. His repentance is, in the end, 'sincere' – Jane says it 'need not be doubted' – but only because it turns out that Mrs Smith would have forgiven him and he could have married Marianne and had enough money after all. Where we hear his repentance in his own words, he is mawkish, self-indulgent; remember that he turns up at what he thinks is Marianne's death-bed intoxicated ('yes, I am very drunk') and demands Elinor's attention, as of right. There's nothing redemptive about the scene. The reviewer in the *British Critic* was forthright in his condemnation of Willoughby, calling him a 'male coquet', 'fickle, false, and treacherous'. This ought to be our conclusion, too. From the very beginning, Jane indicates that we should be suspicious of Willoughby, that he cannot be relied on.

I suggested in the last chapter that Ann Radcliffe's Gothic novel *The Mysteries of Udolpho* was so popular, and so widely-read during the late 1790s, that Jane would have expected her audience to recognise even quite detailed references to it. When Willoughby first appears, he does so almost exactly like Valancourt, the love-interest of Emily, the heroine of *Udolpho*.* And Valancourt proves himself to be a gambler, one who very much enjoys the company of 'captivating' marchionesses and countesses. Though he loves Emily when he's with her, her image fades. He does nothing towards rescuing her from the dangers she's embroiled in. No reader who was familiar with *Udolpho* would have been surprised to discover that Willoughby is a weak-willed, sexually inconstant gambler who gets himself into debt; the difference between him and Valancourt is that Jane doesn't subscribe to the comforting notion that a sinner can be reformed by love – or that they ought to be. She avoids dishing out punishment to Willoughby – 'that he was for ever inconsolable, that he fled from society, or contracted an habitual gloom of temper, or died of a broken heart, must not be depended on', we're told – but she isn't willing to countenance giving him an ending in which everything is resolved and forgiven.

Happy endings, truly happy ones, are in short supply in this novel.

Quite early on, when both Elinor and Marianne are fairly confident of their respective men, they discuss what sort of income would make for happiness. Marianne rebukes her sister for suggesting that 'wealth' is necessary; she wishes only for a 'competence'.

'Perhaps,' said Elinor, smiling, 'we may come to the same point. *Your* competence and *my* wealth are very much alike, I dare say; and without them, as the world goes now, we shall both agree that every kind of external comfort must be wanting [...] Come, what is your competence?'

'About eighteen hundred or two thousand a year; not more than *that*.'

Elinor laughed. '*Two* thousand a year! *One* is my wealth! I guessed how it would end.'

---

* Willoughby enters the novel as 'A gentleman carrying a gun, with two pointers playing round him' – a hunter. Valancourt is first described as 'a young man ... followed by a couple of dogs', 'in a hunter's dress', with a 'gun ... slung across his shoulders'.

Colonel Brandon's income is £2,000 a year, as we know from shrewd Mrs Jennings, who once considered him as a potential son-in-law. When Marianne marries him, she gets her 'competence'. But Elinor doesn't quite get her 'wealth'. Jane tells us that Edward's new job as a vicar will bring in 'about two hundred a year'.* She reminds us that Elinor has £1,000 of her own, Edward £2,000. Assuming that this money is placed in government bonds, the 'five-percents' which is what nearly all of Jane's characters invest in, that will add £150 a year, making an annual income of £350.

This isn't enough to marry on. Mrs Dashwood is in no position to advance them any money; the only way for them to marry is for Edward to appeal to his mother. She, grudgingly, gives him £10,000, the same sum 'which had been given with Fanny'. Edward isn't just made into a younger son; he's made into a daughter. Still, thanks to Edward's mother, he and Elinor will have an extra £500 a year, making £850 altogether. It's a perfectly adequate income. But it falls short of the 'wealth' without which 'every kind of external comfort must be wanting'. They'll be able to afford servants, perhaps a carriage, but they will struggle to send their sons to school or university, to set them up in a career. They're unlikely to be able to provide dowries for any daughters, certainly not extensive ones. And as a vicar, Edward will have no home to leave to his wife and children – just like Jane's own father.

Finances aside, there are other reasons for us to be doubtful about how happy Elinor will be with Edward.

He and Willoughby seem, initially, to be entirely different. Edward is 'not handsome'; nor is he charming, but instead 'diffident' and 'shy'. His 'manners', Jane informs us, 'required intimacy to make them pleasing'. Again, in opposition to Willoughby, he has no taste for poetry, for art, for nature, and is unable to pretend that he does. But then, he isn't particularly intelligent. The most Jane can say of him is that: 'His understanding

---

* For more detail on how careers in the Church operated at this point, see Chapter 5.

was good, and his education had given it solid improvement.' 'Solid' isn't high praise. Jane doesn't ever really explain why Edward was educated by a provincial tutor rather than being sent to Westminster like his younger brother. Westminster is the large London boarding-school that has existed since the middle ages. Robert boasts about the connections he made there, and we should imagine him rubbing shoulders with the rich and powerful. Old boys included prime ministers and poets laureate, playwrights, philosophers, historians, judges, aristocrats – names like John Dryden, Christopher Wren, John Locke, the Duke of Portland, the Earl of Elgin, the Marquis of Rockingham. Lord Mansfield, who we'll encounter in Chapter 5, went there. So too did a man called Warren Hastings – Governor General of India and the godfather of Jane's cousin Eliza.

There must be a reason why this school wasn't deemed suitable for Edward, particularly considering his mother's political ambitions for him. Apparently an uncle ('Sir Robert') persuaded Mrs Ferrars that her eldest son should have 'private tuition'. Was he sickly? Was he bullied? Was his behaviour in some way undesirable, peculiar even? And why send him to Exeter? It's a provincial town in Devon, several days' journey from London, a fact you can hardly escape in this novel, where characters are continually travelling to and from the county. It's further still from Norfolk, which is where the family estate is. Edward would have received a better education from some of the excellent specialist tutors who worked in the capital. And he wouldn't have got engaged to Lucy Steele – his tutor's niece, introduced into the house, one suspects, quite deliberately.

Edward, interestingly, blames his mother rather than his former tutor. He calls his engagement to Lucy 'a foolish, idle inclination', but is quick to point out that any foolishness or idleness was 'the consequence of ignorance of the world—and want of employment'. 'Had my mother given me some active profession', says he, 'I think—nay, I am sure, it would never have happened.' His mother should have chosen a 'profession' for him, or 'allowed' him to 'chuse'; she should have sent him to university sooner. She 'did not make my home in every respect comfortable', complains Edward; his brother was 'no friend, no companion'. It's a tendency Edward shares with Willoughby, this ability to always find someone to blame.

It's not the only similarity between the two characters, in spite of their apparent positioning as opposites. Both have financially independent female relations who attempt to use money to control their behaviour. Both encourage one of the Dashwood sisters to believe that they are interested in marrying them, and Jane makes a point of showing us that it isn't just Marianne and Elinor who are misled, but almost everyone who observes the two couples together. It's arguable as to which man behaves worse in this regard. Whatever Willoughby intended at the beginning, there was a period when, he says, 'I felt my intentions were strictly honourable'. Edward knows, right up until nearly the end of the novel, that he's engaged to another woman. He's not in a position to have proper intentions towards Elinor. Both men indulge their own vanity, and their own feelings, without much regard for the women they claim to love.

Marianne allows Willoughby to cut off a lock of her hair, as a love token (or perhaps a trophy); Elinor assumes – mistakenly – that the hair set in a ring which Edward wears is her own. She is 'conscious', Jane explains, that it 'must have been procured by some theft or contrivance unknown to herself'. Elinor is 'not in a humour [...] to regard it as an affront', but let's just pause a minute – she thinks he's stolen her hair. How? Does she imagine he's pulled hairs out of her hairbrush? Bribed her maid, or a hairdresser? Crept into her room at Norland while she was sleeping, even, with a pair of scissors?*

---

*   Sexual fetishes connected to hair were certainly recognised in the eighteenth century. In the period's most famous work of erotica, *Fanny Hill, Memoirs of a Woman of Pleasure* (1748–9), one of Fanny's customers is 'a grave, staid, solemn, elderly gentleman whose peculiar humour was a delight in combing fine tresses of hair [...] drawing the comb through it, winding the curls round his fingers, even kissing it as he smooth'd it'.

Edward seems to have a thing about scissors, remember. Towards the end of the novel, when he's come to Barton Cottage to explain that his engagement with Lucy Steele is at an end, he finds breaking the news awkward, stressful. He walks across the sitting room to the window 'apparently from not knowing what to do' and helps himself to 'a pair of scissors that lay there'. While he explains that Lucy is now married to his brother Robert, he is 'spoiling both them [the scissors] and their sheath by cutting the latter to pieces'.

It's no wonder that Emma Thompson felt the need to alter this scene in her screenplay for the 1995 film of *Sense and Sensibility*, and have *her* Edward fiddle with the china ornaments on the mantelpiece instead. Just imagine the fun Sigmund Freud would have had. The Latin for sheath is 'vagina', as Jane, with her smattering of Latin, may very plausibly have known. The word was already in use as a medical term during her lifetime.

The sheath, then, is Lucy, or, strictly speaking, Lucy's private parts. The scissors are – what, a penis? Robert's? Edward's? Or something else, even. Jane seldom uses symbolism, but this looks like symbolism, and symbolism of a deeply disturbing, unhealthy, sexually violent kind. Perhaps we don't need to look any further for the reason why Edward was educated privately with a tutor, away from his younger siblings.

'Men were deceivers ever', as the song in *Much Ado About Nothing* has it. Willoughby and Edward are deceivers, capable of lying to mothers, lovers, sisters. All the way through the novel, a careful reader can see that Jane suggests reserving judgement about people. Someone may seem or appear a certain way; what they really are is harder to ascertain. Almost every page reveals sentences which, on a second reading, hesitate, equivocate.

Take Edward; 'he *appeared* to be amiable', 'he *gave every indication* of an open and affectionate heart' (my emphasis). Even Elinor is forced to speak of his virtues in lengthy sentences, complexly structured: 'Of his sense and his goodness […] no one can, I think, be in doubt, who has seen him often enough to engage him in unreserved conversation.

The excellence of his understanding and his principles can be concealed only by that shyness which too often keeps him silent.' It's no accident, I think, that these sentences contain words like 'doubt' and 'concealed'. Over the course of *Sense and Sensibility*, readers learn enough about Edward to doubt his sense, and perhaps his goodness too; we realise that it's more than just 'shyness' concealing his 'understanding and principles'.

Jane reminds us, through the medium of Elinor, how easy it is to misjudge people:

> 'I have frequently detected myself in such kind of mistakes,' said Elinor, 'in a total misapprehension of character in some point or other: fancying people so much more gay or grave, or ingenious or stupid than they really are, and I can hardly tell why or in what the deception originated. Sometimes one is guided by what they say of themselves, and very frequently by what other people say of them, without giving oneself time to deliberate and judge.'

Elinor would do well to heed her own words; so would we. There are far more secrets in *Sense and Sensibility* than in any of Jane's other novels. There are also confessions, and the person who receives nearly all of them is Elinor. The contortions Jane has to go through in order to make this happen suggest that it's important, perhaps because we're meant to be holding this pronouncement of hers in mind. What people 'say of themselves' shouldn't be used as a guide 'without giving oneself time to deliberate and judge'.

Of the four confessions Elinor receives, the first – Lucy's – is obviously intended to be suspect. Lucy has heard that the man who is engaged to her looks like he's courting another woman. She's warning Elinor off. When Willoughby rushes to Marianne's sick-bed, and spends what must be some considerable time haranguing Elinor, he claims that he means 'to open my whole heart' to her. Edward's heart, we're told, is 'open to Elinor', eventually; 'all its weaknesses, all its errors confessed'.

But each speech needs to be sifted for self-justifications and inconsistencies. None should be taken at face value.

And this surely also holds true for the other confession Elinor is forced to listen to; Colonel Brandon's story of his past, of his connection with his cousin, and with his ward, Eliza Williams.

∞

Jane puts three male romantic interests into the novel. Given that two of them spend large portions of time lying, and conceal dark secrets in their romantic and sexual pasts, we're well within our rights to ask a few hard questions about Colonel Brandon. 'No one can be deceived in him!' cries Mrs Dashwood. Well, she's been deceived in Edward and Willoughby too, so let's not give what she says too much weight.

What do other people say about Brandon? He's first mentioned as a 'particular friend' of Sir John Middleton, and as 'neither very young nor very gay'. Sir John drops 'hints of past injuries and disappointments'. Mrs Jennings declares, with complete confidence, that he has fathered a bastard child – 'Miss Williams [...] is a relation of the Colonel's, my dear; a very near relation [...] she is his natural daughter'. She's equally sure that he is in love with first Marianne, and then Elinor. She informs Elinor, and through her us, that Brandon's estate is worth in the region of 'two thousand a year' and that though 'his brother left everything sadly involved', the Colonel 'must have cleared the estate by this time'. Willoughby jokes about disliking him and asserts, at the same time, that he believes 'his character to be in other respects irreproachable'. Both Willoughby and Marianne claim that Brandon tells dull stories about the 'East Indies'. Marianne thinks him, in addition, an 'old bachelor', 'old enough to be *my* father'.

From this mishmash of fact and opinion, we can glean the information that Colonel Brandon isn't particularly young – 35 when we first encounter him – that he is a younger son, that he has substantial assets which have required some careful handling, that he has been in the East

Indies – and that there is some mystery in his background connected with his young ward.

Marianne, in this early part of the novel, thinks that the age difference between them makes any suggestion of romantic interest absurd. An age difference between husband and wife of around five years was most common in this period and the average gap between Jane's heroes and heroines is a little larger; closer to six or seven years.[5]* Colonel Brandon is eighteen years older than Marianne. Unusually for her, Marianne isn't exaggerating when she says that Brandon's old enough to be her father; he is.

The age difference wouldn't have been as troubling for Jane's first readers as it is for us, however. What they were much more likely to be troubled by, is the Colonel's connection with India.

Exactly how long Colonel Brandon has spent in India is unclear, a detail I'll return to in a moment. But he has been there, serving either in the British army or possibly in a private regiment controlled by the British East India Company. The company was one of several European organisations which had started trading with India around 1600. By the end of the eighteenth century, thanks to wars, proxy wars, ethically dubious taxation schemes and worse, it was a dominant force in the sub-continent.

The East India Company essentially gained Britain a vast imperial holding on the cheap. But public opinion was hostile. British men who returned home, having gained fortunes in India, were referred to, scornfully, as 'nabobs', a corruption of the Urdu *nawab*. The Company's rule was seen as corrupt and corrupting, even criminal.

In a 1772 play by Samuel Foote, called *The Nabob*, the title character Sir Matthew Mite is presented in a wholly negative light. He's accused of 'scattering the spoils of ruined provinces', of being someone 'who owes

---

* We can extrapolate larger age differences in the marriages of some of the parents in Jane's novels – between Mr and Mrs Bennet, for example, or between Mr Woodhouse and his wife.

his rise to the ruins of thousands'. His possessions are 'plunder', 'treacherously gained'. At one point in the play, the East India Company's *modus operandi* is described:

> Why, here are a body of merchants that beg to be admitted as friends, and take possession of a small spot in a country, and carry on a beneficial commerce with the inoffensive and innocent people, to which they kindly give their consent [...] Upon which [...] we cunningly encroach, and fortify by little and by little, till at length, we growing too strong for the natives, we turn them out of their lands, and take possession of their money and jewels.

And, alongside accusations of war crimes and general corruption, this was almost exactly what Warren Hastings, old boy of Westminster School and Governor General of India, was charged with in 1787 – that he had stolen the treasury belonging to the women of the royal family of Oudh. The prosecution was, really, less about Hastings and his actions and more about the government of India. It was driven by a man called Edmund Burke, a famous orator and politician, and occasional idealist. We'll talk more about him, and his most famous piece of writing, in the next chapter.

The trial of Warren Hastings took place in the House of Commons, with prominent politicians acting for the prosecution and defence. There was, for a time, enormous popular interest. The interest faded, however. The trial dragged on until 1795, when, in the changed political climate of war with France, Hastings was acquitted on all charges. But the damage was done, both to him and to the reputation of the British in India.

Jane does seem to have been intrigued by India. In a youthful attempt at a novel, called *Catherine, or the Bower*, she sends the heroine's friend, Miss Wynne, to Bengal. A second Wynne sister is sent to Scotland and we're told the heroine corresponds with both; we would almost certainly have seen letters sent from India if Jane had continued, perhaps even scenes set there. In *Mansfield Park*, one of the heroine's many younger brothers is employed on an 'Indiaman', that is, one of the East India Company's trading ships. The fascination is natural. Jane's aunt Philadelphia Austen had sailed to India, to a marriage which had probably been arranged for her before she left. Jane's cousin (and later sister-in-law) Eliza was born there. As I mentioned, Eliza's godfather was Warren Hastings. There were long-standing rumours, possibly true ones, that he was also her biological father.

But whatever Jane's family connections and family loyalties might have been, she can hardly have avoided knowing that, for the majority of her readers, a reference to India would have been a black mark, a reminder of corruption, of avarice. Brandon is tainted by association. She could easily have avoided it, either by not mentioning where Brandon had been, or by substituting the 'East Indies' with somewhere like Canada. She doesn't.

In fact, if we look at Colonel Brandon's tragic history, as narrated by himself, he can't have been in India for all that long. The history consists of the following: Colonel Brandon had a cousin, named Eliza. An orphan, she was brought up in his family 'from her earliest infancy'. He and Eliza were very close in age ('Our ages were nearly the same'), they were 'playfellows and friends' from their 'earliest years'. As they grew, friendship deepened to love. They planned to elope together 'to Scotland', where it was and still is possible to marry without parental consent from the age of sixteen; the plan was discovered, they were separated, and Eliza was coerced into marrying Colonel Brandon's older brother instead.

Here, again, we can see primogeniture at work, can see too the damage it does to natural loyalties, honourable impulses. Eliza is an heiress ('her fortune was a large one'). That Colonel Brandon's father, as her uncle and guardian, should act to stop the planned elopement is entirely proper; without the proper paperwork her fortune would immediately pass out of her hands. An uncle's instinct, a guardian's duty, should be to protect, not to exploit. But by then marrying her off to his older son without drawing up a marriage settlement, he transfers her fortune to his own family; by compelling Eliza to marry 'against her inclination', he has, arguably, committed a crime under the law against 'stealing an heiress'. It was all done for money; for money and the good of the eldest Brandon son. The family estate is 'much encumbered', which is, as the Colonel remarks, 'all that can be said for the conduct of one, who was at once her uncle and guardian'. The action is legally questionable, and morally, wholly reprehensible.

The marriage, as might be expected, doesn't prosper. Eliza is 'lost' to Colonel Brandon – married – 'at seventeen'. That point seems fixed. But inconsistencies start to emerge elsewhere in the Colonel's narrative. It is 'about two years' after Eliza married that he hears of 'her divorce'. Divorce was not, at the time, a quick affair; each required its own bill in parliament. Add to this the fact that the Colonel is with his regiment in India, and that the news had to travel there from England, a journey which, even with favourable weather, was likely to take four months or more, and it begins to look as if the marriage got into serious difficulties very early on. The Colonel tells Elinor that it was 'nearly three years after this unhappy period before I returned to England'. Is that three years since the divorce, or since he heard of the divorce, or since Eliza married? It isn't entirely clear.

Eliza has, to all intents and purposes, vanished. The Colonel tries to find her, but cannot trace her 'beyond her first seducer'. The tiny divorce alimony she was awarded has been signed over to someone else. The Colonel does find her, however, 'at last, and after I had been six months in England'. He finds her in a 'spunging house' – a private debtors' prison – dying of tuberculosis. With her is 'her only child', also called Eliza, 'a little girl, the offspring of her first guilty connection, who was then about three years old'. Born after the divorce, or before? Again, we can't be certain. What Colonel Brandon intends, by mentioning all these dates, is surely to indicate that the child isn't his. He's been six months finding them. Add in the time for the voyage and the three years, however imprecise the starting date, that he's been in India, and it becomes impossible. Nevertheless, the Colonel explains that he took charge of her. He sends her to school, and later, once his brother has died and he's inherited the family estate, he puts her 'under the care of a very respectable woman, residing in Dorsetshire'. He's even had her to stay with him. On a visit to Bath, she is unfortunate enough to meet Willoughby, and to be seduced by him. She vanishes, and has a daughter outside marriage. Like mother, like daughter.

Throughout this version of events, the Colonel's behaviour is impeccable – he falls in love; he removes himself from the scene to try to promote the happiness of Eliza once she's married; tries to find her when he returns; he attends her deathbed; he cares for her child, and for her child's child. He even fights a duel with Willoughby. It's the generosity of deathless love.

Or is it?

Setting aside the insistent egoism apparent in the Colonel's story (just look at all the 'I's and 'my's in it), it never seems to enter his head that perhaps he ought to be saving up as much money as he can to give to his ward – to replace, in some measure, the fortune which was effectively stolen from her mother and used to prop up the estate. John Dashwood is appalled to find that the Colonel hasn't sold the right to serve as priest in his local parish ('for the next presentation to a living of that value [...] he might have got I dare say—fourteen hundred pounds'). That's fourteen hundred pounds which could have gone a little way towards righting the financial wrongs that the Brandon family have committed, and doesn't.

Then there's the small problem of the dates not quite adding up. Colonel Brandon mentions that 'three years ago', his ward 'had just reached her fourteenth year'. By this he seems to mean that she had just turned fourteen. Elsewhere he mentions the mother's death, which took place when the child was three, as a 'subject [...] untouched for fourteen years'. He is 35 when we first meet him, and turns 36 towards the end of the main action of the novel. His age is mentioned no fewer than eight times. Jane really didn't want us to miss it. Did she want us to be able to perform a fairly simple piece of arithmetic?

Colonel Brandon must have been eighteen when the younger Eliza was born, or at the outside, nineteen. Add in the nine months during which her mother was pregnant with her, and all at once we're presented with a question – just when was she conceived? If it was really eighteen months or two years after the Colonel left for India, how young was he precisely when he was planning to elope to Scotland – fifteen? In spite of his careful, coded protestations – in spite of the fact that he describes events to Elinor in such a way as to allow her to conclude that he spent five years in India and so could not possibly be considered as a candidate – it seems that Colonel Brandon is very much in the frame as a potential father to the younger Eliza. In fact he never explicitly denies the relationship. He says that the child is 'the offspring' of his cousin's 'first guilty connection'. He says that: 'I called her a distant relation; but I am well aware that I have in general been suspected of a much nearer connection with her.'

So is she his daughter?

She goes by the name Eliza Williams. Now it's possible that Williams was her mother's maiden name, or that it's a name picked for her at random. But it's also possible that it spells out the identity of her father even though she has no right to use his surname, that she is 'Eliza, William's child'. It's easy then; we just have to look at Colonel Brandon's Christian name. It'll be a pretty hefty clue, one way or another.

Jane never tells us what it is.*

Now she never gives us the first name of Darcy's cousin Colonel Fitzwilliam, either, in *Pride and Prejudice*, so the silence isn't exceptional. But Colonel Brandon is the only central character in the novels whose Christian name isn't mentioned. And names are problematic in *Sense and Sensibility* anyway. For that reason they assume undue prominence.

---

* Emma Thompson's screenplay for the Ang Lee-directed film adaptation of *Sense and Sensibility* (1995) made him a 'Christopher', on absolutely no basis whatever.

We've already looked at the significance of some of the surnames.*
On top of that, quite a number of characters have the same Christian
names, and not always because they're related, but sometimes, seemingly, at random.

We have the two Elizas, mother and daughter. We have Marianne
and her little cousin, Annamaria – both, presumably, named for the same
female relations. There are two Henrys and a Harry. The disagreeable
Thomas Palmer shares his name with the Dashwoods' manservant. We
learn in a throwaway piece of dialogue that Fanny Dashwood shares
hers with a cousin of Colonel Brandon's. We have three grown-up Johns
– John Dashwood, Sir John Middleton, and John Willoughby – and a
little one, the oldest of the Middleton children.

There was a limited pool of names in common use in England in the
eighteenth century, and this kind of coincidence must have happened
all the time. In a novel, though, it's almost too true-to-life, too natural-
istic. It's hard to escape the suspicion that some of this, at least, is Jane's
inexperience as a writer showing. As I've mentioned before, we don't
know when the novel was written, or when or even whether it was ever
substantially revised. But Jane must have read through it before it was
sent to the publishers, and we know she checked through the proofs.

Is there some point to the repetition of names, then?

Let's look at the Dashwoods' cousins, the three named Middleton
children. The daughter is Annamaria, the sons John and William.
Annamaria, I've suggested, is named for the same people as Marianne.
John, though he shares his name with John Dashwood and with John
Willoughby, is surely named for his father. Who is William named for?
Well, plausibly, for a godfather. And a likely candidate for a godfather is

---

* Colonel Brandon's surname carries some fairly negative connotations. As the
Australian critic Olivia Murphy points out, Brandon Hall is the estate where the
virtuous heroine is imprisoned and subjected to attempted rape in *Pamela*, the
first novel by Samuel Richardson, who dominated the genre in the middle of the
eighteenth century.

his father's near neighbour and 'particular friend', Colonel Brandon. So perhaps the Colonel is a William, after all?

It's the only indication we're ever given, as readers. We can't be certain, but there's room for doubt – doubt about Colonel Brandon's morals, his motivations. Doubt, ultimately, about whether Marianne can ever really be happy with a man who, if he doesn't quite steal the bread out of the mouths of his daughter and granddaughter, is happy to enrich himself from the fortune which, morally, ought to belong to his female relations.

Jane herself never seems to really want to convince us about the good sense of Colonel Brandon and Marianne marrying. Why make the age difference so vast? Why have characters think about the age difference as being insurmountable ('thirty-five and seventeen had better not have any thing to do with matrimony together', 'he had little to do but to calculate the disproportion between thirty-six and seventeen')? Why manipulate matters so that, as far as the reader is concerned, the two never once converse with each other?* Why not show us Marianne's feelings gradually altering, rather than telling us that Marianne's mother and sister and brother-in-law wish to promote the match out of gratitude to the Colonel? 'They each felt his sorrows, and their own obligations, and Marianne, by general consent, was to be the reward of all', Jane writes. Marianne marries, with 'no sentiment superior to strong esteem and lively friendship'; she finds herself 'submitting to new attachments'. In all this, Marianne plays an alarmingly passive, even sacrificial role. On a more cheerful note, we're assured that 'Marianne could never love by halves; and her whole heart became, in time, as much devoted to her husband, as it had once been to Willoughby'.

---

* We're never shown the two in conversation together. The one time we see Marianne actually address a comment to the Colonel, he doesn't reply. Even towards the end of the novel, there are no more than a couple of indirect references to them exchanging very basic courtesies.

How long that time might be, we're not told, nor how long this love might last.

For Wollstonecraft, it was self-evident that sensibility, in exciting women's feelings, particularly their sexual feelings, would be a lifelong burden. As she says, 'A husband cannot long pay those attentions with the passion necessary to excite lively emotions, and the heart, accustomed to lively emotions, turns to a new lover, or pines in secret, the prey of virtue or prudence.'

It's an ending which, in its own way, is fully as chilling as Edward's little trick with the scissors.

In the world of *Sense and Sensibility* love and family, honour and duty have hardly any meaning. Promises are made to be broken. Women are exiled from their homes. Guardians don't guard. Brothers ignore their sisters, mothers disinherit their sons, fathers fail to safeguard their daughters. Elinor Dashwood marries a man who we know is an unfaithful liar with (perhaps) troubling sexual inclinations. Marianne Dashwood, having lost her heart to a vicious, selfish scoundrel, marries a man whose morality is suspect, and who she can never be certain of. Edward comes to regret his engagement to the venal – or the practical – Lucy Steele. Colonel Brandon falls in love with a girl he doesn't know.

In a society where unmarried men and women were kept largely separate, and permitted to socialise only when properly chaperoned, how could a woman arrive at any sort of knowledge of a man's character – and how could a man hope to understand the nature of the woman he married?

In *Mansfield Park* and *Emma* the heroines seek safety in quasi-incestuous marriages with men who are closely connected to their families, and who they have known for years. In *Pride and Prejudice*, though, Jane suggests an altogether more revolutionary approach to the problem.

James Gillray, *A March to the Bank* (1787). In topical terms this is a
complaint about the behaviour of a particular group of soldiers who
regularly marched along the Strand in London, but on a deeper level it
is an expression of profound social anxiety about military power.

CHAPTER 4

'All Our Old Prejudices'

Pride and Prejudice

Steventon, Christmas 1798. *

She was to have dined at Deane this evening, with Martha Lloyd, but it is coming on to snow, and she doubts whether a journey – even if it is only to the next village – is altogether to be advised. Martha will not mind it. She is a dear friend, dearer still since the birth last month of little James-Edward, their shared nephew. If only James had married Martha instead of Martha's sister Mary, though. Jane could have loved Martha, who is quite the most appreciative reader that *First Impressions* has had. Since she cannot while away the evening chatting with Martha, however, she has taken out her half-finished letter to Cassandra, at present in Kent. But having passed on the pleasantest news, that their brother Frank is to be made captain, and that their own particular little brother Charles will not have so long to wait before he is promoted, every other topic seems flat and insipid.

They have had cold weather this last little while. Their mother has suffered with it – she who feels the cold far more than other mortals. Jane has already exhausted the ball. That it was thin of company, less than a dozen couples; that she wore her black cap; that she danced twenty dances without the least fatigue; the list of her partners – these facts are already recorded in her letter. Cassandra, it appears from *her* most recent letter, has been at a ball herself and supped with a prince,

---

*   Based on Jane Austen's letter to Cassandra Austen (24th December 1798).

no less. Jane can say nothing of their acquaintance in Hampshire that can compete with princes. Still, there are clothes, and there is ill-health – a perennially fruitful topic with such a mother, and such a brother as Edward.

And charity. She has laid out half a guinea in four pairs of worsted stockings, a shift and a shawl, and distributed them among the poor women in Steventon. Cassandra will be glad to hear of her doings. She is glad herself.

She drums her fingers on the table top. What else is there that can she write of?

Perhaps Cassandra will be amused to hear that, at the very time their father was approaching Admiral Gambier to enquire about the prospects of promotion for Frank and Charles, Charles was attacking another of the Sea-Lords directly. 'The Lords of the Admiralty will have enough of our applications at present', she writes, and, straining for a humorous tone, 'I am afraid his serene Highness will be in a passion, & order some of our heads to be cut off. —'

It does not do, to joke about such matters.

What must it be like to lose one's head? The Irish rebellion is all but defeated now, so she gathers from the newspapers. But all this year, it seems, she has been reading of how the rebel leaders had their hearts taken out, their heads stuck up on spikes in Cork and Wexford. To be sure, it was no more than they deserved, for inviting the French into Ireland. But still, imagine seeing one's father, one's brother or husband, beheaded …

It's too close.

She's sent letters to Cork – to her little brother Charles, when he was on board the *Unicorn*, not two years since.

Her cousin Eliza – clever, fascinating cousin Eliza, heiress to an Indian fortune from her godfather, now married to brother Henry – lost her first husband, the French Comte, to the guillotine during the Terror. Jane dreamed about heads in baskets for months.

And yet, in the beginning, it had all seemed so different. At fourteen, at fifteen, she had believed firmly in the need for liberty and equality – for fairness.

Jane thinks of the women shivering in the cottages around Steventon, of how little her charities will do to warm them. She thinks of her mother, upstairs in bed, with the covers heaped over her and a fire roaring in the grate.

She doesn't know what she believes now.

Everyone – almost everyone – loves *Pride and Prejudice*.* It regularly tops lists of the hundred most important or best-loved novels. The hero and heroine, Darcy and Elizabeth, have developed lives of their own, rather like Conan Doyle's Sherlock Holmes. They've become cultural icons in their own right, their relationship the ultimate in literary romance.

I have a mug that I was given a couple of Christmases ago. It's one of a series that you can buy, 'Classic novels abridged'. This one encapsulates the plot of *Pride and Prejudice*: 'Mr Darcy is a proud man', it reads. 'Elizabeth Bennet doesn't like him. They change their minds and get married. The end.'

There is, of course, rather more to it than that.

More than anything else, it's the 1995 BBC television series of *Pride and Prejudice* which precipitated the current, two-decade-long period of intense, near-global, obsession with Jane Austen. It's this version that entered the cultural consciousness, creating such a strong hold for itself that when a member of the general public hears the title, the first image that appears in their mind is one which has no counterpart in the book: a sweaty Colin Firth stripping half naked and diving

---

*   One notable exception is Mark Twain, who once wrote in a letter that every time he read the book, he wanted to dig Jane up and 'beat her over the skull with her own shin-bone'.

into the lake at Pemberley. And there have been other very popular *Pride and Prejudices* since, lots of them – the 2005 film starring Keira Knightley, the Bollywoodised *Bride and Prejudice*, *Bridget Jones's Diary*, *Lost in Austen*, *Death Comes to Pemberley*, *Pride and Prejudice and Zombies*, Curtis Sittenfeld's *Eligible*. Even the 'biopic' *Becoming Jane* riffed on *Pride and Prejudice*. All these retellings and variations work on the assumption that readers or viewers know the characters and the story very well, an assumption that doesn't get made with Jane's other books. The assumption isn't wrong.

But it's that same knowledge, that same sense of familiarity, which blinds us to much of what *Pride and Prejudice* is actually doing as a text. It makes it, perhaps, the most difficult out of all of Jane's novels for us to read as she intended.

We all know that *Pride and Prejudice* is a happy, cheerful book, even if we haven't read it. There's a degree of truth there, but only a degree.

Jane herself, in one of those passages of her writing which it's almost impossible to fix the tone of, called it 'rather too light & bright & sparkling'.* It wanted, she said, 'shade' and 'to be stretched out here & there with a long Chapter – of sense if it could be had'. Failing long, sensible chapters, she suggests the book might benefit instead from adding in passages of 'solemn specious nonsense – about something unconnected with the story; an Essay on Writing, a critique on Walter Scott, or the history of Buonaparte'.

It isn't that unusual to find long sections in eighteenth-century novels which seem to have nothing to do with anything; theoretical discussions about writing appear too.† There was, for a long time, a pervasive view that the novel, as a genre, wasn't good enough – wasn't sufficiently serious, intellectual, improving. This is something we discussed briefly in

---

* Letter to Cassandra Austen; dated only with 'February 4th', though the year of composition is clearly, from internal references, 1813.

† Henry Fielding's *Joseph Andrews* (1742, sometimes called the first English novel) is a notable, but hardly solitary, example.

the chapter on *Northanger Abbey*, and the 'defence of the novel' which appears there seems, in some respects, to chime with what Jane's saying here. In *Northanger Abbey*, she sets the novel in opposition to other, traditionally better-respected, types of writing – essays, history – and she defends it against literary critics as well.

But any 'history of Buonaparte' would, of its nature, be political, would, in spite of being called a 'history', be in effect current affairs.* Bonaparte, after all, was still very much a present threat in early 1813. And though Walter Scott's poetry, like his later novels, was largely cod-medieval, though it had generally been reviewed very favourably, there had been one particular rather famous criticism – a 'critique'. It had appeared in the *Edinburgh Review* in 1808 and focused on Scott's long poem about wicked knights, villainous nuns, and the Battle of Flodden: *Marmion*.

Marmion ends with an address to 'Statesmen grave', wishing them 'Sound head, clean hand, and piercing wit, | And patriotic heart – as Pitt!' Pitt is William Pitt, the youngest prime minister Britain has ever had, who had died in 1806. It was Pitt who'd overseen the government crackdown on radicalism in the 1790s, the increase in state surveillance, the suspension of habeas corpus, the forced Union with Ireland after the Uprising, the expansion of the navy and the militia. The *Edinburgh Review* 'critique' of *Marmion* ended with a sneering reference to the 'political creed of the author'. Reviews could be an even touchier subject in the early nineteenth century than they are now.

What's the reason that Jane starts to talk politics here, as she seems to be doing? Why does she follow up the references by asserting that her correspondent – Cassandra, as so often – would think differently

---

* One positively glowing 'Memoir of General Buonaparte' had been printed in the magazine of the London Corresponding Society, the group which really did want to have a revolution and overthrow the British government. (*The moral and political magazine of the London Corresponding Society* (1796–1797, Volume 1).)

('– I doubt your quite agreeing with me here – I know your starched notions')? Are politics totally 'unconnected with the story'?

In another letter penned a few days earlier, Jane mentions some printer's errors she's noticed in the text of *Pride and Prejudice*: 'There are a few Typical errors—& a "said he" or a "said she" would sometimes make the Dialogue more immediately clear—'. No matter, though, she continues, 'I do not write for such dull Elves As have not a great deal of Ingenuity themselves'.

This is, roughly, a quotation from the second to last stanza of *Marmion*. In the space of a few lines, the reader is encouraged to imagine how the hero, Wilton, and the heroine, Clara, are united, and how all the stray plot strands will be tied up:

> I do not rhyme to that dull elf,
> Who cannot image to himself,
> That all through Flodden's dismal night,
> Wilton was foremost in the fight [...]
> [...] Nor sing I to that simple maid,
> To whom it must in terms be said,
> That King and kinsmen did agree,
> To bless fair Clara's constancy;
> Who cannot, unless I relate,
> Paint to her mind the bridal's state [...]

This stanza, the stanza which pops into Jane's head when she's thinking about how her newly-appeared novel will be read, deals with what an author can expect a reader to do. It's about the author's desire for readers who can join the dots, follow implications and allusions through to their natural conclusions, who can 'image' for themselves, 'paint' for themselves, who don't necessarily have to see the words set down in order to understand the message.

Jane wants readers who have a 'great deal of ingenuity'. Isn't it possible, then, that *Pride and Prejudice* isn't quite so light and bright and sparkling as we've been led to believe? That there are darker, more serious layers to be uncovered?

∽

In December 1943, on a visit to Tunis, the British wartime leader Winston Churchill fell seriously ill with pneumonia. Later he recalled that, confined to bed, banned from work, he 'decided to read a novel' or, rather, to have his daughter Sarah read one to him. Having 'long ago' read 'Jane Austen's Sense and Sensibility', he thought that he

> would have Pride and Prejudice. Sarah read it to me beautifully from the foot of the bed. I had always thought it would be better than its rival. What calm lives they had, those people! No worries about the French Revolution, or the crashing struggle of the Napoleonic Wars. Only manners controlling natural passion so far as they could, together with cultured explanations of any mischances.*

This wasn't an original idea. Rudyard Kipling, the great writer of empire, had drawn a very similar direct contrast in *The Janeites*, a short story centring on one character's experiences in the trenches of the Great War. In it, Jane's novels are absurd, almost meaningless and, paradoxically, a representation of civilisation, salvation and Britishness, a balm to wounded minds. The names and passages that the main character, the Cockney hairdresser Humberstall, learns to recite – and which get him out of more than one sticky situation – are to begin with all Greek to him. After the war, when he reads the books, he finds 'nothing in 'em' – except the solace of seeing ordinary, everyday peacetime life reflected back to him.

---

* The story appears in more than one place; the museum now in Chawton Cottage, where Jane lived, used to have it in a letter, mounted on the wall in what's supposed to have been Jane's bedroom.

In a novel of 1975 by Paul Scott – *A Division of the Spoils*, the last of the 'quartet' on which the 1980s television series *The Jewel in the Crown* was based – a returned prisoner-of-war recalls discussing with one of his former captors what the experience of coming home might involve. The home in question is in colonial India but the imagined return is both distinctly British and soothing, hypnotic even – 'a comfortable chair in a cosy room', 'reading *Pride and Prejudice*, sipping a glass of special malt whisky, and fondling the ears' of a 'faithful black labrador'. Dog, whisky, *Pride and Prejudice* – all are equally alien to India, and, it's implied, equally unimaginable in war, in its twentieth-century incarnation at least.

The idea that Jane's novels offer a blissful, almost drugged-up, break from harsh reality doesn't hold water, though. Remember that Britain was at war with France from 1793 to 1815, with only two short periods of peace. It's this background that we have to place the books against. The 'emigrant' mentioned in passing in *Sense and Sensibility* is a refugee from the French Revolution. Easy enough to miss the reference out, if you wanted to try to make the war and revolutionary unrest disappear; Jane doesn't.

War is a constant presence in the novels, a buzz of background static which, at times, rises to ear-splitting screeches and whines. Later on, we'll see just how closely the plot of *Persuasion* is built around the 'crashing struggle' of the Napoleonic wars. In that novel, the heroine's family don't object to her marrying a naval officer just because they're snobs, but because there is a very real risk that he will be killed or injured, leaving her without any money. He returns years later with a fortune acquired by seizing enemy ships; hardly a blameless or a bloodless pursuit. While Anne has sat at home, 'quiet, confined' and anxiously poring over the newspapers, Captain Wentworth has been braving sabres, musket fire, and cannon. *Persuasion* ends with 'the dread of a future war'.

Possibly Winston Churchill was familiar with the 1940 Hollywood film of *Pride and Prejudice* starring Laurence Olivier and Greer Garson, which transfers the action to the Victorian era and softens almost all of Jane's jagged edges, even succeeding in the difficult task of making

Darcy's aunt Lady Catherine de Bourgh lovable. Churchill seems to have known what he was going to find in the novel before he ever opened it (he had 'always thought it would be better') – I'd suggest he's very far from being the only reader to approach the book through a haze of preconceptions. Either way, we have to wonder how much of Jane Austen's *Pride and Prejudice* he actually heard, and how much he tuned out, as he dozed.

Because what he doesn't seem to have registered is that, for a novel which is supposedly far removed from any concerns about war, it's crammed with references to soldiers. Its pages are peppered with the words 'regiment', 'militia', 'officers'. *Sense and Sensibility* has one colonel – Colonel Brandon, who seems to have retired from military life.* *Pride and Prejudice* features two, both of whom – so far as we know – are still active. One major character and quite a number of minor ones are pursuing military careers, though, naturally, as officers. The ranks of the militia were supposed to be filled by lot but you could pay to be taken out, so that in practice the landowning, and even middling classes were exempt.†

Both *Persuasion* and *Mansfield Park* have been called naval novels; if Jane ever wrote an army novel, then it's this one.

And it's one which, unlike *Sense and Sensibility*, is definitively set during wartime. At the end of the book, when Jane details the various fates of the different characters, she mentions, explicitly, 'the restoration of peace'. The whole action of the novel, then, takes place during hostilities. But to Jane's first readers this would have been apparent from early on. The 'regiment of militia' which in Chapter 7 takes up its winter

---

* Mr Weston, in *Emma*, we're told, once served for some time in the militia as a captain, some 20 or 25 years before the story starts. It is, as we'll see, difficult to date *Emma*'s setting with any certainty.

† It was possible to insure against being drawn for the militia. A premium of 25 shillings would allow you to evade service if you wished (see, for example, the *Hereford Journal*, 1st February 1797).

quarters in the town of Meryton and, halfway through the book, moves to a larger camp at Brighton, on the south coast, would have been shifted around the country like this only during a time of war. The summer army camps strung along the south coast weren't there just to train recruits in the bracing sea breezes; they were there to defend against invasion.

I grew up near Chatham in Kent, which was for centuries a major naval base. It's ringed with hilltop fortifications built or extensively remodelled during the Napoleonic wars. Throughout Jane's adulthood, people were terrified of being invaded by the French. There was a degree of scaremongering involved. It was far from unusual for newspapers to carry alarmist reports in which invasion was made to seem imminent. But scaremongering wasn't the only reason people were afraid. Fourteen hundred French troops landed at Fishguard in Wales in 1797.* They quickly surrendered, but they landed.

And one of the alarmist reports at least was pretty accurate. It appeared in 1796, and detailed how an escaped prisoner-of-war had seen, with his own eyes, French volunteers massing near Dunkirk, consumed with revolutionary bloodlust, warning that the French had collected 'a number of flat-bottomed boats all along the coast, which are constructed with great convenience for the landing of cavalry from them. Each boat has two field pieces [i.e. artillery guns] belonging to it. The French talk of the Expedition being ready towards the end of November.'†

It was. The French didn't invade the well-fortified south coast; they tried instead to land troops at Bantry Bay, on the sparsely-populated south-west coast of Ireland. They were prevented by a combination of bad weather and the British navy. Among the ships which sailed out from

---

* The story that the French mistook the Welshwomen, dressed in red shawls and tall black hats, for soldiers, is charming, but absent from early sources.

† *Reading Mercury*, 7th November 1796; the report also appeared in at least half a dozen other newspapers.

Cork to mop up the last remains of the French fleet was the *Unicorn*, captained by the man who'd married Jane's first cousin Jane Cooper and having, among its officers, Jane's younger brother Charles.

Ireland, in some ways, was less distant from England then than it is now. Jane never ventures there in her fiction – aware, perhaps, that her scenes would be unlikely to stand comparison with the then more famous novelist Maria Edgeworth, who had lived in Ireland for much of her life. She sends characters there quite often, though, more often than she sends them anywhere else. Jane Fairfax's foster sister, in *Emma*, marries a Mr Dixon and goes to live with him at his Irish 'country seat, Baly-craig'. In *Persuasion*, Admiral and Mrs Croft are stationed for a time at Cork and the heroine, Anne, has family who live in Ireland, the aristocratic but uninspiring Dalrymples. In the unfinished fragment usually called *The Watsons*, the heroine returns home to her birth family because the aunt who brought her up has married again to a man called 'O'brien', and 'is gone to settle in Ireland'.

We don't have to cling to those mysteriously vanished letters, and the idea that Jane was in love with the Irish lawyer Tom Lefroy to explain this. Jane knew a number of people who had spent time in Ireland; Tom Lefroy, yes, but also, as we saw above, her cousin and her younger brother. In 1799 her brother Henry, too, spent the better part of a year in Ireland with the Oxfordshires, the regiment of militia which he had joined in 1793, and for which he became Acting-Paymaster.

Ireland wasn't so distant to Jane, and – though both her brothers had managed to avoid them – the horrors which took place there in the narrow gap between Charles's visit and Henry's must have seemed uncomfortably close to home.

In 1798 French soldiers invaded Ireland, in support of what used to be called the 'Irish rebellion' and is now more often called the United Irish Uprising.

For us Irish nationalism is strongly associated with Roman Catholicism but in the 1790s the Catholic Church was opposed to any suggestion of rebellion in Ireland. Not many of the United Irishmen were Catholic. They were political radicals; most had been directly influenced by the literature and ideas of the French Revolution. Prominent among the United Irish leaders was a man called Lord Edward Fitzgerald, one of the 22 children born to the Duchess of Leinster. Despite being related to half the aristocratic families in the British Isles and serving for a time in the army and as a member of parliament, Lord Edward embraced revolution wholeheartedly. He visited Paris, where he stayed with Thomas Paine, the author whose writings could fairly be said to have inspired both the American and French Revolutions. He repudiated his title and married a woman who was in all probability an illegitimate daughter of the Duke of Orléans, the only member of the French royal family to support – and indeed help to promote – revolutionary change.

The Uprising was more than an expression of Hibernian nationalism – it was a clash of fundamental ideologies, played out over the course of a wet summer across the Irish hills and through the streets of towns like Carlow and Ballynahinch and Enniscorthy. Bullets flew. Buildings were burned. There were brutal atrocities on both sides; the aftermath was no gentler. Fitzgerald was betrayed and shot, dying in prison of untreated septicaemia. His co-conspirator, Wolfe Tone, who held the rank of general in the French army, committed suicide. Jane could have read in the *Hampshire Chronicle* of the fate of another Irish rebel, Henry Munro, hanged opposite his front door. 'After hanging a considerable time', the newspaper reports, 'his heart was taken out and his head being severed from his body was stuck on top of a pike and affixed on the market house.'[1]

What the Uprising revealed was that the British government was willing to turn its troops – including its foreign mercenaries and its militia – against its own people. In 1797, in Haddington in Scotland, a disagreement over call-ups to the militia had resulted in public unrest in which a number of civilians were killed.[2] In the wake of the Uprising, this looked less like an unfortunate incident and more like the unspoken reason for having a militia in the first place. When proposals for expanding the militia were being debated in parliament, a member of the opposition claimed that 'the real object [...] was to [...] extend the influence of Ministers'.[3] The government wanted, he suggested, a large armed force with which to menace the populace; their true intention was to introduce, by stealth, the apparatus of 'an absolute Monarchy' – a tyranny, a dictatorship.

Serving in the militia was rather like being in the Territorial Army – in peacetime you occasionally had to do some training but it wasn't a major disruption to your life. During wartime or national crisis it was different. Militia were purposely stationed away from their homes, in areas where they had no loyalties, no networks of friends and family. Traditionally they had been billeted in towns; the officers in rented lodgings, the men at inns, though this was starting to change. In *Pride and Prejudice* it seems likely that the men, at least, are in barracks, since in one scene the Bennet sisters dine together at the local inn, the George. The officers, however, are in 'lodgings' – and, with their red coats, are a visible presence in the town, a constant reminder of government observation and control. Meryton is, we know, close to the Great North Road – the main arterial route northwards from the capital. When it's thought that Lydia and Wickham have eloped via London to Scotland, a character laments that 'they must have passed within ten miles of us'. From Meryton to London is, Jane tells us, 'a journey of only twenty-four miles', one that can be achieved in a morning. The War Office hasn't quartered the regiment at random; they've put it there so that it can easily march to the north or be used to help suppress metropolitan unrest.

The militia aren't in the novel to provide young men for the Bennet girls to dance with; they bring with them an atmosphere which is highly politically charged, they trail clouds of danger – images of a rebellious populace, of government repression and, more distant but insistent nevertheless, the fear of what might happen if the men in the militia, the troops, mutiny. The militia embody one of the central questions of the age – who should you be afraid of? In evading one danger, do you run straight into the arms of another?

Jane freely admits that men in uniform are glamorous. Even the intelligent, cynical heroine Elizabeth Bennet isn't immune, though she is discerning. When she and her sisters first meet the caddish Wickham, they're delighted to find that he's planning to join the militia – 'the young man wanted only regimentals [i.e. uniform] to make him completely charming'.* Wickham has, in addition, 'all the best part of beauty, a fine countenance, a good figure, and very pleasing address'. He's also – crucially – happy to pull Darcy's character apart. But Kitty and Lydia, the youngest and silliest of the Bennet girls, are entranced even by the 'regimentals of an ensign' – the most junior officer rank, not infrequently held by teenaged boys.

For Jane, though, it's only naivety or extreme youth which enable characters to persist in this kind of attitude. Mrs Bennet can 'remember the time when I liked a red coat myself very well', but, for all she is 'a woman of mean understanding', she can see past the uniforms. She doesn't want her daughters marrying just any officer. Only 'a smart young colonel, with five or six thousand a year' will do.

As I pointed out in both of the previous chapters, we can be certain of next to nothing about the genesis of the early novels. But whenever – and in whatever guise – *Pride and Prejudice* was begun, by the time Jane came to publish it, she had herself lived in what was, for all intents and purposes, a garrison town. The glamour, for her, had worn off.

When the regiment removes to a summer camp at Brighton, Lydia Bennet is invited to go too, by her friend, the wife of the colonel. We're told that she imagines:

the streets of that gay bathing-place covered with officers. She saw herself the object of attention, to tens and to scores of them

---

* In theory militia officers were meant to be landowners – which neither the fictional Wickham nor the real Henry Austen were – but the rule was easily and frequently got round.

at present unknown. She saw all the glories of the camp—its tents stretched forth in beauteous uniformity of lines, crowded with the young and the gay, and dazzling with scarlet; and, to complete the view, she saw herself seated beneath a tent, tenderly flirting with at least six officers at once.

Jane makes it absolutely clear that this is 'the creative eye of fancy' – and the fancy of a fifteen-year-old girl, at that. Jane knew that military camps were anything but 'beauteous', knew that a town full of soldiers was not a pleasant place for women – and she knew that her readers knew that too, or could guess at it.

The camp at Brighton will be dirty and – if it rains – muddy. It will stink. There will be stalls selling alcohol; public drunkenness. There will be women (and girls, and perhaps a few boys) plying their wares as prostitutes. And these kind of problems aren't confined to the large training camps. The militia, who supposedly exist to preserve order and to protect the local inhabitants, are in fact a disruptive force throughout *Pride and Prejudice*.

When Elizabeth first hears of Lydia's wish to go to Brighton, she's appalled. 'Good Heaven!' she thinks to herself, 'Brighton, and a whole campful of soldiers, to us, who have been overset already by one poor regiment of militia, and the monthly balls of Meryton!' We're told that Elizabeth 'did not credit above half of what was said' by the local gossips after Wickham elopes with Lydia but even if he isn't 'in debt to every tradesman in the place', even if his amorous adventures – his 'intrigues' – didn't in fact extend 'into every tradesman's family', we're left to conclude that Wickham really is economically and sexually dangerous, that he has done some damage in the town. And he's only one officer. Are we meant to believe that all the others have been virtuously idle the whole winter through?

Well, in fact, we know they haven't. We see them promenading in the street, flirting, dancing, dining, drinking. We're told that they've been dressing up as women – 'We dressed up Chamberlayne in woman's clothes on purpose to pass for a lady, only think what fun!' – and this with the approval of the Colonel ('Not a soul knew of it, but Colonel and Mrs Forster, and Kitty and me').

There's a nasty underbelly to all this fun and games. Jane lifts the lid on it in one deeply, dizzyingly unsettling sentence, which goes from social niceties to bloody violence and back again: 'several of the officers had dined lately with their uncle, a private had been flogged, and it had actually been hinted that Colonel Forster was going to be married.' There must be plenty of privates somewhere in or near Meryton, but this is the only one we ever glimpse. As an ordinary member of the militia ranks, not an officer, he's unlikely to have been a volunteer; he'll have been selected by lottery and then conscripted. He didn't, evidently, have the money to evade the ballot. He's being flogged, subjected to discipline – the kind of discipline which, if wrongly judged or mistimed, could lead to bad feeling in the ranks; even, on occasion, to mutiny. Flogging took the skin off your back. It scarred you for life. What is this particular man being disciplined for? Laziness, insubordination, drunkenness, theft, handing out seditious leaflets, 'bothering' the local women? All of these options are plausible; none are soothing.

The presence of the militia in the novel, then, introduces layer upon layer of anxiety. There's the anxiety which always attaches to the sudden arrival of large numbers of strange men in a neighbourhood. Elizabeth really isn't wise to walk alone, as she does early in the novel. It's noticeable that she stops doing it. But there are also political anxieties – what if the strange men become radicalised? What, conversely, if a meeting gets a little out of hand, and they start shooting at ordinary people? Meryton isn't so calm and untroubled after all.

Invasions; the naval mutinies at Portsmouth and in the Thames Estuary in 1797; the food riots which periodically erupted throughout the war years – they're there. They're in the background, but they are there.

∽

As I mentioned in the previous chapter, we don't actually know when *Pride and Prejudice* was begun or finished, nor whether it once had another title. It may be pretty much the same as *First Impressions*, the novel Jane mentions in letters in January and June of 1799. It may be the novel that Jane's father thought was good enough to send off to a publisher at the end of 1797. We can't be sure, though. Nor can we be sure when *Pride and Prejudice* is set. More than one eminent literary critic has devoted their time and effort to trying to make the dates Jane mentions match to a particular year or years. It can't be done. Jane explains herself that the manuscript was 'lop't and crop't' before it was published – who knows what was taken out or altered.

But from what remains, it seems that we can't be going too far wrong in identifying the setting as the mid to late 1790s. This chimes with the mention of 'peace' at the end of the novel, with the prominence given to the militia, and with the reference to the large summer army camps at Brighton. The way in which Miss Bingley and her sister talk about Elizabeth's muddy petticoat early in the novel ('six inches deep in mud, I am absolutely certain; and the gown which had been let down to hide it not doing its office') also indicates 1790s fashion rather than anything later.

Elizabeth must be dressed in what was called by dressmakers a *robe à l'anglaise*, a dress which, by even the mid-1790s, was beginning to look dated, and countrified. It had a split overskirt, open at the front, which could be ruched up or let down at the back. The 'petticoat' is the underskirt, often in a contrasting material or colour. If the back of her 'petticoat' has been splashed with mud, Elizabeth may well have stopped outside Netherfield and done her best to hide the dirt by undoing the loops which hold her overskirt gathered up at the back. By 1813, this style was pretty much confined to the wardrobes of working women.

Miss Bingley and her sister aren't just criticising Elizabeth for walking alone through the muddy fields, they're bitching about how unfashionably she's dressed, a point the modern reader misses.

If the 1790s setting is the right one, then we probably need to reassess the book's title, because it should have been suggesting rather more to Jane's first readers than it does to us.

For the first nine-tenths of the eighteenth century, 'pride and prejudice' was a fairly standard, fairly innocuous phrase, like 'love and friendship', which Jane used as the title for one of her teenage pieces. It appears three times, all in capital letters, in the final chapter of *Cecilia*, a novel by the extremely popular author Fanny Burney, published in 1782.

Jane certainly read and enjoyed Burney's books and *Pride and Prejudice* echoes, faintly, some elements of both *Cecilia* and the earlier *Evelina*. Jane gives her readers a short lecture on pride early in the novel, using the only plain Bennet, Mary, as her mouthpiece.* But from 1790 onwards, the word 'prejudice' took on a very particular frisson, one which it simply didn't have when Burney was writing *Cecilia*. And that frisson was intimately associated with the French Revolution and with radical politics.

The initial reaction in Britain to the French Revolution of 1789 was for the most part mutedly positive. Before the revolution, the French had had an absolute monarchy – not one balanced by parliament, like Britain had. They'd had imprisonment without trial; England had habeas corpus, which insisted that detention had to be publicly justified. If France was becoming more like Britain, that was really the best thing they could do. It wasn't until heads started to roll that British public opinion recoiled. By the time the French royal family were guillotined, the revolutionaries inspired horror and disgust in almost every stout

---

* "'Pride,'" observed Mary […] "is a very common failing, I believe. By all that I have ever read, I am convinced that it is very common indeed; that human nature is particularly prone to it, and that there are very few of us who do not cherish a feeling of self-complacency on the score of some quality or other, real or imaginary. Vanity and pride are different things, though the words are often used synonymously. A person may be proud without being vain. Pride relates more to our opinion of ourselves, vanity to what we would have others think of us."'

British heart. Some people, though, had seen nothing but danger in the French Revolution from almost the very beginning. One of the most prominent of these was Edmund Burke.

We've encountered him already. It was Burke who led the prosecution of Warren Hastings – the godfather (and reputedly the biological father) of Jane's cousin and sister-in-law Eliza. Hastings was tried in the House of Commons for extortion and corruption in his management of British affairs in India.

Burke had been born in Ireland sometime around 1730. His mother was Catholic; so was his sister. But his father wasn't, and Edmund and his brothers were raised outside the Catholic faith. This, at the time, was very normal in Ireland. There was a lot of legislation deliberately geared towards making life difficult for Catholics and easier for everyone else. Almost everything was made problematic – property ownership, inheritance, entry to the universities and to many of the professions, even owning a nice horse. For women, whose lives were anyway hugely circumscribed, the anti-Catholic laws made little real difference; for men they did, and so you ended up with generations of families in which religious loyalties were neatly divided by sex.

After training as a lawyer, and turning his hand to writing philosophy and history, Burke had ended up in parliament, where he'd quickly found fame as an orator. Though not a Catholic, he chose to marry into a Catholic family. He had been prepared for university, conversely, at a Quaker school. It's no surprise to find that, as well as being prominent in the hard-fought repeal of anti-Catholic legislation, he was sympathetic to religious dissenters of all kinds. During the anti-Catholic 'Gordon Riots' of 1780, a mob gathered in front of his house – not an occurrence to be taken lightly in a bout of civil disturbance which saw buildings set on fire, people killed, and the breaking open of Newgate Prison and the Bank of England.

But for several years after this, his instincts remained reformist ones, not just in questions of religion, but in economic and constitutional matters as well, and in legal ones. Burke called some of his economic proposals 'radical'. He disliked how much power remained in the hands of the Crown. Having been able to appreciate the arguments of both sides in the American revolutionary war, he was critical of how imperial expansion was being handled elsewhere. He pushed for the trial of Hastings. He spoke out against the prevalence of capital punishment. On one occasion he even involved himself in a case where a man convicted of sodomy had been killed in the stocks.

Events in France, though, brought out a strongly reactionary streak in him.

'— what Spectators and what actors!' wrote Burke in a letter of August 1789, a few weeks after the revolution had begun; 'England gazing in astonishment at a French struggle for Liberty and not knowing whether to blame or to applaud'. Burke decided soon enough. Within months, he was openly criticising developments across the Channel in parliament. In 1790, he published *Reflections on the Revolution in France*, the book which was to become the touchstone of British conservatism – and a target for criticism by radicals – for the next decade, if not longer.*

Reflections on the Revolution purports to be a letter to a young man who has been caught up in revolutionary fervour. It's one long, anguished cry for the past, for certainty, for the way things have always been done.

'We know that we have made no discoveries', writes Burke. (The 'we' here, it soon emerges, is the English, an odd identity, you might think, for this particular author to adopt.) There are, he continues, 'no discoveries [...] to be made in morality'. The 'great principles of government' and the 'ideas of liberty' were 'understood long before we were born'. It is, Burke suggests, almost a racial characteristic of the English to 'cherish and cultivate' their 'inbred sentiments'. They 'preserve the whole' of their 'feelings still native and entire'. And what does that lead

---

*   This turnabout, though genuine, seems very abrupt. Burke's behaviour was at times erratic through the 1780s and it has been suggested, both by historians and by his contemporaries, that he was suffering from mental health issues.

the English to do? 'We fear God; we look up with awe to kings, with affection to parliaments, with duty to magistrates, with reverence to priests, and with respect to nobility.' Burke insists that this is as it should be – 'natural' – and that 'all other feelings are false and spurious'.

'You see', he goes on, a few lines later:

I am bold enough to confess that we are generally men of untaught feelings, that, instead of casting away all our old prejudices, we cherish them to a very considerable degree, […] we cherish them because they are prejudices; and the longer they have lasted and the more generally they have prevailed, the more we cherish them. We are afraid to put men to live and trade each on his own private stock of reason, because we suspect that this stock in each man is small, and that the individuals would do better to avail themselves of the general bank and capital of nations and of ages.

'Prejudice' then, in the 1790s, isn't simply bias or judging without all the facts – it's tradition, 'inbred sentiments', unquestioned cultural assumptions. It's the entire edifice of society. The monarchy, the government, the judicial system, organised religion, the class system: all are to be upheld simply because they've been around for a long time. 'Awe', 'duty', 'reverence', 'respect' – these are the 'old prejudices'. They are to be clung to, a raft swirling in the maelstrom of revolution.

So far as Burke was concerned, any criticism of the way things had always been done would lead inevitably to the chaos and madness which, according to him, was already engulfing revolutionary France. It bordered on treason to question any element of the status quo. The poet William Wordsworth, who travelled to France to observe the revolution at first hand, later came to agree with Burke, writing in *The Prelude* – the epic poem in which he describes his youth and how he became a poet – that, having dragged 'all precepts, judgments, maxims, creeds, like culprits to the bar', all that was left to him was confusion and darkness.

But that's what radicalism was, and still is, about – questioning unexplored assumptions, getting, quite literally, down to the root, the 'radix'. It's about reassessing the way society works on a fundamental level, about challenging, in the process, every single one of Burke's 'prejudices'.

∽

If Jane wasn't familiar with Burke's *Reflections on the Revolution* she would have been in a minority among the educated, literate Englishmen and women of her time. We know she read at least some of the other influential political writers of the period – we saw that she probably borrowed the set-up for *Sense and Sensibility* directly from Wollstonecraft's *A Vindication of the Rights of Woman*, and there are indications in *Northanger Abbey* that she was also familiar with some of the writing of the anarchist philosopher William Godwin. If *Pride and Prejudice* had been published with that same title in the 1790s, it could scarcely have avoided being seen as consciously political, as deliberately attaching itself into radical discourse.

And even though it didn't appear until 1813, there are clear links to Burke's wholly impassioned, irrational defence of prejudice, and to the revolution.

For a start, the names of the hero (Darcy) and of his aunt (De Bourgh) sound and look French. The first is occasionally printed as 'D'Arcy' in nineteenth-century editions of the novel. 'De Bourgh' isn't even vaguely anglicised. Why make characters with French names aristocrats and the owners of large land holdings if you don't want to bring up what had happened in France – the abandoning of titles, the confiscation of estates, the guillotining?

Jane's novels are unusual for their period in that they seldom feature members of the 'nobility', the titled aristocracy. Her near-contemporaries – Maria Edgeworth, Fanny Burney – love a lord or a lady. Jane doesn't, an aspect of her work which was remarked on by more than one early critic. 'Her characters', suggests an essay of 1830, 'are for the most part commonplace people [...] of secondary station, and hardly ever exhibited through that halo of rank and wealth which makes many an ill-drawn sketch pass ... with a credulous public'.[4]

It's rare that Jane ventures higher than a baronet. This is the rank held by Sir John Middleton in *Sense and Sensibility*, by Sir Thomas Bertram in *Mansfield Park*, and by Sir Walter Elliot in *Persuasion*. Baronets are the lowest hereditary title; they're technically still 'commoners' rather than 'nobles'. There is a noblewoman, a viscountess, in *Persuasion*, but she is in no way a prominent character, not least because we hardly ever hear her speak.

Pride and Prejudice is the exception – something which, again, was picked up early on. One review of Jane's next-but-one novel, *Emma*, laments that it lacks the 'highly-drawn characters in superior life which are so interesting in *Pride and Prejudice*'.[5] Sir William Lucas, the Bennets' officious though friendly neighbour, may only have risen to 'the honour of a knighthood' (not a hereditary title). Lady Catherine de Bourgh's late husband may only have been a baronet, perhaps no more than a knight. But – as is indicated by the use of her Christian name – Lady Catherine herself is the daughter of a high-ranking nobleman; as it turns out, an earl.* The hero, Fitzwilliam Darcy, is that same earl's grandson. His cousin, Colonel Fitzwilliam, a minor character, is the younger son of the current earl. Earls are the third-highest rank of nobility. There are no more than a handful of them in England; a few more in Scotland and Ireland.

---

* In one of many aristocratic peculiarities, the daughters of a duke, marquis, or earl are, for example, Lady Mary Crawley, Lady Edith Crawley, and Lady Sybil Crawley. Marriage alters only their surnames, unless they marry a man who has a superior noble title of his own. Younger sons of an earl, though, are 'The Honourable', a title which they can share with their wives but which only ever really appears on letters. I've come across sneers that Jane made a mistake with Lady Catherine de Bourgh's title; she didn't. Colonel Fitzwilliam's apparent lack of a title is also entirely correct.

In *Pride and Prejudice* Jane employs a convention quite common in earlier eighteenth-century fiction but which she hadn't used in her own writing since her youthful 'novel' *The Beautifull Cassandra*, that of coyly referring to her fictional earl as 'Lord —'. This usually serves the dual purpose of steering well clear of any possible action for libel while at the same time encouraging your readers to wonder if you might not actually be referring to a real live earl. Here, however, we're also told several times that the family name is Fitzwilliam. It's Darcy's Christian name, as well. And there was a real live Earl Fitzwilliam – Lord Fitzwilliam – at the time *Pride and Prejudice* was published. He was the nephew of one prime minister and grandson of another. He was a prominent politician in his own right. He'd also been the patron of Edmund Burke – Burke was occupying one of the parliamentary seats owned by Lord Fitzwilliam when he published *Reflections on the Revolution*.★

So does this novel – with a title which seems to direct our attention towards Burke, and featuring characters with names which do likewise – look up with awe to kings, with affection to parliaments, with duty to magistrates, with reverence to priests, and with respect to nobility? Not so much.

Colonel The Honourable Fitzwilliam is a fairly inoffensive chap – 'not handsome, but in person and address most truly the gentleman'. His greatest fault is a tendency to gossip; he's the one who spills the beans about Darcy's role in crushing the promising romance between Bingley and Elizabeth's older sister. Now in Jane's novels gossip isn't always seen negatively. In *Emma*, as we'll discover, Miss Bates' relentless gossiping frequently exposes the truth, and the truth, for Jane, is necessary. Similar revelations arise from gossip in *Persuasion*. Here, though, it does look as if we're meant to think a little less of Colonel

---

★ Perhaps emboldened by the fact that Lord Fitzwilliam appeared completely unaware or unconcerned that she'd made use of his name, Jane appears to have borrowed more from him – Lord Fitzwilliam lived at the vast Yorkshire mansion called Wentworth Woodhouse.

Fitzwilliam. The affair is nothing at all to do with him and besides, he barely knows Elizabeth.

But, in this first half of the novel at least, he's the best representative of the nobility we get. Darcy, in his first proposal to Elizabeth, is justly accused of having behaved in a manner which is less than 'gentleman-like'. And the behaviour of Lady Catherine isn't remotely lady-like.

Lady Catherine is a looming presence in the novel from early on, because Mr Collins, the distant cousin who is set to inherit the Bennet estate, owes his recent employment as a clergyman to her.* He's very proud of the association, and drags her, and her many carriages and her ludicrously expensive chimney-pieces, into every possible conversation. We hear about her, as well, from Wickham, and from Elizabeth's friend Charlotte Lucas, who suffers the fate worse than death – that of marriage to Mr Collins. Charlotte's letters back home to her family and friends, once she's married, 'mentioned nothing which she could not praise'. She is determined to like her new home, the 'furniture, neighbourhood, and roads', determined too to find Lady Catherine's behaviour 'most friendly and obliging'. Charlotte has a gift for attempting to make silk purses out of sow's ears.

Elizabeth has begun to form her own view of Lady Catherine long before she travels to Kent and meets her in person. As she explains to Mr Wickham early on, though her cousin 'speaks highly both of Lady Catherine and her daughter', she has her own ideas: 'from some particulars that he has related of her ladyship, I suspect his gratitude misleads him, and that in spite of her being his patroness, she is an arrogant, conceited woman.'

The reader, too, at this point, is likely to have their own suspicions about Lady Catherine, based chiefly on her choice of parish priest. There's rarely much Burkean 'reverence' in Jane's attitude to the clergy; in *Pride and Prejudice* there's none at all.

---

* For an explanation of how the system of employing clergymen worked, see Chapters 5 and 6.

The letter in which Mr Collins invites himself to stay with his cousins, and which precedes his appearance in the novel, is 'a mixture of servility and self-importance'. When he does appear, he's 'absurd'. It's impossible to take him seriously as a man, still less as a moral shepherd carefully guiding his flock. He hardly seems to think about religion. The closest we see him come to a sermon is when he reads to his cousins from 'Fordyce's Sermons', which isn't church sermons, but an old-fashioned book of lectures on how young ladies ought to behave. Tact, social grace, these are alien concepts to Mr Collins. He proposes to two young women within the space of 48 hours. He actually writes down 'such little elegant compliments as may be adapted to ordinary occasions'. He can't even dance well. That Lady Catherine can bear to be in his company, that she can think him fit to serve as a clergyman, says very little for her character, or for her sense.

Wickham assures Elizabeth that her suspicions chime with his own experiences. He has, he says, not seen Lady Catherine 'for many years, but I very well remember that I never liked her, and that her manners were dictatorial and insolent'.

It's worth just dwelling on this for a moment. Wickham and Elizabeth bond over their shared dislike of Darcy. Wickham's dislike of Lady Catherine is, really, just an extension of his feelings about Darcy (he suggests that her 'reputation of being remarkably sensible and clever' is the creation, in part, of 'the pride of her nephew'). But Elizabeth's impression of Lady Catherine is, so far as we can tell, completely unconnected to Darcy; she's only just discovered that the two are related. What Jane is offering her readers here is a potent and, for some, terrifying cocktail – a dash of personal and class resentment, a measure of clear-eyed judgement. A young, unmarried woman with connections in trade, and a lieutenant of militia, the son of a steward, an estate manager, sit and shred the character of a much older woman, a lady, a member of the nobility, who has the power to pick a clergyman to serve her local parish and who we're meant to imagine might be related to prime ministers.

This, right here, is a revolutionary moment.

And by the same token *Pride and Prejudice* is a revolutionary novel. A conservative novel would show its readers how wrong Elizabeth was, or at the very least introduce a truly positive aristocratic character by way of counterweight. Darcy could have been made into this counterweight, but, as we'll see, he isn't, or not in any straightforward way. Instead, Elizabeth's suspicions (and ours) turn out not to have gone far enough. In spite of her title and her lineage, Lady Catherine isn't just conceited, she's shockingly ill-bred, far worse than the vulgar Mrs Jennings in *Sense and Sensibility* who, if she sometimes blunders tactlessly, has a kind heart.

On the very first occasion that Lady Catherine meets Elizabeth, she interrogates her, without, seemingly, any awareness of how impolite she's being: 'She asked her, at different times, how many sisters she had, whether they were older or younger than herself, whether any of them were likely to be married, whether they were handsome, where they had been educated, what carriage her father kept, and what had been her mother's maiden name?' She demands to know Elizabeth's age. She criticises the way she's been brought up.

And she's like this with everybody. When she condescends to visit Mrs Collins and Elizabeth at the vicarage, we're told that she 'looked at their work' – their needlework – and 'advised them to do it differently'. The furniture is wrongly arranged, the housemaid has neglected some part of her duties. She even criticises the food she's given to eat and, with it, Charlotte's housekeeping.

Lady Catherine was born into luxury, remaining in it all her life. A self-anointed expert on almost every subject, she never exerts herself to acquire new knowledge. She claims at one point that there are 'few people in England, I suppose, who have more true enjoyment of music than myself, or a better natural taste. If I had ever learnt', she declares, laughably, 'I should have been a great proficient'. Her total lack of experience doesn't stop her offering advice on Elizabeth's piano-playing. Nor, Jane tells us, does Lady Catherine's lack of experience of poverty prevent her from sallying forth 'into the village' 'whenever any of the cottagers were disposed to be quarrelsome, discontented, or too poor', confident in her ability 'to settle their differences, silence their complaints, and scold them into harmony and plenty'.

Jane's not exactly showing her readers a perfectly functioning system here, is she, any more than she is with the militia? Not only are the cottagers 'poor' and 'discontented'; Lady Catherine doesn't do anything for them, apart from scolding them. She's not a Lady Bountiful. There is, for her, no sense of *noblesse oblige*, no feeling that noble rank entails any sort of responsibility. From the corner of our eyes we can see the shadow of the guillotine.

There's no unthinking respect for the nobility in *Pride and Prejudice*, any more than there's reverence for Mr Collins.

In fact Jane makes it clear that titles and blood count for very little. In this novel, being 'gentleman-like' has almost nothing to do with your social position. Colonel Fitzwilliam is; Darcy, for much of the novel, isn't. Mr Bingley is, and his money 'had been acquired by trade'. Elizabeth's uncle Mr Gardiner, too, is 'a sensible, gentlemanlike man [...] well-bred and agreeable', though he lives 'by trade'. It isn't always a reliable measure of true moral worth – Wickham, after all, is also described as 'gentlemanlike' – but it's open to almost everyone. In this self-consciously politicised text, 'breeding' isn't about your lineage, it's about what you think and how you behave. Lady Catherine de Bourgh exhibits 'ill-breeding', while the social efforts of Georgiana Darcy's lowly companion, Mrs Annesley, 'proved her to be [...] truly well-bred'. Elizabeth is eventually persuaded to respect not Darcy's 'noble' pedigree, but his actions in saving her sister Lydia's reputation and his 'feelings', which were 'always noble and just'.

Elizabeth, in common with most of Jane's heroines, has inadequate parents. They have made no financial provision for her, nor can she apply to them for moral guidance or advice. But there are characters who perform this second function – her uncle and aunt, Mr and Mrs Gardiner. Mr Gardiner is a considerate man, far more so than

Mr Bennet. Mr Bennet barely bothers to write to his wife and daughters during his attempts to discover Lydia in London; Mr Gardiner, by contrast, makes a point of keeping them informed. He does all the things that Lydia's own father ought to be doing. His wife, too, is as close to an exemplary character as Jane allows us to come in *Pride and Prejudice*. Mrs Gardiner is 'an amiable, intelligent, elegant woman'. She's kind; she takes the oldest Miss Bennet back to London with them to help her get over her romantic disappointment. She's tactful; we see that she will turn a conversation 'out of compassion', and she cautions Elizabeth against developing feelings for Wickham 'punctually and kindly'. What's more, she does so in such a way that Elizabeth not only agrees, but thanks her for her intervention, 'a wonderful instance', remarks Jane, 'of advice being given on such a point, without being resented'.

It's a significant departure, this, to make the characters who live by trade not only so much the most agreeable of the older generation, but also the novel's moral arbiters. Jane makes no effort to soften the realities of their social position. The Gardiners live in London, but it's a very different London to the fashionable western end of the city, which is where Jane took us in *Sense and Sensibility*. Their house is in Cheapside, 'in view of their own warehouses', at what is still, nowadays, the heart of the financial district, the 'City'. Mr Gardiner is the son of a country attorney; his wife has no relatives that we know of, though we're told that before she married she lived for a time in Derbyshire, near Pemberley, that she has seen the place (from outside, it seems), and has many acquaintances in common with Wickham. That, we gather, was her original social position – she belonged with the stewards and attorneys. She, at least, did not quit the sphere in which she had been brought up when she married. Mr Gardiner can afford to travel for pleasure – he and his wife propose taking Elizabeth on holiday with them to the Lake District – but his priority is his work, and business requires him to substitute a shorter journey to Derbyshire instead, with life-altering consequences for Elizabeth and Darcy.

More importantly, Mr Gardiner's still very active interest in whatever trade he carries on distinguishes him from, for example, the Bingleys – Miss Bingley and her sister manage most of the time to forget 'that their brother's fortune and their own had been acquired by trade'. The social hierarchy during this period fetishised the ownership of land, as we've seen, but it was just about willing to overlook the fact that money had come from trade provided that there was enough of it, and that the source was decently concealed. In *Pride and Prejudice*, by contrast, we're encouraged to think far more positively of Mr Gardiner than we are of Sir William Lucas, whose knighthood 'had given him a disgust to his business' and led him to abandon it, although he is by no means rich (he can afford to give Charlotte 'little fortune' when she marries, and he appears to have at least five children).

In the other novels Jane's readers would have known, city characters – characters involved in trade – are included for broad comedy or to create embarrassment for heroines. In one novel we know Jane liked – *Emmeline*, by Charlotte Smith – the character who started his career as 'a clerk to an attorney in the city' is 'cunning', interested in only 'place or profit'. The heroine has suitors who are engaged in business – and are, clearly, meant to be repellent. The only men she seriously considers are noblemen. In Burney's *Evelina*, our beautiful young protagonist fairly writhes under the humiliation of having relations in trade. She's constantly 'chagrined', filled with 'mortification', apprehensive that an acquaintance might hear one of these people 'call me cousin'. She sets down on paper that she is 'ashamed' of her 'near relationship' with her own grandmother. And Burney's novel never questions Evelina's snobbery. Her city cousins are uniformly quarrelsome and unappealing, their speech filled with grammatical solecisms. Her grandmother is appalling. Evelina is better than them and after her splendid marriage to Lord Orville, she abandons them without a backward glance.

In *Pride and Prejudice*, though, Darcy's mindless snobbery isn't allowed to stand. It can't be justified. For the first half of the novel he is certain both of his own place in the social hierarchy and of everyone else's, viewing status less as opinion than fact. For him, it's immutable, self-evident. It's an idea which is so obviously right that it has never occurred to him to question it. It's a prejudice, in Burkean terms – something that has to be correct because everyone's thought it for ages. When Miss Bingley and her sister take the opportunity to laugh over the 'vulgar relations' the Bennet girls are saddled with, ones who actually work for a living, the good-natured Bingley objects (as well he might, given the origin of his own fortune). And he tries to defend them as individuals – '"If they had uncles enough to fill *all* Cheapside," cried Bingley, "it would not make them one jot less agreeable."' Darcy disagrees; that's not how it works. He doesn't dispute that the eldest Miss Bennets are 'agreeable', but having those family connections 'must very materially lessen their chance of marrying men of any consideration in the world'. 'Must', note, rather than 'will' or 'is likely to' – this isn't about likelihood, it's about the rules which govern 'the world', the world that Darcy knows.

Darcy's first proposal to Elizabeth continues down the same – prejudiced – path. Jane withholds most of the proposal itself. 'You must allow me to tell you how ardently I admire and love you', Jane has him declare, before promptly shifting into summary, and stopping him telling the reader much at all. Now it's rather a feature of her novels that successful proposals aren't written down in full, to the frustration of generations of scriptwriters. The exception is *Persuasion*, Jane's last (more or less) complete novel, and that's rather a unique proposal anyway, since the heroine indirectly declares her love first. We know that it involved some fairly major editing, as well as clever stage-managing to make it work. What we are given, much more fully, is unsuccessful proposals – Mr Elton's offer to Emma Woodhouse, for example, or Mr Collins' cringe-making one to Elizabeth.

Here we're told only that Darcy 'spoke well'. There are, though, 'feelings besides those of the heart to be detailed and he was not more eloquent on the subject of tenderness than of pride'. Jane informs us that he speaks about Elizabeth's 'inferiority—of its being a degradation—of the family obstacles' which had stood in the way of his 'inclination', and this with 'a warmth which seemed due to the consequence he was wounding, but was very unlikely to recommend his suit'. Exactly what he said, though, to rouse Elizabeth first to 'resentment' and then to 'anger', isn't clear. After Elizabeth has, to his astonishment, turned him down, Darcy insists that there is no reason for him to be 'ashamed of the feelings I related'. On the contrary they were 'natural and just'. The insistence on naturalness might, again, recall Burke to mind. The reader, though, is unable to agree or disagree, because we don't know what the feelings were. Who is he objecting to? On what basis? Their birth, or their behaviour?

Now, it may be that this is one of the scenes that was 'lop't and crop't', edited out. Artistically, it makes a certain amount of sense, because the whole of the next chapter is taken up by Darcy's letter to Elizabeth, and the less he says here the greater our interest, as readers, in what he goes on to reveal there. But later it appears that Darcy has talked specifically, disparagingly, about Mr and Mrs Gardiner. Two-thirds of the way through the novel Elizabeth, holidaying with her aunt and uncle in Derbyshire, ends up visiting Pemberley. She can't really get out of it without making an embarrassing admission and she's been assured that Darcy is away from home. He turns up, of course, a day early, while Elizabeth and the Gardiners are being shown around the estate.

Tourism within Britain, to places with interesting historical associations or particularly picturesque scenery, became increasingly common during the period of the Napoleonic wars, for obvious practical reasons. Big houses – the kind of places that are now run by the National Trust – were also a draw for tourists. But it wasn't the case that just anyone could turn up and be granted access. You didn't buy a ticket – it wasn't a financial transaction. You paid, in effect, with social capital; you had to be confident that you would be allowed in by, usually, the upper servants. It was a question of 'passing', socially. And the Gardiners do.

They pass with Darcy, as well. He asks Elizabeth 'if she would do him the honour of introducing him to her friends'. We'll talk more in a minute about the significance of introductions. What Jane makes obvious here is that Darcy doesn't for a moment suspect who the Gardiners are. Elizabeth, Jane explains, 'could hardly suppress a smile at his being now seeking the acquaintance of some of those very people against whom his pride had revolted in his offer to herself.' A few pages further on, we have the moment where Elizabeth's heart really begins to soften towards Darcy: 'When she saw him thus seeking the acquaintance and courting the good opinion of people with whom any intercourse a few months ago would have been a disgrace—when she saw him thus civil, not only to herself, but to the very relations whom he had openly disdained.'

Critics queue up to accuse the heroine of *Emma* of being a snob, with, as we'll discover, only partial justification. They don't do it for Darcy, though, and his snobbery is far more overt and disruptive, for the first part of the novel at least.

∞

If I were to ask you when Darcy and Elizabeth are first introduced to each other I can almost guarantee that you'll begin by visualising a scene that owes a lot to one or other of the adaptations. The Meryton assembly rooms; wood-panelled, candle-lit. Music, couples dancing in the background. In the foreground, Mrs Bennet, on the catch for rich suitors, forcing her five daughters on the notice of Mr Bingley and Mr Darcy, and practically thrusting the oldest into Mr Bingley's arms. All very necessary, in an adaptation, and all very helpful in making sure that the viewers start getting to know the names of the characters. But that's not what happens in the book.

Introductions are a lot less important in English society than they used to be. Few people now care who's meant to be introduced to whom or are troubled about getting titles exactly right. No one worries unduly about the approved way of visiting a new neighbour for the first time.

Etiquette is by far more fluid. But it used to take up a lot of time and attention. And in *Pride and Prejudice* it's something that, as readers, we ought to be particularly attentive to.

Social introductions are referred to 30 times in *Pride and Prejudice*. To compare this to the other novels of slightly greater length, there are nineteen incidences in *Mansfield Park*, 23 in *Emma*, and fifteen in *Sense and Sensibility*. In several scenes, the exact form and correctness of introductions is explicitly addressed, as when Mr Collins introduces himself, very improperly, to Mr Darcy. The first two chapters of the novel are taken up with the question of whether or not Mr Bennet will 'visit' Mr Bingley, the rich newcomer to the neighbourhood. Mrs Bennet is very keen that he should. She has an eye to her daughters' marriage prospects, and optimistically announces that Bingley 'may very likely fall in love with one of them'. She tells her husband that he 'must go, for it will be impossible for *us* to visit him if you do not'.

A visit involves going to a house and sending in your card, after which you might expect to be admitted to see the master or mistress. The visit should then be returned within a few days. Fifteen minutes was the hard limit for these initial meetings, indeed for all social calls which were formal rather than genuinely friendly and relaxed – when Bingley returns Mr Bennet's visit, he sits 'about ten minutes with him in his library'. Visiting, as the word suggests, is all about seeing. By turning up on Mr Bingley's doorstep, Mr Bennet is declaring his equal or roughly equivalent social status; by returning the visit, Bingley can see whether he agrees with that assessment. It's also a way for Mr Bennet to check how the newcomer is living (the furniture, the servants, whether Bingley is dressed, or unacceptably hungover, whether he has a mistress with him). Once the visit has been paid and reciprocated, to everyone's satisfaction, normal social intercourse can begin.

Mrs Bennet is unable to begin the process herself – there is at this point no hostess in Bingley's household (he collects his sisters from

London only just before the Meryton assembly). Women can't pay these first, ceremonial visits to single men, only to women. You can see why Mrs Bennet gets so frustrated when Mr Bennet keeps telling her that he won't go.* By not visiting, Mr Bennet would be indicating either that he doesn't consider himself to be of an equivalent social status to Bingley, or that he's unwilling to permit his wife and daughters to socialise with him. A death-knell, either way, to Mrs Bennet's matrimonial ambitions. The visit isn't an empty gesture; it has a purpose. And that purpose is exactly what Mr Bennet is joking about when he tells his wife that, 'I will send a few lines […] to assure him of my hearty consent to his marrying whichever he chooses of the girls'.

'Visiting' was one of the few occasions when it was deemed acceptable to introduce yourself to a stranger. Usually introductions required a third person, someone who was acquainted with both parties – a guarantor, if you like, of each side's good faith and good character. Places like Bath, where it could be difficult to find someone to do this, had a Master of Ceremonies to carry out the role instead. It was all quite formalised. It also required a decision as to the relative social status of the parties, because generally the party who was lower in status was introduced to the party who was higher or who had more to lose, so young people to older people, single people to married people, untitled to titled, men to women. Once you had been introduced, you could dance, converse, and so on. It was possible, though, for either party to reject the introduction, to show their unwillingness to be acquainted.

---

* We ought, I think, to read a touch of malice into Mr Bennet's behaviour over Bingley. As soon as Mrs Bennet realises that the visit has been paid, she invites Bingley for dinner so that he can meet her daughters. He has to turn the invitation down in order to go to London. When the day of the Meryton assembly comes round, does Mr Bennet accompany his wife and daughters, so that he can introduce them, naturally and easily? No, he stays at home, in his study, reading. Luckily, Bingley seeks an introduction to Jane.

Look in almost any late-eighteenth- or early-nineteenth-century novel and you'll see how introductions worked:

Lionel eagerly begged permission to introduce his sisters and cousin to Mrs Arlbery, who readily consented to the proposal [...]

'Mortimer,' said Mr Delvile, 'I understand you have already had the pleasure of seeing this young lady?' 'Yes, Sir,' he answered, 'I have more than once had that happiness, but I have never had the honour of being introduced to her.' [...]

Mrs Berlinton declined being introduced to that lady [...]*

In Jane's novels, too, introductions are almost always mentioned specifically, particularly between the main characters. *Emma* is an exception, because Emma and Knightley have known each other all her life, they're near-neighbours, but we're usually shown the other heroes and heroines meeting. In *Northanger Abbey* we're told of Catherine's excitement when 'the Master of Ceremonies introduced to her a very gentlemanlike young man as a partner; – his name was Tilney'. In *Sense and Sensibility* Edward Ferrars appears as 'a gentleman-like and pleasing young man, who was introduced to their acquaintance soon after his sister's establishment at Norland'. The peculiar circumstances of Willoughby's meeting with Marianne mean that he has to introduce himself – a warning sign, perhaps. In the first chapter of *Mansfield Park* even the children (ranging in age from ten to eighteen) are formally introduced to each other, and it is formal – the entire family is assembled, and the heroine's aunt revels 'in the importance of leading her into the others, and recommending her to their kindness'. The hero and heroine of *Persuasion*, who haven't seen each other since their engagement was broken seven years earlier, go to some trouble to

---

* These examples are from Fanny Burney's *Camilla*.

avoid the embarrassment of being introduced to each other again – 'he had inquired after her, she found, slightly, as might suit a former slight acquaintance, seeming to acknowledge such as she had acknowledged, actuated, perhaps, by the same view of escaping introduction when they were to meet'.

Introductions were an important moment.

Which makes it all the more remarkable – and all the more obviously deliberate – that Elizabeth and Darcy aren't ever, so far as we can see, introduced to each other. In fact, they actively resist the efforts of other characters to make them formally acquainted.

The first occasion is a memorable one, though we tend to miss the real significance of it. It takes place early on in the novel, at the Meryton assembly, the first occasion on which we, as readers, meet Darcy. Bingley and Darcy, we discover almost immediately, have very different personalities. While Bingley 'had soon made himself acquainted with all the principal people in the room', Darcy stalks about, managing to offend almost everyone. He dances twice with Bingley's sisters and, we're told, declines being introduced to 'any other lady'.

For us, Darcy's refusal to dance – at a dance – appears socially awkward, but almost endearingly so. As we learn, he doesn't like dancing. 'I detest it', says he, and later, 'It is a compliment which I never pay to any place if I can avoid it'. Instead, he refuses to do anything that is socially expected of him. It's hard to counter the effect of his 'fine, tall person, handsome features, noble mien', still more of his 'ten thousand a year', but he manages it. He makes a spectacle of himself. Even Bingley, who rarely criticises his friend, is exasperated to see Darcy, as he says, 'standing about by yourself in this stupid manner'.

Is it deliberate, on Darcy's part? Well, the indications are that, yes, it is. Bear in mind, Darcy could have stayed away, as Bingley suggests he do if he wants to avoid the Netherfield ball – 'he may go to bed, if he chooses, before it begins'. He could have gone to the card room, with the older men. Assembly rooms almost always had one. He could have made conversation with the older, married women. Instead, we find him creating some rather unpleasant situations.* He sits 'close' by one lady, 'for half-an-hour without once opening his lips'. When she, in desperation, or defiance, asks him a question, it's reported that 'he could not help answering [...] but she said he seemed quite angry at being spoke to'. When Bingley assures Darcy that there are many 'pleasant girls', points out Elizabeth, and offers to arrange an introduction – 'Do let me ask my partner to introduce you' – Darcy 'looked for a moment at Elizabeth, till catching her eye, he withdrew his own and coldly said: "She is tolerable, but not handsome enough to tempt *me*; I am in no humour at present to give consequence to young ladies who are slighted by other men."'

Elizabeth, we're told, is 'sitting down just behind' him. Presumably he turns to look at her. He catches her eye. He means her to hear him. The consensus among the good people of Meryton is that Darcy is 'above his company', or, as Mrs Bennet puts it 'eat up by pride'. What we can say for certain, at this point in the novel, is that he's being obnoxious on purpose. Does he deserve to be treated with the 'respect' Burke would insist on? On this behaviour, no. It appears that he's willing to interact with the men. They are, of course, almost all of them his social inferiors. He's prepared to address Sir William Lucas, who has been knighted, with due respect – he calls him 'sir'. He doesn't encounter Mr Bennet until almost the end of the book; one rather wonders how that particular introduction would work – what's the top trump? Age, or annual income? But by refusing to be introduced to any of the women, Darcy makes it clear not only that he doesn't wish to dance, but that

---

* Darcy's refusal to interact with his perceived social inferiors leads to some strangulated, triangulated conversations, as when Mrs Bennet, taking offence at a comment which Darcy addresses in front of her, but to Miss Bingley, is forced to refer to him as 'that gentleman'. Her apparent rudeness at the end of the novel, when she speaks to Darcy only in the shortest of sentences, is in fact an attempt at socially correct behaviour under circumstances which Darcy has made extremely problematic.

he considers them all to be his social inferiors – so much so, perhaps, that he's unwilling to grant them the courtesy traditionally given to women, that of treating them, temporarily, as the higher-status party in an introduction.

One person at least seems to think so. Let's move on to talk about the scene in Chapter 6. A fortnight has gone by. Elizabeth and Darcy are still, at this point, not formally acquainted, they've not been introduced. We know this because Jane tells us: Darcy has been looking at Elizabeth, he's attracted despite himself, he 'began to wish to know more of her, and as a step towards conversing with her himself, attended to her conversation with others'. They're not yet on speaking terms. There's been no mutual social recognition. Elizabeth notices the eavesdropping, and declares that she 'shall certainly let him know that I see what he is about'. Speaking to him at all, of course, without an introduction is 'impertinent' – Elizabeth admits as much. Her friend, Charlotte Lucas, defies her to bring the subject up with him, 'which immediately provoking Elizabeth to do it, she turned', and addresses a challenging remark. But even with her own determined impertinence, even with all that defying and provoking, Elizabeth manages only a few short sentences. The situation is, undoubtedly, socially uncomfortable, and Charlotte produces an easy out for her friend by insisting that Elizabeth should sit and play the piano.

A little later in the evening, Sir William Lucas is talking – with difficulty – to Darcy. Arriving at a conversational hiatus, he notices Elizabeth, 'at that instant moving towards them'. He is 'struck with the action of doing a very gallant thing' and decides, on the spur of the moment, to introduce the pair so that they can dance. He does it the wrong way round, though – 'My dear Miss Eliza, why are you not dancing? Mr Darcy, you must allow me to present this young lady to you as a very desirable partner.' The clear implication is that Elizabeth is the inferior one, socially. This is – surely – at least part of the reason why Darcy is 'extremely surprised'. Sir William may have been presented at the royal court, but this introduction breaches normal etiquette.

Elizabeth refuses the introduction – 'she instantly drew back, and said with some discomposure to Sir William: "Indeed, sir, I have not the least intention of dancing. I entreat you not to suppose that I moved this way in order to beg for a partner."' She is 'determined'. Sir William's 'attempt at persuasion' and Darcy's 'grave propriety' – recently acquired, one gathers – are equally 'in vain'. It isn't simply that Elizabeth doesn't want to dance with Darcy; she doesn't want to be formally acquainted with him, or at least not like this. She doesn't once address Darcy here; she speaks through Sir William. So far as she's concerned, the message she's sending is clear – she isn't prepared to acknowledge Darcy as her social superior.

It's a moment that radical thinkers would have recognised, a stripping back to essentials, the propounding of a problem. What happens with something as apparently everyday and straightforward as an introduction if the two parties can't agree on their relative social status?

Jane's been preparing her readers for this. Not only does she open the novel with the lengthy disagreement between Mr and Mrs Bennet about visiting, but when Mrs Bennet, made almost incoherent with frustration about the whole business, cries out 'Nonsense, nonsense!', her husband chides her: 'What can be the meaning of that emphatic exclamation?' He then poses a question. It's directed not just at his wife but I think at us, too: 'Do you consider the forms of introduction, and the stress that is laid on them, as nonsense?'

Well, Jane doesn't consider them nonsense, quite, but she is interested, I think, in exploring what happens when you start examining them more closely, and in what happens when you take them away altogether.

So she sets up a situation where, first of all, Darcy refuses to be introduced to Elizabeth, and then Elizabeth refuses to be introduced to Darcy. And she has the two of them embark on a relationship that takes place, almost entirely, outside social norms; one in which all kinds of set ideas and traditional concepts – prejudices – are uprooted.

She puts their relationship alongside other, more traditional, socially-sanctioned arrangements. There's the carefully sex-segregated visiting and activities that take place (the shooting, the fishing, the gentlemen going to dine with the officers). There's the staid romance between Bingley and Elizabeth's older sister. Bingley obtains a very proper introduction to the eldest Miss Bennet: 'he inquired who she was, and got introduced, and asked her for the two next [dances]'. Even Bingley's admiration is textbook. His praise of Miss Bennet is lifted straight from Burney's *Evelina*. 'She is the most beautiful creature I ever beheld!' he declares, having known her perhaps an hour, and 'as to Miss Bennet, he could not conceive an angel more beautiful'.*

Jane tells us exactly what the relationship between Miss Bennet and Bingley consists of. It's all exceedingly correct, and it doesn't amount to very much. The two 'meet tolerably often', but 'never for many hours together' and 'they always see each other in large mixed parties'. Miss Bennet has 'danced four dances' with Bingley, 'she saw him one morning at his own house, and has since dined with him in company four times'. Subsequently, she spends five days at Netherfield, but she's ill in bed for most of that time and even when she's well again, there are other people around. The pair then bump into each other very briefly in Meryton, and dance together at the Netherfield ball. At this point, Bingley leaves Hertfordshire and is persuaded, by the combined forces of his sisters and Darcy, to stay away, and that's it. Miss Bennet doesn't see Bingley again until the following autumn, whereupon they almost immediately get engaged. Their interactions are nothing like enough to make them understand each other's character; it's a shaky foundation for married life, for all its decorum.

---

* Burney's novel *Evelina* features the following conversation in praise of the eponymous heroine: '"By Jove," cried the man, "she is the most beautiful creature I ever saw in my life!" Lord Orville, as he well might, laughed; but answered, "Yes, a pretty modest-looking girl." "O my Lord!" cried the madman, "she is an angel!"'

In comparison, Darcy and Elizabeth have, during an identical time-frame, danced once, dined together several times, argued a lot, walked alone together, sat alone in rooms together, debated, corresponded, and insulted each other's family (him) and manners (her). Darcy has proposed and been rejected. He's detailed the sexual peccadilloes of his younger sister. Darcy is the first person Elizabeth encounters after receiving the news of Lydia's elopement; he's the first person she tells about it. He rushes off to sort it out. The longest they go without seeing each other is about three and a half months. The pair of them have changed their minds, and their behaviour. They've acknowledged their mistakes, and even introduced their relations to each other – this last, one imagines, with a particular consciousness of the fact that, according to the social rules, they themselves aren't formally acquainted.

We're so familiar with what happens between them that we fail to register quite how wholly improper much of their behaviour is. Theirs is an astonishingly frank, astonishingly intense relationship, and almost no one, except for the two of them, knows that it's happening at all, certainly not the true extent of it. The news of their engagement comes as a complete shock to Elizabeth's family; it's met with flat incredulity.

Elizabeth, we know, is impatient of convention and established modes of behaviour, not for the sake of being contrary, but when she considers that they're being clung to for no good reason. Her 'lively, play-ful disposition [...] delighted', Jane informs us, 'in anything ridiculous'. 'I dearly love a laugh', Elizabeth admits early in the novel, but when Darcy, instinctively recoiling, accuses her of mindless, unthinking mockery, she contradicts him. No. Her laughter has direction, purpose, even: 'I hope I never ridicule what is wise and good. Follies and nonsense, whims and inconsistencies, *do* divert me, I own, and I laugh at them whenever I can.'

The wisdom of the ages is, for Elizabeth, as open to doubt as any-thing else. Darcy at one point brings Shakespeare into a discussion about poetry. 'I have been used to consider poetry as the *food* of love', he says, half-quoting from *Twelfth Night*. But Elizabeth thinks otherwise: 'Of a fine, stout, healthy love it may. Everything nourishes what is strong already. But if it be only a slight, thin sort of inclination, I am convinced that one good sonnet will starve it entirely away.'

Elizabeth is, fundamentally, a radical. She knows her own mind; she reserves the right to decide questions for herself. There are plenty of kinds of authority that she doesn't recognise, or tolerates only as far as it suits her. On occasion we see her all but disciplining her own mother – 'For heaven's sake, madam, speak lower', she says. This is not what dutiful daughters do. Elizabeth views even her father, the head of her family, with a critical eye. She had, Jane tells us, 'never been blind to the impropriety of her father's behaviour as a husband', deeming it 'highly reprehensible'. At one point, when she's trying to persuade him not to let Lydia go to Brighton, she tells him, in essence, what an incompetent parent he is: 'Excuse me, for I must speak plainly. If you, my dear father, will not take the trouble of checking her exuberant spirits, and of teaching her that her present pursuits are not to be the business of her life, she will soon be beyond the reach of amendment.'

When, towards the end of the novel, Lady Catherine appears on Elizabeth's doorstep and demands that the younger woman undertake never to marry Darcy, her demands are couched in language that Burke would have recognised and approved, the kind of language he used himself in *Reflections on the Revolution*. It's all obligation, obedience, claims, 'honour, decorum, prudence', 'duty', and 'gratitude'. And it comes up against a completely different kind of language. 'You have no right', announces Elizabeth. 'What is that to me?' she asks. She is, she says, 'only resolved to act in that manner, which will, in my own opinion, constitute my happiness.' Society be damned – Darcy and Elizabeth's relationship is nothing to do with anyone else.

Elizabeth's undutifulness as a daughter, her laughter, her lack of reverence for Mr Collins, her lack of respect for Lady Catherine de Bourgh, they're all of a piece. Elizabeth is, in short, constructed to be a conservative's nightmare.

∽

Elizabeth transgresses almost as much as Marianne Dashwood does, perhaps even more, but Jane never devises any punishment for her. There's no illness, no betrayal, no watching the man she loves marry someone else while she makes do with second best. All Elizabeth is made to do is change her mind about Darcy when she's presented with new evidence, which is completely in line with radical thinking. Jane seems, indeed, to have been very attached to Elizabeth – her comments on the character are the only definitive record we have of what she thought about any of her heroines.* '*I* think her as delightful a creature as ever appeared in print', she writes, in the first of her two letters penned straight after the novel's publication, '& how I shall be able to tolerate those who do not like her at least, I do not know'. The majority of readers over the past 200 years have tended to agree with the author, but the approval has by no means been universal.

In common with both *Northanger Abbey* and *Sense and Sensibility*, the evidence points very much to *Pride and Prejudice* never having obtained the readership it was intended for, to its having been published out of its time. The literary magazines didn't, in 1813, discuss Elizabeth as a radical heroine, though the *Critical Review* remarked on her 'quickness of perception' and 'strength of mind' and identified her as the 'Beatrice of the tale' – comparing her to the heroine of Shakespeare's *Much Ado About Nothing*, another strong-willed, self-assured woman with determined ideas of her own and a tongue sharp enough to puncture any inflated ego she encounters. The reviewer was convinced, however, that Elizabeth's 'independence of character […] is kept within the proper line of decorum'.

But there was at least one contemporary reader who thought Elizabeth shockingly indecorous, badly judged – a woman called Mary

---

*   The often-quoted comment about Emma Woodhouse ('a heroine whom no one but myself will like') is unsubstantiated family tradition, while we can't be entirely sure which heroine Jane is referring to as 'almost too good for me' in a letter which seems to belong to 1817. Probably it's Anne Elliot, the heroine of *Persuasion*, but we can't say for certain.

Russell Mitford who was herself a writer and so perhaps more attuned to exactly what Jane was doing in the novel. Mitford rather admired Jane, as a novelist, but she couldn't stand Elizabeth:

> It is impossible not to feel in every line of Pride and Prejudice, in every word of 'Elizabeth', the entire want of taste which could produce so pert, so worldly a heroine as the beloved of such a man as Darcy. Wickham is equally bad. Oh! they were just fit for each other, and I cannot forgive that delightful Darcy for parting them. Darcy [...] is of all characters the best designed and the best sustained.*

Darcy is, though, by no means the paragon that Mitford seems to be suggesting here. As he says himself, 'I have faults enough'. Certainly he isn't a conservative paragon, and though he resolves the difficulties of the plot, he doesn't do so in a way conservatives would have been able to really approve of. He has pride in his birth, he has prejudices in favour of rank, he appeals, at times, to recognised authority, and to 'natural' – generally accepted, time-honoured – ideas, but Jane makes it apparent from early on that he is 'clever', too clever, ultimately, to reject the justice of Elizabeth's criticisms and arguments.

In fact there are indications that he's receptive to new ideas even before he begins to be seriously attracted to Elizabeth. Darcy is, we learn, 'always buying books'. He cannot, he says, 'comprehend the neglect of a family library in such days as these'. What books does he buy? He is, we learn in this scene, guardian to a very much younger sister. Rather endearingly, and rather radically, too, he buys books about bringing up young women, written by older women. Not for him the

---

*   Mitford was writing to a man called Sir William Elford, who had been a friend of Pitt and had also served as a lieutenant-colonel of militia. This letter, dated 20th December 1814, is the only one to survive from a longer correspondence. It's interesting that Mitford seems to anticipate that Elford will agree with her negative judgement of Elizabeth.

old-fashioned, male-authored conduct books such as Fordyce's *Sermons to Young Women*, which Jane mentions elsewhere in *Pride and Prejudice*. Darcy ends the lengthy discussion about female accomplishments, which takes place in the drawing room at Netherfield, by pronouncing that dancing and modern languages are all well and good, but that a truly accomplished woman 'must yet add something more substantial, in the improvement of her mind by extensive reading'. It's a clear reference to a work by Hester Chapone called *Letters on the Improvement of the Mind*, which details how girls can educate themselves through a proper programme of reading. Jane herself was presumably aware that Chapone had been praised by no less a radical than Mary Wollstonecraft in her *Vindication of the Rights of Woman* and many of Jane's readers would have been aware of that too.

Darcy is excited by Elizabeth's unconventionality – it speaks deeply to some hidden, largely repressed part of his own character. He can't stop himself arguing with her, about women's accomplishments, about poetry, about Scottish dancing, about music, about other people, about themselves. In Kent, he deliberately and repeatedly seeks her out. He visits her at the parsonage house and walks alone with her in the park at Rosings. As Elizabeth crossly summarises these occasions in her own mind, 'it was not merely a few formal inquiries and an awkward pause and then away, but he actually thought it necessary to turn back and walk with her'. After her rejection of his proposal, and their subsequent furious argument, he again accosts her privately, and hands her a long letter. It takes up the best part of a chapter; it's more than 2,500 words long. He hands it to her, we're told, 'soon after breakfast'. He began to write it 'at eight o'clock in the morning' – that's when it's dated. Earlier on, Bingley jokingly explains that Darcy doesn't write 'with ease', that he 'studies too much for words of four syllables'. But this letter is written in far too short a period of time to have been 'studied'. It's written from the heart. Giving it to Elizabeth at all is a terrible idea, shockingly risky, both in that he might be seen handing it to her, giving rise to all sorts of gossip, and in that it talks frankly about the reputation-destroying conduct of his own sister. Darcy wants – he needs – to explain himself.

A more conservative character, in a more conservative novel, wouldn't accept that his behaviour needed to be explained. Nor would he be open to being reformed. The conduct of a character like Darcy wouldn't be open to criticism in a conservative novel. Darcy is older than Elizabeth by seven or eight years. He is 'a landlord, a master' with 'many people's happiness [...] in his guardianship' and the 'power to bestow' either 'pleasure or pain', just as he chooses. He is rich, he owns a great estate, he's descended from a noble house and, Jane invites her readers to imagine, related to influential political figures.

But he listens to Elizabeth – the second daughter of a country gentleman, with no fortune, with a silly vulgar mother, with a host of low-status relations. He makes himself vulnerable to her. He learns from her – 'What do I not owe you! You taught me a lesson, hard indeed at first, but most advantageous. By you, I was properly humbled.'

Eighteenth-century writers were deeply uneasy about making their upper-class characters marry out.* There are few exigencies to which they aren't reduced, in their desperation to achieve social parity between hero and heroine. Children are switched at nurse; villainous uncles hide the rightful heirs; foundlings turn out to be related to the local landowner after all; fortunes appear; marriage certificates are discovered; guardians marry their wards; cousins marry each other.

Jane doesn't do this in *Pride and Prejudice*.

The marriage between Darcy and Elizabeth is not, as her father fears it might be, 'unequal'. Each comes to admire and respect the other. Their relationship begins with a refusal to accept social inequality, and it ends with it, too.

---

* The only really convincing exception is Samuel Richardson's *Pamela*, and even then the heroine's social status remains problematic to the end of the novel and most of the way through a very lengthy sequel. The unequal marriage was mocked viciously by other writers.

True, Elizabeth is, when they're first engaged, a touch hesitant about being herself with Darcy – 'he had yet to learn to be laughed at, and it was rather too early to begin' – and, too, she feels the need to 'shield' Darcy from her mother and her aunt Mrs Phillips, trying anxiously 'to keep him to herself, and to those of her family with whom he might converse without mortification'. But she needn't have worried. Darcy's reform is complete. Elizabeth soon returns to her 'lively, sportive manner', taking 'liberties with her husband'.

Is it coincidence that Jane, at the end of *Pride and Prejudice*, mentions 'liberties' and equality in marriage as well as giving huge prominence to sibling and sibling-in-law relationships – thus echoing, faintly, the French revolutionary call for liberty, equality and fraternity? I don't think it is. She informs us specifically that the personalities of Wickham and Lydia 'suffered no revolution'. She leaves her readers to decide which, among the other characters, *do* experience it. And Jane wanted, remember, readers who were not 'dull elves', as Scott put it in *Marmion*, readers who were both able and willing to follow the clues in the text through to the obvious conclusion.

Darcy refuses, for the sake of his sister, to accept Wickham as a guest, and one imagines he avoids offering frequent invitations to his mother-in-law, but all the other relations he was originally so reluctant to acquire – Elizabeth's father, her younger sisters, even Lydia – they are welcomed to his house. Lady Catherine, by contrast, is admitted only on sufferance, and because Elizabeth wishes it. Of the new, extended family that Elizabeth and Darcy create, the family members that Darcy is happiest with, apart from his sister, the ones he is 'on the most intimate terms' with, the ones he is 'sensible of the warmest gratitude towards' are, in the end, the Gardiners, the low connections in trade. Pemberley isn't 'polluted', as Lady Catherine fears. Instead, it keeps the best of the old, and welcomes the best of the new.

Almost every reader who encounters Darcy and Elizabeth finds them wonderfully attractive characters. Their independent personalities, their wit and intelligence, their occasional wrong-headedness, their ability to examine their own behaviour and where it stems from, and to try to do better, their mutually supportive and rewarding marriage, these are aspects that accord almost perfectly with modern Western ideals of self-expression and happiness within marriage. But they are wonderful. Jane never, in her other novels, offers us such a perfect marriage between hero and heroine as she gives us here. Elizabeth and Darcy were written to be not just characters, but symbols as well.

Any reader fully sensitised to the loaded language of revolution and counter-revolution would have read *Pride and Prejudice* for what it is – a revolutionary fairy tale, a fantasy of how, with reform, with radical rethinking, society can be safely remodelled. Darcy, who represents both the politically powerful nobility and the landed gentry, has to embrace change – to embrace Elizabeth and her laughter. He has to be, as he says, 'properly humbled'; he has to recognise that worth lies in morality and behaviour, not in bloodlines. His pride set aside, his prejudices, for the most part, dismantled, it's Darcy who, symbolically, removes the threat represented by the militia when he buys the militia officer Wickham a transfer into the regular army, stationed in Newcastle, in the far north of England, and liable to be sent overseas.

If society were reformed, and the revolution to take place bloodlessly, then there would be no need to worry that popular disaffection would flourish, and no way the government could justify retaining an armed force to subdue its own people. Once peace returns, as it does – duly, symbolically – at the end of the novel, Elizabeth and Darcy can continue their radical marriage, freed from senseless or inconsistent rules and conventions. Together they will read, and debate, and remain open to new ideas, ready to cast off prejudices which no longer fit. It's a fairy-tale ending; it's a sweet-natured one. No one – not even Wickham, not Lady Catherine – is punished.

It's a fairy tale.

Back in the real world, with two novels published, Jane had her sights set on a subject that was by far less sweet. Her next book, *Mansfield Park*, was to shock some of her readers immeasurably.

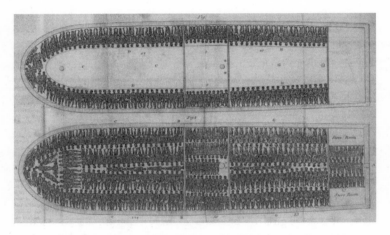

Drawing of the slave ship *Brookes* from Thomas Clarkson's book *The History
of the Rise, Progress, and Accomplishment of the Abolition of the African
Slave-Trade by the British Parliament* (1808). Jane greatly admired Clarkson.

CHAPTER 5

'The Chain and the Cross'

Mansfield Park

London, 1813.[*]

The little girls, who had hoped for an evening at one of the theatres, are indulging in a fit of the sulks. It is only the mildest of fits, however. Jane has been determinedly ignoring them this past half hour, and is encouraging her eldest niece Fanny to ignore them likewise. Fanny is not always wise where her sisters are concerned. And after all, Jane is sure she would be rather sulky herself, if she had been compelled to subject her teeth, as they had earlier in the day, to the tender mercies of Mr Spence – filing and extractions and gold stops and the dear knows what else besides. And those frowns, those gusty sighs, might well be a sign, not that the girls feel themselves hardly-used, but that their letters to their brothers and sisters, at home in Kent, are proving difficult to write. No one knows better than she does that words do not always flow easily.

Jane loves a play well enough, but what with the shopping, and the wearing hour they spent at the dentist, she is glad of a quiet evening with only their own company. Her eyes are troubling her again. A trip to town often takes her this way. It is the late nights, and the smoky lamps, and the dust in the streets forever agitated by carriages and crossing-sweepers. It is pleasanter to sit round the circular table in this snug inner room in Henry's house, even if the girls are being a trifle

---

[*]   Based on Jane Austen's letter to Cassandra Austen (16th September 1813).

tiresome. It is pleasant to be wearing her new cap and to know that her hair is dressed more or less according to the fashion.

The arrival of the tea things seems a good moment to put an end to her letter. The girls evidently think so, too; they laughingly drag Fanny from the table, complaining that they're fainting from hunger, and that some of those little cakes will be just the thing—

Fanny, struggling to maintain her seniority, begins to read them a lecture on all the trash and sweet things they eat and to threaten them with a return visit to the dentist. Perhaps Marianne will have to have *all* her teeth taken out!—

Marianne turns white. The drops of laudanum which she took with her wine and water have not made her forget her ordeal at the hands of Mr Spence, poor child.

Fanny, says Jane, folding her letter, this is hardly helpful—

—And, replies Fanny, as if she has not heard her aunt, as if producing a winning card, sugar is made by slaves and so it is the most immoral, unchristian thing for her sisters to eat as much of it as they do.

Is that true? the little girls ask. And, is that true, Aunt Jane – I thought we didn't have slaves any more in England?

We don't, says Fanny. You must know that sugar comes from the Sugar Islands, from Jamaica, and Antigua, and places such as those. And it is a shocking thing to eat it in such quantities – practically heathenish. Mr Plumptre says that sugar might as well be soaked in blood—

—Oho! crows Lizzy, in delight. Mr Plumptre!

Jane frowns her down, but not before a tide of colour has begun to mount in Fanny's cheeks.

Marianne, putting her hot little face close to Jane's ear, proffers the whispered information that Mr Plumptre is Fanny's *particular* friend.

Edward appears in the doorway, his looks severe, Henry trailing behind, embarrassed. The little girls fall silent. Fanny too. Her father does not altogether approve of Mr John Plumptre.

The younger girls dismissed to bed, Fanny and Edward nibbling on cake, avoiding one another's eyes, Jane asks Henry in an undertone whether he is unwell.

Henry, grimacing all the while, at last confesses to a disordered stomach. He will be much the better for some tea, with sugar, if Jane would be so kind.

Jane stares down at the delicate cup and saucer, the spoon poised, the sugar powdered into dust.

Her other hand strays to the topaz cross which her brother Charles bought her, oh, years since, and which is still her very prettiest ornament. She put it on when she was dressing for dinner, in compliment to the cap and the hair.

How many souls, she wonders, suffered to make this spoonful of sugar?

Mansfield Park was published in May 1814, to almost total silence. There were no reviews at all in the literary magazines – Mansfield Park is the only one of Jane's novels which wasn't reviewed when it came out. Both Sense and Sensibility and Pride and Prejudice had won praise in the press. The Critical Review said that Sense and Sensibility 'reflects honour on the writer'. The British Critic picked out a few 'trifling defects' but pronounced it a 'very pleasing and entertaining narrative' and lamented that there wasn't room to discuss it more prominently. In 1813, it judged Pride and Prejudice 'very far superior to almost all the publications of the kind'. The Critical Review, too, thought the novel 'very agreeable'. These responses indicate how carelessly literary critics tended to read the work of lady novelists, quite as carelessly as Crosby had. They indicate, too, that a lot of the force of these novels was lost by publishing them when memories of the texts and events which had helped to inspire them were beginning to grow vague.

Both these journals were conservative, allied to traditional, establishment views. The British Critic had actually been set up as an Anglican journal and was part-owned by clergymen and part by the Rivingtons, a printing firm which had specialised in religious publications for decades. The reviewers for both magazines enjoyed Jane's characters and her writing, but they were interested – openly so – in lessons, and in what they call 'sober and salutary maxims for the conduct of life'. That they didn't find lessons or 'salutary maxims' in *Mansfield Park*, or at least any they wanted to promote, gives us the first hint that, in this novel, Jane had gone further than was, perhaps, altogether wise.

In the autumn of 1815 Jane left Egerton, the firm which had seen three of her novels into print, and moved to John Murray. Murray – who also published Lord Byron's poetry – was a highly professional publisher, bred to the trade. Jane describes him to Cassandra as 'a rogue, of course, but a civil one'.[1] As had become usual, Henry Austen began the negotiations – perhaps as early as the end of 1814 – but he fell ill and Jane took over the business herself.* It was the first time she had dealt with a publisher directly since her disastrous attempt to manipulate Crosby in 1809. More cautious, and more considered, her correspondence with Murray displays none of the word tricks or empty threats that she had employed with Crosby. But she did, as part of the agreement for *Emma*, insist that Murray produce a second edition of *Mansfield Park*. Her insistence was, as it turned out, ill-judged; the second edition made a heavy loss, eating up most of the profits from *Emma*.†

But the fact that she insisted at all suggests that she thought *Mansfield Park* hadn't reached the audience it deserved.

Murray did his duty by *Emma*, which was reviewed in no fewer than five journals, including Murray's own 'house journal' the *Quarterly*

---

* Kathryn Sutherland, in her article 'Jane Austen's Dealings with John Murray and his Firm', *Review of English Studies* (2012), points to references in letters in the Murray archive which indicate a tentative approach quite soon after the publication of *Mansfield Park*.

† 750 copies of the second edition of *Mansfield Park* appeared in February 1816. Five years later more than 400 still hadn't been sold.

Review, edited by his friend and close collaborator William Gifford. The reviewer selected was Walter Scott, the author of *Waverley* and *Ivanhoe*, who was at this point still known chiefly for his poetry. The review is a serious one – thoughtful, attentive. It takes the form of a twenty-page essay which begins by discussing the emergence of a new kind of novel, dealing not with long-lost heirs and brigands and adventures but with 'such common occurrences as may have fallen under the observation of most folks'. As far as this newer type of novel is concerned, Jane is, for Scott, in a class of her own. A writer himself, he appreciates not only the end product ('sketches of such spirit and originality') but the work which has gone into producing it; the 'neatness' and 'precision', and the 'peculiar tact' with which she reveals character through 'quiet yet comic dialogue'.

At one point in the essay, Scott explains that he's including 'a short notice of the author's former works' as a way of illustrating the kind of novels she writes. The plots of both *Sense and Sensibility* and *Pride and Prejudice* are duly summarised. *Mansfield Park* isn't even mentioned.

Jane questioned this when she wrote to Murray, returning the copy of the magazine he'd sent to her: 'I return you the Quarterly Reveiw [*sic*] with many Thanks', she writes. 'The Authoress of *Emma* has no reason I think to complain of her treatment in it — except in the total omission of Mansfield Park. — I cannot but be sorry that so clever a Man as the Reveiwer of *Emma*, should consider it as unworthy of being noticed.'

What does this indicate? That Jane wanted to know what a 'clever man' ('a reading man', to quote *Persuasion*'s Captain Wentworth) thought of her third, difficult, disappointing novel? Did she consider the omission deliberate? I think so – she sees it as a cause for complaint. She was 'sorry'; was she surprised?

∽

What was it that made the literary reviewers shy away from *Mansfield Park*?

So far as we know it was the first novel Jane had started – and finished – in years, perhaps nearly a decade or even longer. We can't be sure how much she reworked *Sense and Sensibility* and *Pride and Prejudice*, but there are enough indications remaining in the texts to suggest that the family tradition that they were originally written in the 1790s isn't entirely wide of the mark. Redrafting and revising are – as every writer knows – different, very different, to writing something from scratch.

And *Mansfield Park* is very different from the novels which were begun when Jane was young, even if the first page seems like a sort of sequel to *Pride and Prejudice*, picking up where that novel ended, with three sisters marrying into different social classes, the second oldest making a brilliant match while the youngest elopes and lands in comparative poverty. If *Pride and Prejudice* is, as Jane joked, 'too light and bright and sparkling', then *Mansfield Park* is its dark and sombre reflection.

It is a sober novel, even more so than *Sense and Sensibility*. There are few moments of comedy to vary the tone. The two weddings at the end of *Mansfield Park* are neatly cancelled out by a divorce (extraordinarily rare at the time) and a death, two marriages finished, dissolved. The book is filled with infidelities, with not-so-genteel poverty, with bullying and threats of violence. The heroine, Fanny Price, is sent away from her birth family as a child of ten. Her much-loved brother William, little older, joins the Royal Navy and is sent to sea, in wartime. Another of the Price children enters the service of the East India Company, sailing half-way round the world with cargoes worth a king's ransom, exposed to the dangers not only of the sea, and of piracy, but of the Indian climate and diseases – malaria, dengue fever – to which European settlers had absolutely no natural resistance. Another of Fanny's siblings dies as a child. Fanny's uncle, the Reverend Mr Norris, dies at the beginning of Chapter 3. The gluttonous clergyman, Dr Grant, 'brings on apoplexy and death' a few pages before the end of the novel. Even Fanny's favourite horse, the 'old grey poney', dies.

Then there are the parents. In all the novels except for this one either the hero or heroine has lost at least one parent. This is true in *Northanger*

Abbey, in *Sense and Sensibility*, in *Pride and Prejudice*, in *Emma*, and in *Persuasion*. In *Mansfield Park*, by contrast, the heroine has almost too many parents, and all of them are terrible. Perfection, for Jane, belongs only to the dead, and the living parents she writes are, without exception, flawed human beings – just as her heroes and heroines are. But though the parents in Jane's other novels may be tyrannical, like General Tilney, dangerously inept, like Mrs Dashwood, or a social embarrassment, like Mrs Bennet, they are motivated by what they believe is best for their children. Not so for Fanny Price. There are her own father and mother – the one a drinker, 'dirty and gross', the other 'a partial, ill-judging parent, a dawdle, a slattern'. Then there are her foster parents, her uncle and aunt, Sir Thomas and Lady Bertram. Lady Bertram is 'indolent', 'dozing' her life away on the 'sopha'. Sir Thomas Bertram is 'cold' and 'injudicious', anxious about the implications of allowing Fanny to enter his household ('he thought of his own four children, of his two sons, of cousins in love, etc.'). Fanny's other aunt, Mrs Norris, a deeply unpleasant individual whose mind is a mystery even to her creator ('perhaps she might so little know herself'), only ever notices Fanny to scold her.

Both of the heroine's 'fathers' behave in ways which are, on the kindest interpretation, ill-judged.

Meeting his eldest daughter for the first time in years, Mr Price gives her a 'hug', the only one in all of Jane's novels. A 'hug', for Jane, meant something slightly different than it does nowadays. It was more than an embrace, it was close, rough, forcible. It's a pressing together of bodies. Implicit in it is threat, and physicality – even sexual intimacy. And there's more. When Mr Price reads in his newspaper that Fanny's cousin Maria has left her husband for another man, he announces that, if he were Maria's father, he would whip her for it: 'I don't know what Sir Thomas may think of such matters; he may be too much of the courtier and fine gentleman to like his daughter the less. But, by G—! if she belonged to *me*, I'd give her the rope's end as long as I could stand over her.'

It has, we gather, been a while since Mr Price was in gainful employment, but when he did work it was as an officer of marines – the soldiers who served as part of the Royal Navy. He will have seen men flogged until their backs were nothing more than a mass of soft bloody flesh. The word 'sadist' hadn't been coined when Jane was writing, but that's undoubtedly what Mr Price is.

What should we make of the fact that Fanny's two sisters fight over possession of a silver knife, and that one of Fanny's first actions after arriving back in Portsmouth is to make sure they each have one? Does she suspect – does she know – that they might need to protect themselves?

Fanny's other father, her uncle, admires her 'person', her 'complexion' and 'figure' – that is, her body, lightly covered by the flimsy dresses which were in fashion in the early years of the nineteenth century. He watches closely, almost vicariously, as Henry Crawford courts Fanny. He discusses her looks with his son, Fanny's first cousin – the man Fanny loves and eventually marries. The idea of a man of 50 noticing his wife's niece in this way, a girl brought up in his house, should, I think, make us feel uncomfortable. It makes Fanny feel uncomfortable.

It's worth noting that she's the only one of Jane's heroines who, it seems, has short hair – 'a queer fashion', her brother William remarks, and one which he 'could not believe' when he 'first heard of such things being done in England'.* Short hair was quite modish for a time, but it was daring – an odd choice of hairstyle for the painfully shy Fanny to adopt, unless one views it as an attempt to avoid male attention, to evade 'being worth looking at'.

---

* The intensity of William's reaction suggests that we are dealing here with cropped hair and not just short front ringlets. In a letter of 1808 which has since disappeared, Jane seems to refer to a niece – Anna – having cut off her hair, a decision 'much regretted' by some of the family, though Jane herself took the philosophical view that hair grows and that 'two or three years will restore it again' (Wednesday 15th–Friday 17th June 1808).

Fanny Price's family is not like the other ones Jane creates. We'll see another possibly ill-advised, quasi-incestuous relationship between the hero and heroine of *Emma*, but we come closer to incest in *Mansfield Park* – threatened and real. Marriage between first cousins was legal in England and in fact remains so. Indeed, Jane's brother Henry married their first cousin Eliza. True, Henrietta Musgrove marries her cousin Charles Hayter in *Persuasion*, but it's something Jane otherwise goes out of her way to avoid in her writing. Mr Darcy doesn't marry his cousin Anne de Bourgh. Even with more distant cousins – William and Anne Elliot, Mr Collins and the Bennet girls – Jane prevents any marriage from getting near to happening.

In *Mansfield Park*, she not only marries first cousins to each other but does so after she has made it clear that adding a sexual element to pre-existing relationships is a horribly messy and undesirable thing to do. When Fanny finds out that her cousin Maria has run off with Henry Crawford – the very man who has proposed to *her* – her first reaction is visceral disgust:

> A woman married only six months ago; a man professing himself devoted, even *engaged* to another; that other her near relation; the whole family, both families connected as they were by tie upon tie; all friends, all intimate together! It was too horrible a confusion of guilt, too gross a complication of evil, for human nature, not in a state of utter barbarism, to be capable of!

From the very first chapter of the novel, the possibility of a sexual or romantic relationship between Fanny and either of her male cousins has been acknowledged, and acknowledged as an evil. Mrs Norris announces that it will be 'morally impossible' if Fanny is brought up with them, 'always together, like brothers and sisters', and it ought to be so. It isn't, as it turns out, impossible; whether it's moral, or psychologically healthy for either party, is another question altogether.

Jane doesn't gloss over these issues; we get to see Fanny being brought up with her cousins, with all the intimacy of siblings. The action of *Mansfield Park* is set over a far longer time period than is covered by Jane's other novels. Fanny is ten when we first meet her. By the time the novel ends she must be nineteen or twenty if not a little more (Jane announces her intention to 'purposely abstain from dates'). *Sense and Sensibility*, with the next longest action, is set over three years. The norm is a year or thereabouts.

Mansfield Park really isn't like Jane's other books.

Even the title is a departure from her normal practice; from her childhood onwards she tended to pick for her titles either names (*The Beautifull Cassandra, Frederic and Elfrida, Susan*) or set phrases (*Love and Freindship, First Impressions, Sense and Sensibility, Pride and Prejudice*). Jane's next novel, *Emma*, returns to this. There seems to be something quite fundamental, quite important, about the words 'Mansfield Park' – something Jane wants library subscribers to *see* when they're looking through the catalogue, something she wants to confront her readers with every time they pick the book up, and to have printed alone, in large lettering, at the beginning of each of the three volumes in which the novel was published.

There's a tantalising scrap of a letter which turned up in the 1960s, date and addressee both unknown. On one side are a few lines that make little or no sense out of context, and on the reverse is a postscript:

Perhaps before the end of April, *Mansfield Park* by the author of S & S. — P. & P. may be in the World. — Keep the *name* to yourself. I sh[d] not like to have it known beforehand. God bless you. — Cassandra's best Love. Yours affec:[ly]

J. Austen

If this really is part of a letter written by Jane, then perhaps we ought to read this as a fit of assumed or real modesty, or a desire to do things in the proper, professional way. Or perhaps it's a sensible precaution in an age when pressure was often brought to bear on publishers to prevent politically or personally damaging material ever seeing the light of day.

As a number of critics have remarked over the years, there had been a person called Mansfield, a prominent person: Lord Mansfield, the man who – without quite intending to – succeeded in making slavery illegal in England.

Lord Mansfield – William Murray – was born into an aristocratic family in Scotland in 1705.* His father and two of his numerous siblings were attached to the Catholic Stuart cause, opposing the usurpation of the British throne by the Protestant, Hanoverian Georges. This was a handicap for a young man of ambition, and William took an unusual way of dealing with it, leaving for England at the age of fourteen and cutting off contact with his more embarrassing relations. He was a scholar at Westminster School and went from there to Christ Church Oxford, making a number of useful acquaintances at both. After toying with the idea of the Church, he went in for law, and did extremely well. He rose to the very top of the legal and political trees, closely intertwined in England, holding in turn the positions of Solicitor-General, Attorney-General, and chief justice of the King's Bench – Lord Chief Justice. He became a privy councillor, a member of the body which advised the king. He occasionally filled, for short periods, the offices of Lord Chancellor, of deputy speaker and even speaker of the House of Lords. He was an influential and powerful man.

Mansfield and his wife had no children of their own, but they informally adopted three of his great-nieces, Anne and Elizabeth Murray, and Dido Elizabeth Belle – illegitimate, mixed-race, the daughter of an African woman and Mansfield's nephew, John Lindsay. Mansfield seems to have been fond of Dido. He gave her a generous allowance and left her money in his will. Someone – perhaps Mansfield – also commissioned a portrait of Dido with her cousin Elizabeth. It's rather charming. Granted, Dido is holding an armful of leaves and fruit (nature) while her

---

*   Apparently no relation to the publisher John Murray.

cousin sits with a book open on her lap (culture), and she's pointing to her own brown, dimpling face with one finger, but she's beautiful – vital, smiling. She's dressed in white silk, with what look like pearls round her neck and sparkling earrings in her ears. She's hurrying somewhere (a gauzy scarf billows behind her), and her cousin reaches out a hand to restrain her. The eyes of the two girls are almost identical. Just the way the artist painted brown eyes, or a family resemblance, faithfully depicted? *

Jane met Elizabeth Murray several times. Elizabeth had married, becoming Lady Finch-Hatton and a Kentish neighbour of Jane's brother Edward. The Finch-Hattons also owned Kirby Hall in Northamptonshire, where the 1999 adaptation of *Mansfield Park* was filmed. Kirby Hall is entirely the wrong period to have served as a model for 'spacious, modern-built' Mansfield Park, but it's another connection between the book and Lord Mansfield. Mansfield Park, Jane tells us, is not far from the town of Northampton.

In his long and varied legal career, Mansfield would have come across a number of cases relating to slavery in one way or another.†
There were plenty of cases to be had.

Dozens upon dozens of West Indian islands belonged to Britain – Jamaica, Bermuda, Grenada, Barbados, Antigua, the Bahamas. Until 1775, Britain also owned most of the eastern seaboard of America. British-owned slaving ships endlessly traced the Atlantic 'triangle', taking rum and sugar and cotton to Britain, manufactured goods from Britain to the west coast of Africa, and slaves from Africa to the West Indies and America. Merchants from the ports of Plymouth, Liverpool,

---

* Dido married a man called John Davinier, a 'steward', and gave birth to three sons. For more information see Paula Byrne's *Belle*. The 2013 film *Belle*, directed by Amma Asante, compresses events together and takes considerable liberties with the few facts we have.

† Simon Schama's *Rough Crossings* gives a comprehensive overview; so does Adam Hochschild's *Bury the Chains*.

Bristol and London grew rich. Britain grew rich. The historian Adam Hochschild estimates that around the turn of the century 30 per cent of British imports came from the West Indies. On average, more than 40,000 people were transported across the Atlantic every year.

The Atlantic crossing was dangerous, but that didn't stop the people who owned estates and businesses in the West Indies from travelling to Britain. Often they brought slaves with them. Some of those slaves had children of their own. Some ran away. By the time Jane was born, London's black population was large enough to hide in – 5,000 strong at least, and probably closer to 10,000.[2]

In 1769, a man called Charles Stewart came to Britain from Virginia, bringing with him a slave, James Somerset. Stewart settled in London, in Cheapside; in what was then and still is the heart of the business district. Cheapside is where Elizabeth Bennet's favourite uncle Mr Gardiner lives in *Pride and Prejudice*, though Jane makes a point of stating that his is a 'respectable line of trade', presumably not connected with slavery, or not directly, at least. In September 1771, Somerset vanished. Stewart, with difficulty, traced him. Somerset was abducted while walking through Covent Garden and taken, shackled, to a ship that was about to set sail for Virginia, where he was to be sold. Anti-slavery activists managed to obtain a writ of habeas corpus, meaning that Somerset's jailers had to produce him, in court, and explain precisely why they were holding him. The case was heard early in 1772, before Lord Mansfield.

Mansfield's Jacobite parents and siblings had been a source of embarrassment for most of his life. Now his great-niece was to become another. A year earlier, in 1771, Mansfield had refused to make any formal judgement in a case very similar to Somerset's. The decision of a jury didn't bind any later court, but any formal pronouncement by so senior a judge would have been at least strongly persuasive to any-one coming afterwards. Mansfield really didn't want to have to make a judgement this time round, either. But at length (the case was dragged out for months) he cut through some of the tangle of contradictory statutes and case law and most unwillingly pronounced that: 'Contract for the sale of a slave is good here; the sale is a matter to which the law properly and readily attaches, and will maintain the price according to the agreement. But here the person of the slave himself is immediately the object of inquiry, which makes a very material difference.'[3] Stewart had rights, but so did Somerset. The imprisonment was illegal; Somerset must be released.

Mansfield didn't intend to outlaw slavery in England. He hadn't actually done so, but what Mansfield had intended and what he had done paled into insignificance alongside what everyone thought had happened. Even the fiercest defenders of slavery, people like Edward Long, author of the *History of Jamaica*, bewailed the Mansfield judgment as putting an end to slavery not just in England, but everywhere the British ruled: 'I cannot well comprehend', wrote Long, 'how the master can exercise a right of perpetual service, without restraining the Negroe [*sic*] of his personal liberty, his power of locomotion, or of removing his person wheresoever his inclination may direct.'[4] How could slavery function when the law – in the person of Lord Mansfield – had removed the practical basis on which it rested?

In vain did Mansfield protest that the judgment had been misunderstood. In vain did he insist, in the later case of the ship *Zong*, that the deliberate drowning of dozens of slaves could be tried only as insurance fraud. The abolitionists celebrated the Somerset case as a triumph. In America, escaped slaves fled to the coast, to claim sanctuary on British ships. When war broke out, the British commanders, ever expedient, promised freedom to any slave who fought for them. It was too late – the genie was out of the bottle.

∽

It would have been unforgivably careless of Jane to attach Mansfield's name, out of all the names she could have chosen, to *this* novel unless she meant her readers to think about him and about slavery. There are brief references to the slave trade in *Emma*, and to property in the West Indies in *Persuasion*. But in *Mansfield Park* two characters –

the forbidding Sir Thomas Bertram and his oldest son Tom – actually travel abroad to the Caribbean. And they go, Jane tells us specifically, to oversee the management of their estate in the sugar island of Antigua.

Slavery wasn't some distant, abstract notion for Jane. It couldn't be. Jane's own family had ties to the Caribbean. Her oldest brother, James, had a slave-owning godfather: James Nibbs, an Oxford acquaintance of the Reverend George Austen.* Nibbs sent his son to the little boarding school which Jane's father ran at Steventon, indicating a close and continuing relationship between the families. James Austen went on to marry a woman whose father had been born in Antigua. Charles, the baby of the Austen family, married a pair of sisters from Bermuda – Frances and Harriet Palmer.† One of Jane's aunts – the wife of her mother's brother, James Leigh-Perrot – had been born in the West Indies, in Barbados, and was shipped to England as a child. The Leigh-Perrots, we know, kept a black servant called Frank. Jane mentions him in a letter of 1799, and again in 1801.

But what did Jane herself think? We know that she had read Thomas Clarkson's *History of the Abolition of the Slave-Trade*, detailing his experiences over decades of campaigning against slavery. She even describes herself as having been 'in love' with Clarkson – a love which tells us far more about her than her feelings for any of her supposed suitors do.[5]

She paid Clarkson a peculiar compliment. Mrs Norris – Fanny's vicious, bullying aunt – shares her name with a real-life slave-trader

---

* One biographer, Claire Tomalin, includes this information in an appendix about attitudes to slavery, almost as if she thinks the issue doesn't really have anything to do with Jane or her writing.

† Frances Palmer died in 1814; Charles later married her sister Harriet. This was not illegal at the time in England (though it became so in 1835, and continued to be illegal until 1905), but it was frowned upon. Mr and Mrs Palmer attested to Jane's will, which had been unwitnessed, meaning that her signature had to be sworn to. As a former Attorney-General of Bermuda, Mr Palmer presumably enjoyed high standing.

and anti-abolitionist: Mr Norris of Liverpool, the man Clarkson cast as chief villain in his book.

Norris first appeared when Clarkson was touring the port towns, trying to find someone who had experience of slave-trading but was willing to testify against it in front of a forthcoming parliamentary committee. Norris offered himself, appeared an enthusiast for abolition, asserted that his former way of life, his former employment, made him sick to the soul. He then entered the committee hearing as a witness for the other side, and started lying through his teeth. In his book Clarkson recounts some of the evidence given by Norris.

> [...] Mr Norris had painted the accommodations on board a slave-ship in the most glowing colours. He had represented them in a manner which would have exceeded his attempts at praise of the most luxurious scenes. Their apartments, he said, were fitted up as advantageously for them as circumstances could possibly admit: they had several meals a day; some, of their own country provisions, with the best sauces of African cookery [...] After breakfast they had water to wash themselves, while their apartments were perfumed with frankincense and lime-juice. Before dinner they were amused after the manner of their country: instruments of music were introduced: the song and the dance were promoted: games of chance were furnished them: the men played and sang, while the women and girls made fanciful ornaments from beads, with which they were plentifully supplied. They were indulged in all their little fancies, and kept in sprightly humour.

It's laughable, or it would be if we had no idea of the horrors that lie beneath it – the clinking of chains, the stench of bodies pressed together in their own urine and faeces and vomit, the ceaseless movement of the sea, what waited at journey's end.

Even before Clarkson's character assassination of him, Norris seems to have been an unpopular individual. Some of the short notices of his death which appear in the papers are positively gleeful. The *Chester*

Chronicle, a newspaper local to Liverpool where Norris lived, announced with spiteful enjoyment that Norris' death 'was in consequence of having lain in a damp bed, on his return from London, where he had been *in favour of the slave-trade!*' (their italics).[6] Once Clarkson's book had appeared, Norris was a name associated not just with slavery, but with the lies and blatant hypocrisy which surrounded it.

Most critics stop with the observation that Mansfield and Norris are both names connected with slavery, that the estate owned by the Bertrams in Antigua is presumably run on slave labour, and that we're told that Fanny asks her uncle about 'the slave trade'. Most of them seem to feel that this is all there is, that the 'dead silence' that meets Fanny's question means that there is, quite simply, nothing else to see, or say.

But remember, this is a novel of Jane's maturity, a novel written over a much shorter space of time than the ones we've looked at so far. If Jane *is* a great writer, a talented artist exercising her craft at its fullest power, shouldn't there be more? Wouldn't a reader of 1814 have expected more, in this book which trumpets its subject on the title page?

They would have done, and they'd have found it – just as we can, if we look properly.

Mansfield Park opens with the words, 'About thirty years ago', and over the course of the first few chapters Jane runs us through the first twenty of those thirty years quickly and – apparently – without much thought for precise dating. But all of this is less vague than it looks. Jane doesn't begin the novel with, 'about twenty-five or thirty years ago' or 'about thirty years or so ago'. She writes 'about thirty years ago'. There's not much more than a year's flexibility in either direction, certainly not more than two. In this novel published in 1814, then, the reader is directed to begin by casting their mind back to 1783–5. In 1783 the British were finally driven out from their American colonies. In fact a lot of the novel's early incidents map closely onto major world events. The 'half a dozen years' which intervene between Lady Bertram's marriage and the marriages of her sisters take us to the period of the French Revolution. The 'eleven following years' of estrangement between Fanny's mother and her family runs up to the temporary peace between Britain and France.

And Jane's first readers, primed by the title, might remember other dates in those decades, milestones on the long, slow struggle towards abolition. 1783 saw British troops leave New York with liberated slaves, who they took to Nova Scotia. These were slaves who had run away to join the British army because of the Somerset judgment.* It also saw Mansfield's ruling in the *Zong* case. In 1785 the abolitionist poet William Cowper published his long, mock-epic poem *The Task* – a poem which contains some of the most eloquent and moving lines written against slavery. The Society for the Abolition of the Slave Trade was established in 1787; in 1791 – around the time, according to the novel's chronology, that Fanny must be born – the French slaves in Haiti revolted. They held the island for years against overwhelming military force. With the outbreak of war with France in 1793, the abolitionists lost some of the momentum they had been gaining. Little progress was made for the next fifteen years or so – and these are years which are, for the most part, skimmed rapidly over in *Mansfield Park*. The Act of Parliament which made slave-trading illegal for British-owned ships was passed in 1807, and it is around 1807 that Sir Thomas leaves for Antigua – to future-proof his estate, we understand. It's at this point that the novel slows down, and the main action begins. The effect is subtle, but sustained.

But Jane doesn't confine herself to subtle hints. In *Mansfield Park* she doesn't use the miniaturist's tools she's usually credited with, but a broader brush and more definite strokes.

∽

Fanny, the heroine of *Mansfield Park*, is a reader, like lots of Jane's heroines. She's quiet, studious, finding an escape from the petty tyrannies

---

* Simon Schama's book relates what happened to them afterwards.

of Mansfield in books. Her favourite poet, or at least the only one she quotes from, is William Cowper. When her cousin Maria's betrothed, the stupid but fabulously rich Mr Rushworth, is explaining the planned landscaping improvements at his estate, Sotherton, Fanny is saddened that an avenue of trees is to be sacrificed. She turns to her cousin Edmund and quotes some lines from Cowper's *The Task*: 'Cut down an avenue! What a pity! Does not it make you think of Cowper? "Ye fallen avenues, once more I mourn your fate unmerited."'

Now, Cowper, as I've already mentioned above, was a poet – the poet – of abolition. He wrote about the subject constantly. His poem *Charity*, published in 1782, asks, 'Canst thou, and honour'd with a Christian name, | Buy what is woman-born, and feel no shame? | Trade in the blood of innocence, and plead | Expedience as a warrant for the deed?' The poem *Pity for Poor Africans* was written to support the sugar boycott of the 1790s.* With its thumping rhymes it seems designed for mass readership, or to be set to music:

> I own I am shock'd at the purchase of slaves,
> And fear those who buy them and sell them are knaves;
> What I hear of their hardships, their tortures, and groans
> Is almost enough to draw pity from stones.
>
> I pity them greatly, but I must be mum [i.e. silent],
> For how could we do without sugar and rum?
> Especially sugar, so needful we see?
> What? give up our desserts, our coffee, and tea!

Both here and in *The Negro's Complaint* of 1788 Cowper condemns slavery explicitly as unchristian: 'Is there, as ye sometimes tell us, | Is there

---

* Adam Hochschild has a detailed discussion of the boycott – so early an example of organised consumer pressure that it predates the coining of the word.

One who reigns on high? | Has He bid you buy and sell us, | Speaking from his throne, the sky?'

But it was *The Task* which made Cowper famous. It was popular, extraordinarily so. The first edition sold out. Why was *this* poem so popular? In part, perhaps, because, unlike many of Cowper's other poems, it allowed – even encouraged – its audience to see Britain, contrary to almost all the facts, as a beacon of liberty and morality:

> I would not have a slave to till my ground,
> To carry me, to fan me while I sleep,
> And tremble when I wake, for all the wealth
> That sinews bought and sold have ever earned.
> No: dear as freedom is, and in my heart's
> Just estimation prized above all price,
> I had much rather be myself the slave
> And wear the bonds, than fasten them on him.
> We have no slaves at home—then why abroad?
> And they themselves, once ferried o'er the wave
> That parts us, are emancipate and loosed.
> Slaves cannot breathe in England; if their lungs
> Receive our air, that moment they are free,
> They touch our country and their shackles fall.
> That's noble, and bespeaks a nation proud
> And jealous of the blessing. Spread it then,
> And let it circulate through every vein
> Of all your empire; that where Britain's power
> Is felt, mankind may feel her mercy too.

The Task brought all Cowper's poems to a wider audience; his complete poems were republished five times in the space of a decade. Thinking of Cowper, then, for most of the first readers of *Mansfield Park*, would have meant thinking, at least for a moment or two, about slavery. Indeed, Jane doesn't let them forget about it for long.

When Fanny, together with the other young people and the omni-present Mrs Norris, goes to visit Sotherton, the description of the gardens – of the wilderness, with its locked gate – recalls another passage from *The Task*.* And it makes Fanny's cousin Maria think of a passage from Laurence Sterne's novel of 1768, *A Sentimental Journey*.

The party has drifted into groups and become separated; Fanny has been abandoned on a bench by Edmund, who's eager to make the most of some unchaperoned time with Mary Crawford. Maria appears, accompanied by Mr Rushworth, her betrothed, and Henry Crawford; all are talking firmly about landscape improvements. Mr Rushworth is dispatched to locate the key to the locked gate and Fanny watches while Henry Crawford attempts to flirt with an unresponsive Maria. He asserts, slyly, that Maria, soon to be married and become mistress of Sotherton, has 'a very smiling scene before' her. Maria's response is sharp:

'Do you mean literally or figuratively? Literally, I conclude. Yes, certainly, the sun shines, and the park looks very cheerful. But unluckily that iron gate, that ha-ha, give me a feeling of restraint and hardship. "I cannot get out," as the starling said.' As she spoke, and it was with expression, she walked to the gate: he followed her. 'Mr Rushworth is so long fetching this key!'

In a foreshadowing of the adulterous affair the two will embark on later in the novel, Maria is persuaded to abandon propriety and to strike out with Henry Crawford. The two of them clamber over the fence (with its 'spikes') and the 'ha-ha' (a concealed ditch into which Fanny is worried her cousin will 'slip') and wander away together. It turns out that, unlike the starling, Maria can get out.

Sterne, who also wrote *The Life and Opinions of Tristram Shandy*,

---

*   The one which begins, 'Now we are passed into a cooler clime ...'

isn't read much these days; his writing, with its endless digressions and laboured *double entendres*, isn't to modern tastes, but the passage Maria quotes from was among the best-known in eighteenth-century English literature.

The narrator of *A Sentimental Journey* (Sterne himself, thinly disguised) is travelling through France. Stopping at an inn, he hears a voice in the corridor, complaining that 'it could not get out'. It turns out to be 'a starling hung in a little cage':

> I stood looking at the bird: and to every person who came through the passage it ran fluttering to the side towards which they approach'd it, with the same lamentation of its captivity. 'I can't get out,' said the starling.—God help thee! said I, but I'll let thee out, cost what it will; so I turned about the cage to get to the door: it was twisted and double twisted so fast with wire, there was no getting it open without pulling the cage to pieces.—I took both hands to it.
>
> The bird flew to the place where I was attempting his deliverance, and thrusting his head through the trellis pressed his breast against it as if impatient.—I fear, poor creature! said I, I cannot set thee at liberty.—'No,' said the starling,—'I can't get out—I can't get out,' said the starling.

The next paragraph but one begins with the words, 'Disguise thyself as thou wilt, still, Slavery! said I,—still thou art a bitter draught! and though thousands in all ages have been made to drink of thee, thou art no less bitter on that account.'

Jane would have been safe in assuming that her readers knew that this was how the passage continued. The whole section, including the reference to slavery, is reproduced in the *Elegant Extracts*, the two collections, verse and prose, which were continually reprinted through Jane's lifetime. The selected passages ('useful and entertaining') were intended to be set as recitation exercises for children, both at school and in the home. The starling extract would have been part of the mental furniture of every educated or even half-educated person.* The leap from starling to slavery is one that readers' brains would have made on their own, almost without any conscious thought.

If these are coincidences then they're two among many.

Early in the novel the youthful Maria and Julia Bertram are lamenting how poorly educated Fanny is. 'I am sure I should have been ashamed of myself, if I had not known better long before I was so old as she is', says one.

> 'How long ago it is, aunt, since we used to repeat the chronological order of the kings of England, with the dates of their accession, and most of the principal events of their reigns!'
>
> 'Yes,' added the other; 'and of the Roman emperors as low as Severus; besides a great deal of the heathen mythology, and all the metals, semi-metals, planets, and distinguished philosophers.'

Clearly the girls haven't learned a complete list of the Roman emperors (they've only gone 'as low as Severus') and so Jane presents her reader with two questions – which of the girls is speaking here, and which of the three Roman emperors called Severus are they referring to? The second and third ruled only for very short periods of time, late in the imperial age. The first, Septimius Severus, ruled for far longer. He came to Britain intending to subdue Caledonia (Scotland) and died at York. He had a wife called Julia – it's presumably she who is speaking, and not Maria. And, as a reference book of the period mentions, Severus 'was by birth an African'† – a black African, as is obvious from statues and coins.

---

* In *Emma*, Harriet Smith's suitor, the largely self-taught Robert Martin, often reads aloud from the *Elegant Extracts* of an evening.

† See the entry for Septimius Severus in *A biographical history of the Roman Empire; from its foundation to the final overthrow of that once great and memorable commonwealth* (Bath, 1790). The fact is also remarked on in Edward Gibbon's vast *Decline and Fall of the Roman Empire* (1776 onwards).

Why mention the name Severus at all? It doesn't add anything, other than making the image of a black man appear in the reader's mind.

There's a continual drip of these kind of reminders, of this sort of mind manipulation.

When the idea of performing a play at Mansfield is first raised there's much discussion as to which play should be chosen. Two of the three Shakespeare plays to feature explicitly non-white characters are suggested – *Othello*, with its 'Moorish' tragic hero who refers in Act One, Scene 3 to having been sold into slavery, and *The Merchant of Venice*, in which a 'Moorish' prince courts the heroine Portia. 'Moor', in Shakespeare's writing, can mean a Muslim person from North Africa. It's also, of course, short for 'blackamoor', someone of, more specifically, black African extraction. It's worth keeping the point in mind.

One of the more modern plays considered is *The Wheel of Fortune*, by Richard Cumberland, first performed in 1795, which features a character called Tempest, governor of the fictional 'Senegambia'. The French and British struggled for control of the Senegal and Gambia rivers for decades. Hundreds of thousands of people – perhaps millions – were sold into slavery from the local markets.

The play finally chosen is *Lovers' Vows*, an English translation of *Das Kind der Liebe* ('The Love-Child') written by the prolific German dramatist August von Kotzebue. It's what would, in Jane's time, have been called 'warm', with one character an unmarried mother and another a young lady who propositions her clergyman tutor. It's also revolutionary; the faithless baron is obliged to marry the servant he ruined, the bastard son is recognised, the peasant woman condemns the lax morals of the upper classes. Sir Thomas Bertram, on his return, burns every copy of the play he can lay his hands on. What, one wonders, would have been his reaction if he'd discovered one of his children blacking up to perform Shakespeare or *The Wheel of Fortune*, or if they'd chosen to perform another of Kotzebue's plays, perhaps the one in which the abolitionist William Wilberforce is mentioned by name, *Die Negersklaven – The Negro Slaves*?

The references, large and small, are everywhere.

The only time that the fashionable, frivolous Mary Crawford ventures on a quotation, she selects an oddly obscure poem. 'Do you remember Hawkins Browne's "Address to Tobacco", in imitation of Pope?—' she asks her sister, before reciting a couple of lines and then composing her own parody of them. The poem may be obscure, but the name of the poet – Hawkins Browne – is a memorable one, and it's one that, like the name Norris, appears in Thomas Clarkson's *History of the Abolition of the Slave-Trade*. Clarkson, invited to dinner at the house of an abolitionist, finds a party there that includes 'Mr Wilberforce', the artist Sir Joshua Reynolds, and Boswell, the friend and biographer of Samuel Johnson. Also there is 'Mr Hawkins Browne', Isaac Hawkins Browne, the son of the poet, a member of parliament. 'After dinner', Clarkson tells his readers:

> the subject of the Slave-trade was purposely introduced. Many questions were put to me, and I dilated upon each in my answers, that I might inform and interest those present as much as I could. They seemed to be greatly impressed with my account of the loss of seamen in the trade, and with the little samples of African cloth, which I had procured for their inspection. Sir Joshua Reynolds gave his unqualified approbation of the abolition of this cruel traffic. Mr Hawkins Browne joined heartily with him in sentiment; he spoke with much feeling upon it, and pronounced it to be barbarous, and contrary to every principle of morality and religion.

It's probable that Hawkins Browne, who had married into a West Indian family and repeatedly voted against abolition, was merely being polite; but it's this passage that Jane's audience would have recognised the name from.

When Maria marries Mr Rushworth, the newlyweds take a house in

London, in Wimpole Street. We're told this a number of times – ten, in fact. It's clearly a detail Jane didn't want her readers to miss. According to Mary Crawford it's 'one of the best houses in Wimpole Street'. In a letter intended as much for Edmund as for Fanny, to whom it's addressed, Mary remarks airily that she has seen the house before: 'I was in it two years ago, when it was Lady Lascelle's.' Lady Lascelles existed. She had married into a notorious slaving family, and though she didn't actually live on Wimpole Street, other members of the family did. It was a street which attracted West Indian families and people with connections in the West Indies. A family called the Pinneys, who had estates in St Kitts and Nevis, lived there; so too did the Beckfords, who owned huge swathes of Jamaica. William Beckford, who inherited the majority of the family money, was at one point the richest man in England. He wasted a good deal of the money on building Fonthill Abbey, before he was disgraced by a same-sex scandal and forced into exile with his wife Margaret.* A cousin of Margaret Beckford was for a time a neighbour of Jane's, renting Edward's house at Chawton. Admiral Cornwallis, who had served in the Caribbean, lived on Wimpole Street; Jane's brother Francis had sailed with Cornwallis as a midshipman. The Knatchbulls, cousins of Edward Austen's adoptive mother, also owned a house on Wimpole Street. It's not impossible to imagine that Jane might have visited there herself. She puts Maria, the daughter of a West Indian plantation owner, among her own kind.

In this novel even an apricot tree works to remind readers of slavery. In Volume 2 Mrs Norris, wife of the former vicar of Mansfield, gets into an argument with the new vicar, Dr Grant, over an apricot tree in the parsonage garden. Mrs Norris is very insistent that Dr Grant should understand that the apricot is 'a Moor Park, we bought it as a

---

* The kinder among Beckford's biographers make much of the fact that no prosecution for sodomy was ever brought against him, but the relationship between him and the sixteen-year-old William Courtenay was, by any standards, wildly inappropriate.

Moor Park, and it cost us—that is, it was a present from Sir Thomas, but I saw the bill—and I know it cost seven shillings, and was charged as a Moor Park'.

'Moor Park' is a particular type of apricot tree – one you can still buy now. A gardener's catalogue of 1795 lists no fewer than nine kinds of apricot.[7] 'Moor Park' is also known as Dunmoor, Peach, or Lord Anson's. Is Jane really using this name, and this kind of apricot tree, out of all the alternatives, by accident? Is it just coincidence that it's the same word Shakespeare uses to describe the ethnicity of black Africans, and that 'Moor Park' echoes 'Mansfield Park'?

Jane is never sloppy with her writing, but she becomes ever more sensitive to the freight attached to certain words. In *Pride and Prejudice* Elizabeth Bennet casually and contemptuously dismisses the easy-going Mr Bingley in her own mind as 'the slave of his design-ing friends'; in *Mansfield Park* it is only the unlikeable characters, the repellent Mrs Norris or the amoral Mary Crawford, who can treat the issue so lightly, the one talking about how she has been 'slaving' herself, the other unwilling to be 'the slave of opportunity'. In the earlier novels Jane uses a word like 'plantation' neutrally; by the time she gets to *Emma*, it appears only when Mrs Elton – a character from the port town of Bristol who is quite extraordinarily sensitive about slavery – is speaking.

The word 'plantation' is used five times in *Mansfield Park*, more often than in any of Jane's other novels. *Mansfield Park* includes repeated refer-ences to 'pheasants', game birds which were difficult to buy and which (like slaves) couldn't be legally recovered if they got away, and so had to be carefully kept and carefully bred to maintain an adequate popu-lation. Jane barely mentions pheasants elsewhere in her writing. When Edmund gives Fanny a glass of wine as a pick-me-up for what sounds like a migraine, he picks Madeira – a fortified wine from the island of that name, the first European slave plantation. This wine is men-tioned only in *Mansfield Park* and *Emma*. Jane repeats the joke she had made in the opening of *Pride and Prejudice*, about men being considered 'property' – repeats it twice. The joke is, of course, at heart entirely unfunny in a world where women, and some men too, could be owned.*

The word with the darkest and most inescapable connotations, though, is one which comes up once in *Sense and Sensibility*, once in *Emma*, not at all in *Northanger Abbey*, *Pride and Prejudice* or *Persuasion*, and no fewer than thirteen times in *Mansfield Park*. This is a novel weighed down – with chains.

It's not a word which Jane ever treats neutrally. In *Sense and Sensibility* it appears explicitly as the reverse of liberty ('Her mind was inevitably at liberty; her thoughts could not be chained elsewhere'). In *Emma* it's associated, like 'plantation', with Mrs Elton (Mr Weston's attention is 'chained' while she talks about his son).

So the title, the literary and historical references, the pointed vocabulary Jane selects – all of them point in one direction, and one direction only. *Mansfield Park* is about slavery. The subject isn't just brought up once or twice; it appears over and over again. It's relentless. The effect, on any reasonably acute reader of 1814, would have been to produce a state of hyper-awareness, to get them anxiously looking for the point that all of this is building towards.

∞

How, though, do we square this with the letter in which Jane seems to say that the novel is about 'Ordination'?

Jane mentions *Mansfield Park* in quite a few of her letters. What appears to be the first reference comes in a letter of January 1813, written to Cassandra, one we've glanced at already. Jane has just received *Pride and Prejudice* ('my own darling child') from London. She tells

---

* 'Miss Bertram's engagement made him in equity the property of Julia, of which Julia was fully aware'; 'Sir Thomas Bertram's son is somebody; and now he is in their own line. Their father is a clergyman, and their brother is a clergyman, and they are all clergymen together. He is their lawful property; he fairly belongs to them.'

Cassandra all about the copies which are to be sent to relations, and how 'the Advertisement is in our paper to day for the first time'. She gloats that she has read 'half the 1st vol.' aloud to an unsuspecting neighbour. The edition itself comes in for some writerly anxiety – there are one or two 'errors' in the printing and 'the 2d vol. is shorter than I could wish'. Having filled a side and a half of paper, Jane announces she 'will try to write of something else; — it shall be a complete change of subject — Ordination. I am glad to find your enquiries have ended so well. — If you cd discover whether Northamptonshire is a Country of Hedgerows, I shd be glad again.'

The tendency has been to read this as a reference to *Mansfield Park*, which is set in the county of Northamptonshire and features a number of clergymen, including one of the central characters, Edmund Bertram. Paula Byrne, in her recent biography of Jane, suggests that it's a joke – that Jane, realising her whole letter has been about *Pride and Prejudice*, picks a subject at random, as far away from that novel's sparkling lightness as she can get.

It's true that Jane does jump around in her letters. Paragraphing, of course, was a waste of expensive paper and added to the cost of postage, but I think there is some association of ideas here, some connection between 'ordination', Cassandra's 'enquiries', and 'hedgerows' – a connection too to Northamptonshire-set *Mansfield Park*. The hedgerows we'll come back to, in much more detail, in the next chapter. For the moment let's stay with ordination.

Ordination is the process by which clergymen become clergymen. The rules are strictly observed in the modern Church of England – prospective members of the clergy have to be at least 24 years old, are first ordained as a 'deacon', a sort of junior position, and, after a year, 'promoted' to become a full priest.

The Church of England that Jane knew was more flexible. It was not unheard of for the age limit to be ignored, and for the full year that was supposed to intervene between becoming a deacon and becoming a priest to be overlooked. A sense of vocation wasn't at all necessary.

The Church was a career and if you knew the right people it could be a very lucrative career indeed. 'Livings' – that is, the right to be a priest in a certain parish – were handed out or sold by bishops, by Oxford and Cambridge colleges, and by ordinary landowners who had no connection with the Church. Jane's own father, for example, was given his 'livings' (one in Steventon, and one in the neighbouring village of Deane) by a distant cousin – the same cousin who later adopted Jane's brother Edward. The livings were passed on to Jane's brother James, then to her brother Henry, and later to one of her nephews. We find similarly cosy arrangements in a number of Jane's novels. Henry Tilney gets his living from his father. Edward Ferrars is given one by Colonel Brandon, the two marrying a pair of sisters not long afterwards. The Mansfield Park estate includes two livings, both of which, by the end of the novel, belong to Edmund Bertram. The two exceptions are Mr Collins and Mr Elton, neither of whom seems to have been given a leg up by their relatives.

What with nepotism and widespread pluralism – holding multiple livings at once, and putting poorly-paid curates into them to do the work required – it's scarcely any wonder that non-conformist churches like the Methodists, Baptists and Quakers had an increasingly widespread following during Jane's lifetime.

But all this seems to be rather a long way from slave plantations and the Atlantic trade. Can *Mansfield Park* really be about both ordination and slaves? What has the Church of England got to do with slavery?

Rather a lot, actually.

In 2006, the then Archbishop of Canterbury, Rowan Williams, issued a formal apology for the Church of England's involvement in slavery. At the beginning of the eighteenth century an Antiguan landowner – and slave-owner – called Christopher Codrington died. He left his collection of books to All Souls Oxford, which still boasts a Codrington Library, and he left his estate on Barbuda – a small island off the coast of Antigua – to the Society for the Propagation of the Gospel, to be held in trust for the furthering of the Society's aims. These were, broadly speaking, to promote the Church throughout the British colonies. The Society was part of the Church of England; among its committee members were senior Church of England clergy. Rowan Williams' apology was made necessary by the publication of Adam Hochschild's book *Bury the Chains* which offered up a number of damning revelations about the Society, including the fact that it didn't just keep the slaves it had inherited, but regularly bought new ones, and that it branded its slaves with the word 'Society' to show that they were Church property. None of this would have been revelatory for Jane, though, or for her first readers; it was common knowledge.

For a long time, the Society saw nothing to be ashamed of in its slave plantation. But as the efforts of the abolitionists began – slowly – to gain traction, the Society became vaguely apologetic, just a touch sensitive about the whole thing. The Bishop of Chester, in a sermon published in 1783, felt it necessary to inform his readers 'that where mention is made of *estates in the West Indies belonging to the Society*, it must not be supposed that we are possessed of any property there *in our own right*'. No – 'we are only holders of certain lands in Barbadoes'.[8] The Society (apparently) 'has always shewn a most laudable solicitude both for the temporal and eternal welfare of the slaves employed on their plantations'. The managers are instructed to treat the slaves 'with the utmost tenderness and humanity'. The plan is for Codrington to be 'a model for all the West Indian islands to imitate' – not now, not soon, but at some misty, as yet undetermined point in the future.

The Bishop dwells fondly on this imaginary model plantation, and on the idea of 'a little society of *truly Christian* Negroes' who will go about

> their daily tasks with alacrity and fidelity; looking up to their masters as their friends, their protectors and benefactors; and consoling themselves for the loss of their liberty and their native land, by the care taken to 'make their yoke easy, and their burden light', to civilize their manners, to enlarge their understandings, to reform their hearts, and to open to them a prospect into a better and a happier country, where

all tears shall be wiped from their eyes, and where sorrow and *slavery* shall be no more.

A decade later, Bryan Edwards – an able special pleader who had spent much of his life in Jamaica before becoming MP for a rotten borough in Cornwall – suggested that some slave-owners, including the Society for the Propagation of the Gospel, were almost to be pitied:

> [M]any persons there are, in Great Britain itself, who ... find themselves possessed of estates in the West Indies which they have never seen ... the Reverend Society established in Great Britain for propagating the Gospel in foreign parts, are themselves under this very predicament. That venerable society hold a plantation in Barbadoes ... and they have found themselves not only under the disagreeable necessity of supporting the system of slavery which was bequeathed to them with the land; but are induced also, from the purest and best motives, to purchase occasionally a certain number of Negroes, in order to divide the work, and keep up the stock.[9]

For the anti-abolitionists, the existence of the Codrington plantation was an absolute godsend. As Robert Norris – Clarkson's old *bête noire* – pointed out in his book *A short account of the African slave trade*, slave-owners had no reason to suppose that they were doing anything wrong:

> The Adventurers in this Trade, who have seen for near a Century past, the Society for propagating Christianity, composed of the Archbishop of Canterbury, the Bishop of London, and many pious Doctors of the established Church, deriving, as Masters, a yearly income from the Labour of their Negroe Slaves in the West Indies, could not consider it as contrary to the Spirit of the Scriptures, or to the Principles of Morality.[10]

For Gilbert Francklyn, the fact that 'my Lords the Archbishops, Bishops, Noblemen, and Gentlemen, who are members of the Society for

Propagating the Gospel in Foreign Parts' are among those 'who purchase negroes in the West Indies' casts a cloak of decency over the whole trade. Clarkson is upbraided by name, painted as a 'rash and arrogant young man' who verges on blasphemy in attempting 'to attribute the hurricanes and tempests in the West Indies to the anger of God against the inhabitants of those islands, for possessing slaves ... although you do not produce a single command of God by which it is forbidden'.[11]

The Church of England – the Society for the Propagation of the Gospel – saw slavery as perfectly godly, as perfectly Christian, as, at any rate, an inevitable evil. For many ordinary citizens, it was a case of out of sight, out of mind; there were no slaves in Britain any more, and the Caribbean, the West Indies, were other countries, far away and seldom to be thought about. But for plenty of people, increasing numbers of people, slavery stained everything and everyone it touched, it made a web of moral contagion – sugar and rum, the fine carriages and the London houses bought with the coin of human suffering, the merchants and slave-owners, the members of parliament and every Church of England clergyman who stood up in the pulpit to preach morality to his English congregation knowing full well what his colleagues and superiors were responsible for in Codrington.

It's into these muddy, churned-up waters that we find Jane wading in *Mansfield Park*.

What she builds up to, with all those references to slavery, is, unusually for her, a symbol. It's not a difficult one to interpret. On the contrary, it's clear as daylight. She puts slavery and the Church right next to each other – quite literally. Her heroine, Fanny, dressing for her coming-out ball, joins together 'the chain and the cross' – a gold chain and an amber cross. They are, Jane reminds us, in case we miss the significance of the moment, 'memorials' and 'tokens'; they stand for something, they are there to remind us. For Fanny, they represent her favourite brother and her favourite cousin, 'the two most beloved of her heart'. For the reader, the associations are, or should be, by this point in the novel, very different.

The juxtaposition of the chain and the cross – of slavery and the Church – might have been jarring (or tactless) for the first readers of *Mansfield Park*, but they couldn't very well deny its truthfulness.

They could hardly, in 1814, have been ignorant of the existence of the Society for the Propagation of the Gospel in Foreign Parts. The SPG and its sister-society, the Society for the Promotion of Christian Knowledge, which worked to promote Anglicanism within Britain, were engaged in a very public turf war with the new and energetic Bible Society. The Bible Society welcomed Christians of most denominations. Prominent among its members were establishment figures – bishops, members of parliament – but also Methodists, Baptists, and Quakers. It was ecumenical, evangelical. Its aim was to give the greatest number of people access to the Bible, across the world, and to that end it printed and distributed translations into a whole variety of languages. It recruited – actively. There was scarcely a town in the country which didn't have a branch.

For the SPG and the SPCK, the Bible Society was a dangerous mix of naive do-gooders and those who actively wanted to undermine the authority of the established Church for their own ends. Chief among their concerns was that giving people unmediated access to the Bible, without any priests to explain it to them properly, or any comforting hierarchy of bishops and archbishops to keep control, might lead to blasphemous misinterpretations – among which, of course, was included anything which didn't happen to suit the Church of England, British commercial interests, or the government. If the Bible Society started shipping Bibles off around the world, wasn't there a very real risk that – for example – slaves in the Caribbean and the West Indies might get tired of waiting for merciful death and the shores of Beulah, and look to other parts of the Bible for guidance instead – to the Book of Exodus, perhaps, in which Moses leads the Hebrews out of slavery?

The Church of England had reason to be anxious about attacks on its influence and power. Almost from the very beginning, it had been subjected to numerous challenges as an institution. In the 250 years since its foundation by Elizabeth I, it had faced the English Civil War, a Roman Catholic monarch, one Calvinist usurper, and one Lutheran one. During Jane's lifetime its status was being threatened again, by the rise of non-conformist religion, by the gradual relaxation of anti-Catholic legislation, by farmers complaining bitterly about the tithe system, under which priests were entitled to a tenth of everything produced in the parish. Questions were beginning to be asked about exactly how priests – and for that matter bishops and archbishops – were chosen, and about the practice of holding numerous parishes simultaneously. Yet again, the Church was on the defensive.

And its chief defender, its attack dog against the incursions of the Bible Society, of would-be reformers and evangelicals, was a man called Henry Handley Norris.*

This Norris was born in Hackney, now a very urbanised area of east London, but occupied in the eighteenth century largely by people who had made their fortunes in trade and moved a little way out of the city in order to enjoy them in a quasi-rural setting. Norris' father was a merchant who traded with Russia and left his son very well off. The young Henry, however, chose to follow his maternal grandfather into the Church. Not for him, though, the quiet life of a parish priest. He became private chaplain to the Earl of Shaftesbury, a member of the chapter of Llandaff cathedral and, finally, of the chapter of Westminster cathedral. He enjoyed the patronage of the prime minister, Lord Liverpool. Norris was a great one for organising things. He sat on the boards of the Russia Company and the Eastland Company (which was interested in trade with Scandinavia and the Baltic), was active in the establishment of Church of England schools, and was a prominent member of the

---

* Both Norrises – Robert and Henry Handley – seem to have had links to shipping and to the financial district of London, so there may have been some distant family connection between the two. There is, however, a degree of uncertainty about the identity of Robert Norris' parents.

committees for the Society for the Promotion of Christian Knowledge and for the Society for the Propagation of the Gospel.

Norris was also a philanthropist, never, it seems, happier than when he was paying money out to those less fortunate than himself, or organising other people into paying it. His name was constantly in the newspapers as a subscriber to good works. From around 1812 Norris was one of the owners of the literary journal the *British Critic*, and even after editors had been appointed he continued to take a close personal interest. He was a writer himself. *The Influence of the Female Character upon Society*, published in 1801, complains about female fashions. He kept up a full and busy correspondence with all sorts of people, much of it, in the 1810s, connected to what he saw as the dangers of the Bible Society. In 1813, he published a whole book made up of letters on the subject – *A practical exposition of the tendency and proceedings of the British and Foreign Bible Society*, later described as 'a farrago of illiberality, bigotry, and ill-nature'.[12] It's a thorough and determined attack on every aspect of the Bible Society, approaching from every angle. Norris objects to the structure of the Society (identical, he says, to that adopted by the Puritans before the English Civil War, or the rebel Irishmen of the 1790s); he objects to its membership; he objects to the fact that it takes money which might otherwise have been donated to the societies he himself was closely involved with, the SPCK and the SPG. He also objects to the Bible Society's decision to publish and distribute Bibles without any explanatory notes, and to neglect the authorised Anglican prayer book.

Coming back to Jane and to *Mansfield Park*, we can pick out quite a number of correspondences between the real-life Reverend Mr Norris and the fictional Mrs Norris, widow of a clergyman. Like her namesake, Mrs Norris disapproves of modern female fashions ('That Mrs Whitaker is a treasure! ... she has turned away two housemaids for wearing white gowns'). Then too, Mrs Norris fancies herself as a philanthropist, 'projecting and arranging' the 'expensive ... charity' of adopting Fanny. 'As far as walking, talking, and contriving reached', Jane tells us, Mrs Norris 'was thoroughly benevolent, and nobody knew better how to dictate liberality to others; but her love of money was equal to her love of directing, and she knew quite as well how to save her own as to spend that of her friends'.

There are – surely – shades of Norris here.

Jane also shows her Mrs Norris thinking about the distribution of prayer books. Fanny, sent home to Portsmouth in disgrace for rejecting the approaches of Henry Crawford, hears her mother complaining that the youngest daughter Betsey doesn't have 'such a good godmother' as Mary, another of the Price children, had. Betsey's godmother is of course Mrs Norris. Fanny – and Jane – both evidently agree:

> Fanny had indeed nothing to convey from aunt Norris, but a message to say she hoped that her god-daughter was a good girl, and learnt her book. There had been at one moment a slight murmur in the drawing-room at Mansfield Park about sending her a prayer-book; but no second sound had been heard of such a purpose. Mrs Norris, however, had gone home and taken down two old prayer-books of her husband with that idea; but, upon examination, the ardour of generosity went off. One was found to have too small a print for a child's eyes, and the other to be too cumbersome for her to carry about.

The joke here is Mrs Norris' almost pathological meanness – mentioned elsewhere in the novel – but it also looks a lot like a reference to the real-life Norris, and to his energetically-expressed anxieties about prayer books. Norris' societies – the SPCK and the SPG – had had decades to organise the distribution of Bibles and prayer books and they hadn't really done it very well. The message Mrs Norris sends, via Fanny, to say that she hopes Betsey 'learnt her book', means her prayer book; she says that it's of vital importance for Betsey to familiarise herself with Anglicanism, but doesn't actually do anything to make it happen.

∽

Quite where Jane's own religious beliefs lay, whether, as Henry declared in his first – and occasionally downright dishonest – biography, 'her opinions accorded strictly with those of our Established Church', is difficult to pin down. At different times, and when writing to different people, she expresses directly contrary views. In 1809 she announces to Cassandra, 'I do not like the Evangelicals'.[13] In 1814, in a letter of advice to her niece Fanny about her relationship with Mr Plumptre, a Bible Society member teetering on the verge of evangelicalism, she remarks that she is 'by no means convinced that we ought not all to be Evangelicals, & am at least persuaded that they who are so from Reason & Feeling, must be happiest & safest'.[14] But in 1816, not long after she made Anne Elliot, clearly one of the quieter sort of evangelicals, the heroine of the novel we know as *Persuasion*, she wrote a letter explaining that 'We do not much like Mr Cooper's new Sermons, — they are fuller of Regeneration & Conversion than ever — with the addition of his zeal in the cause of the Bible Society'.[15] Though we know that Jane didn't much like 'Mr Cooper' (her cousin Edward), these views might not be her own. Elsewhere 'we' sometimes indicates that she is quoting a third party; perhaps, here, her mother.

All three of the Austen women, 'Mrs Austen', 'Miss Austen' and 'Miss Jane Austen', are included in the list of subscribers drawn up at the first meeting of the Basingstoke chapter of the SPCK. So far as we're aware, it's one of only three occasions that Jane's name appeared in print during her lifetime. Edward, we know, attended the meeting, together with the local priest, Mr Papillon.* Did he subscribe on behalf of his mother and sisters? He may well have done so; he might not even have asked. And even if he did ask, even if he was acting with Jane's full approbation, this could easily be one of her outbreaks of queer humour – like signing her letter to the publisher Crosby with the initials 'M.A.D.',

---

* Fanny Austen mentions her father going to the meeting in her journal, though she makes no reference to her grandmother and aunts attending.

or (as we'll see in the next chapter) sneaking some less than complimentary references to the Prince Regent into *Emma*, a novel which she had been invited to dedicate to him.

Whatever the truth behind Jane's subscription to the SPCK, whatever her real ideas about evangelicals, these were not matters she was ignorant of. Her two favourite nieces, Fanny and Anna, were both romantically involved with men who were keen members of the Bible Society; if the subject wasn't openly debated within the family then it must have been rather a large elephant in the room.* Just as with her choice of the name Mansfield for her title, and her selection of loaded vocabulary, just as with her decision to use literary references which bring up slavery and race, we have to assume that Jane is alluding to Norris and his societies on purpose. Otherwise we're dealing with a truly impossible number of coincidences.

Readers in 1814 would, I think, have registered Norris as a name from Clarkson's *History of the Abolition of the Slave-Trade*, but it would have been more immediately familiar to them as a name they frequently saw in their newspapers – the subscriber to and organiser of charity, the opponent of the Bible Society, the defender of the Church. Jane chooses the name Norris as a way of reinforcing her central symbol, her central point – the chain and the cross, the Church and slavery. Norris, for Jane and her readers, means both a man who claimed to be an abolitionist but in fact lied to support the slave-trade, and a churchman who was, in his role as a leading light of the Society for the Propagation of the Gospel, *a slave-owner*.

---

* A 'J. Plumtree, Esq. of Fredville, Kent' – either Fanny's 'Mr Plumptre' or perhaps his father – gave an annual donation of 5 guineas to the Bible Society in 1815. The younger Plumptre was a lifelong member of the Bible Society, later serving as treasurer of the Canterbury branch. (See *Summary Account of the Proceedings of the British and Foreign Bible Society*.) Ben Lefroy, who had become engaged to Anna Austen in the summer of 1813, was active in the Hampshire branch of the Bible Society, as were other members of his immediate family (*Hampshire Chronicle*).

Christianity itself is not to blame – Fanny's 'amber cross', a gift her brother William has brought back for her from Sicily, is, in itself, guiltless; it remains guiltless on the occasion when, we're told, Fanny ties it round her neck with 'a bit of ribbon'. It would remain guiltless still even if she wore it with the necklace which Mary Crawford slyly offers her as a way of facilitating Henry Crawford's courtship. That necklace may in fact be a chain but Jane is careful always to call it a 'necklace'. The morality of the Crawfords is suspect, it's damaging, but it isn't the only – or the most – damaging morality in this novel.

It's the Church of England which is tainted; the Church which taints. Edmund is only days away from his ordination as a clergyman when he buys 'a chain for Fanny's cross'; the item is never particularised in any other way – at one point Jane even calls it 'the real chain'. From the moment Edmund makes the decision to embark on his career in the Church, he is guilty by association.

But Edmund – Edmund is surely the hero of *Mansfield Park*, isn't he?

Well yes, but only really in the sense that he marries the heroine. Like his near-namesake Edward Ferrars in *Sense and Sensibility*, Edmund is, frankly, not much cop. He is – supposedly – 'uniformly kind' to Fanny, 'true to her interests, and considerate of her feelings'. He makes sure there is a horse in the stables which she can ride – so necessary for her health – and he recommends books to her, and talks to her about them. But his kindness for Fanny doesn't go so very deep. Nor does his consideration. Almost as soon as Mary Crawford appears on the scene, Edmund ceases to think much about Fanny at all. Mary expresses a desire to learn to ride, and straightaway Edmund co-opts the horse which was originally meant for Fanny. Fanny wants to go stargazing, but Edmund would rather listen to Mary singing with his sisters. At Sotherton, Fanny wants to see the avenue of trees which is to be cut down in the planned landscape improvements, but Edmund abandons her to sit entirely on her own while he goes walking with Mary. He knows that he's the only friend Fanny has at Mansfield, the only person she can confide in – but Fanny, like Anne Elliot in

Persuasion, is one of those people whose 'convenience was always to give way'.

Edmund is a truly terrible judge of character, just like his father, and like his father he tries to browbeat Fanny into marrying Henry Crawford. But Edmund – who, remember, admits to having had doubts about Henry's behaviour, and who's had the opportunity to watch Henry playing the Bertram girls off against each other – goes on at Fanny for pages, longer than Sir Thomas does, longer even than Henry does himself.

Edmund is easily persuaded to act in a way contrary to his beliefs and morals – though at the same time clinging to the belief that his morals put him in a position to judge others. He allows Mary Crawford to influence him – he is powerfully attracted to her – he intends to marry her – but all the while he continues to dissect her faults of character with Fanny. 'How many a time have we talked over her little errors!' he says. Having protested vehemently against the acting plan, he changes his mind. He does not 'like being driven into the *appearance* of such inconsistency', but his motivation is (of course) purer, different. He is not like other people.

He's a towering hypocrite, perfectly suited to a career in the Church of England. He admits that he chose the Church not out of any deep sense of vocation, but because he knew he would be well provided for:

[T]he knowing that there was such a provision for me probably did bias me. Nor can I think it wrong that it should. There was no natural disin-clination to be overcome, and I see no reason why a man should make a worse clergyman for knowing that he will have a competence early in life [...] I have no doubt that I was biased, but I think it was blamelessly.

Fanny protests that it is 'the same sort of thing ... as for the son of an admiral to go into the navy, or the son of a general to be in the army', but in a novel which includes detailed discussions about the problems that patronage and nepotism create within the navy, Jane doesn't mean us to read this as an excuse.

She doesn't give Edmund an easy ride. She doesn't make him likeable or heroic. Rather, she deliberately associates him with the sins of the Church – with slavery, and also with lesser errors.

Before Edmund is ordained, both he and his father take it for granted that he will live in the parsonage house at Thornton Lacey. Jane has Sir Thomas expound on the advantages – even the necessity – of a clergyman being 'constantly resident', on the idea that 'human nature needs more lessons than a weekly sermon can convey' and that if Edmund 'does not live among his parishioners, and prove himself, by constant attention, their well-wisher and friend, he does very little either for their good or his own'. This necessity, though, appears to vanish at the end of the novel. When Edmund reacquires the Mansfield living, nothing is said of giving up Thornton Lacey, or of exchanging from one living to the other. The parishioners in Thornton Lacey do not, after all, seem to need Edmund's constant attention and example.

Jane's first readers couldn't have missed this – just as they couldn't miss the fact that the Thornton Lacey parish has recently been subjected to enclosure: the removal of access to common land, constraining and impoverishing Edmund's parishioners. When we go on to look at *Emma* in the next chapter we'll see what a destructive effect enclosure had on the rural economy, and on living standards.

In *Mansfield Park*, enclosure and pluralism are there as additional pointers, if any are needed; they're Jane's reassurance to her readers that they really haven't misunderstood, that she really is criticising the Church directly – for many things, but more than anything for the unforgivable sin, for throwing a veneer of Christian respectability over slavery, for making it acceptable to own slaves, provided those slaves are kept out of sight.

Jane grew up in a Church of England vicarage. Her father was a Church of England clergyman, as were two of her brothers, her godfather, cousins, the man her sister would have married, had he lived.

But, still, she could see the Church for what it was. Only one out of all the clergymen in Jane's novels is presented as an actively *good* man – Captain Wentworth's brother in *Persuasion*, who, we're told, refused to prosecute a local man who broke into his orchard. Most readers will barely recall him.

Jane – perhaps frustrated by the apparent critical indifference to *Mansfield Park* – collected the opinions of her acquaintance on it, and on *Emma*. This is how we know that some of Jane's readers thought that her portraits of clergymen were deliberately incendiary. Mr Sherer, vicar of Godmersham, was 'displeased with my pictures of Clergymen'. A Mrs Wroughton 'thought the Authoress wrong, in such times as these, to draw such Clergymen as Mr Collins and Mr Elton'. And this is also how we know some, at least, of Jane's readers recognised that *Mansfield Park* was about the hypocrisy of the Church of England, and the Society for the Propagation of the Gospel. Readers mention the 'moral Tendency' and 'higher Morality' of the novel, talk of its 'pure morality', and how it is preferred by 'all who think deeply & feel much'. 'Pure morality' is a phrase with a distinctly evangelical flavour – one seldom found outside evangelical writing. Evidently the references to Henry Norris, and to the hypocrisy of the Church, hadn't passed these readers by.

It's possible that it was Jane's references to Norris in *Mansfield Park* which drew the attention of the Prince Regent. The 'Regent' had, according to his personal librarian, 'read & admired all' of Jane's publications, but it was only at the end of 1815 that she was invited to dedicate her next novel to him.[16] The Prince Regent was frequently at odds with his prime minister, Lord Liverpool, and might perhaps have enjoyed taking the opportunity to publicly show his approval of the authoress who had made such uncomplimentary allusions to Liverpool's protégé Henry Handley Norris.

And what of Norris – philanthropist, apologist for slavery, magazine-owner and editor? The *British Critic* reviewed five of Jane's six novels when they were first published. It's the only literary journal that did so, making its omission of *Mansfield Park* all the more pointed.

The owners, editors, and printers of the *British Critic* were all heavily invested in the Church of England – none of them, Norris least of all, had a reason to promote a novel which exposed the Church.

That they were aware of the fact isn't, I think, in doubt. The *British Critic* review of *Emma* is short, faintly praising the novel as 'inoffensive'; a 'pleasing tale' constructed from 'slender materials'. The final paragraph of the review, though, changes tack, announcing abruptly: 'We are not the less inclined to speak well of this tale, because it does not dabble in religion; of fanatical novels and fanatical authoresses we are already sick.'

'Fanatical' usually at this point implied non-conformist, critical of the Church of England. Leafing back through the pages of the *British Critic* for 1814 and 1815 we find an occasional reference to novels by women which deal with religion. *Discipline* has 'some slight tinge of fanaticism' while *Display* by Jane Taylor reveals the workings of religious conversion and 'accomplished fanaticism'. But the *British Critic* is much taken by *Rosanne, A Father's Labour Lost*, which details the awakening to Christianity of a girl who has been raised as an atheist, finding in it 'no fanaticism' but only 'pure, affectionate, and genuine Christianity'.

So far as the *British Critic* is concerned, then, women *can* write novels which 'dabble in religion', provided the religion is entirely in line with Church of England thinking. But there hadn't been some great rush of women writing religiously-themed novels. There's no reason at all for the reviewer of *Emma* to start writing about 'fanaticism' or religion. The final paragraph of the review has nothing to do with *Emma*; but the talk of 'fanatical novels' and 'fanatical authoresses' applies very much better to Jane's previous book. The reviewer seems to want Jane to know that he has understood – and heartily disapproved of – what she was doing in *Mansfield Park*.

It's fitting, perhaps, that the reviewers refused to discuss a novel which points out the 'dead silence' that opens up around slavery in polite drawing rooms, which aimed to show that however much Britain might plume itself on abolishing the slave trade, slavery was still wound tightly about the whole structure of society. Jane's intention, in *Mansfield Park*, was to force her readers to face what they already knew, to see what had been hiding in plain sight.

Fanny Price never manages to do this. It's part of what makes *Mansfield Park* such a deeply troubling novel.

The heroine is happy – 'very happy' – at the end only because she refuses to acknowledge the truth of what has happened, and is still happening, around her. She insists on seeing her uncle, Sir Thomas, as a benevolent patriarch, rather than a cold, distant man who looked on while she was bullied, who admired her body, and attempted to force her into a marriage against her will. She doesn't ask about slavery any more. She forgets that she's her husband's second choice, and that the house in which she ends the novel, Mansfield Parsonage, had previously been home to two women – her aunt and her love rival – who disliked her and tried to do her harm.

Earlier in the novel, moved to vexation against Edmund, Fanny exclaims that: 'He is blinded, and nothing will open his eyes; nothing can, after having had truths before him so long in vain.'

The tragedy of *Mansfield Park* is that Fanny wilfully – willingly – blinds herself. The parsonage house at Mansfield, always a source of 'some painful sensation of restraint or alarm', soon becomes 'thoroughly perfect in her eyes'.

Thoroughly perfect, though two of her cousins have been driven out, though she has married a man who doesn't love her, who is a fool and a hypocrite.

Thoroughly perfect, though the Moor Park apricot tree is still in the vicarage garden, a reminder of the evil that everyone knows about and no one is willing to discuss, a tree not of knowledge, but of forgetfulness. With every spoonful of apricot jam, every apricot tart that's served up on the parsonage table, Fanny will eat the fruits of slavery.

And the tree will keep on growing.

J.M.W. Turner, *Hedging and Ditching* (ca. 1808). An enclosure in progress.
© Courtesy of Tate

CHAPTER 6

Gruel

Emma

Chawton, June 1814. *

The day is hot and airless, the sky like pewter. It strikes her that no author – and no authoress either – would ever have written weather like this for the summer of 1814. In a novel, rain and storm would never threaten these first days and weeks of summertime and peacetime together. And, that being so, it seems strange to her that real life should take a different course. An absurd fancy, but there it is.

But real life is absurd enough. Mrs Browning has a daughter who will make an admirable maid, Miss Benn's poor hand is going on as well as possible, and it seems almost certain that Alexander, Emperor of All Russia, will pass by this road on his way to attend the peace celebrations in London.†

Peace, after all these years. She cannot accustom herself to the idea.

Jane stops under the shade of an elm tree to dab a handkerchief over her damp forehead, but she can do nothing about the prickling under her arms, or the beads of sweat that gather and trickle down her back. She will look sadly inelegant, she fears, but she is only going to meet Fanny and Edward. And if her brother expects her to traipse up to the great house and write down memoranda for him of everything that

---

* Based on Jane Austen's letter to Cassandra Austen (13th–14th June 1814).

† In the event, it appears that the emperor took a different route, but it was at one point considered a very strong possibility locally.

needs to be done in order to shut the house up for the summer, then he must take her as he finds her. Item one, the holland covers. Item two, the trunks to be corded. Item three, the carrier to be written to. Item four ...

She would have resented her task, once upon a time. She understands her brother better now. She has come to love him better. And besides, with *Mansfield Park* launched upon the world, she has at present nothing in hand and nothing much to do.

She tramps along the lane, the dust rising, the heat shimmering ahead. Under a hedge is a young woman, a gipsy, picking the wild strawberries that grow by the side of the road. The bright dark gaze that turns on her is astonishingly like her own. This girl is of an age with her niece Fanny, or thereabouts. But what a life she must lead! Jane bids her good day, and before the gipsy girl can reply, turns in at the gates, walks slowly up the long straight drive towards the great house. To the right, across the lawn, is the wilderness, where she imagined that Lizzy and Lady Catherine de Bourgh stood and argued over Darcy.

And here is Edward, with a pencil and a sheaf of papers. Jane takes them from him, and he begins to complain about how much is still to be done.

Well then, says Jane, we had better make a beginning.

Edward frowns in the direction of his kitchen garden. The nurseryman comes tomorrow from Alton, he says, and I must speak to the gardener about it.

The nurseryman? echoes Jane, writing it down.

Yes, to value the crops. He is impatient, as if she ought to have thought of it for herself.

What, she asks, are you selling all the garden stuff?

Of course, he replies. There is nobody here who wants it. The children and I will spend the summer in Kent. It will only go to waste.

But perhaps, says Jane, greatly daring, our mother might wish for some of it. (Or Miss Benn, or Mrs Browning. Mrs Browning's daughter, her other children. We are not all emperors, brother.)

No, no, says Edward, she has her own. And then, you know,

Cassandra is in London with Henry, and you are for Bookham, are you not? To stay with our cousins?

Yes, murmurs Jane, yes, I had thought of it. For a week or two. They are very kind, very pressing.

So you see, there is no call for it here, smiles Edward. It had much better go to market.

❧

'There is no story in it', declared one perplexed early reader of *Emma*, 'except that Miss Emma found that the man whom she designed for Harriet's lover was an admirer of her own – & he was affronted at being refused by Emma ... And smooth, thin water-gruel is according to Emma's father a very good thing.'

These are the words of Maria Edgeworth, who despite living most of her life on an isolated family estate in Ireland and helping to educate her numerous younger siblings, was the best-selling author of the day. Jane made a point of sending her a copy of *Emma* when it was published in December 1815 – then, as now, it was quite a common way of drumming up publicity. If Jane had hoped that Edgeworth would help to promote her, she was in for a disappointment. Edgeworth hated *Emma* and doesn't seem to have got past the first volume. But even on her cursory examination, she registered the novel's interest in food. In *Emma* Jane devotes an extraordinary amount of time and attention to what people eat – far more than in any of her other novels.

Wedding cake, chicken, oysters, eggs, apple tarts, roast pork and roast mutton, Stilton cheese, pigeon pies and cold lamb, baked apples, rice pudding, walnuts, gingerbread, strawberries, cold meat, turnips, carrots, parsnips, beetroot, celery, bread and butter, apple-dumplings – *Emma* covers food for every appetite and every budget, from 'nice smooth gruel' for rich hypochondriacs to broth handed out to the poor.

Unlike Jane's other heroines, Emma Woodhouse is 'handsome, clever, and rich' – we learn these things about her in the first line of the first chapter of the novel that bears her name. At the age of nearly 21, Emma has had, her creator tells us, 'very little to distress or vex her'. Her personal fortune is enormous: £30,000, a sum that, cautiously invested in government funds, would bring in around £1,500 a year. Even if she didn't stand to inherit Hartfield along with her sister, Emma could very well afford her own home, and still live comfortably. In an era of war and uncertainty, Emma is secure, unassailable. But, as we've seen, Jane isn't really writing books about the romantic lives of the upper classes. *Emma* may be named for its rich heroine, but she's no more than a focal point.

Emma is rich enough that the only anxieties about food that ever intrude into her 'comfortable home' come courtesy of her elderly, querulous father, who worries that there might be too much of it. When it comes to food, we're told, 'poor Mr Woodhouse's feelings were in sad warfare'. He likes to 'have the cloth laid' – the tablecloth, that is – but is 'rather sorry to see any thing put on it'.

Few, during the war years, would have shared his sorrow. Not many were in a position to.

With a rapidly increasing population, and years of poor harvests, the cost of putting meals on the table kept rising and rising. Wages couldn't keep pace. The price of bread more than doubled between 1793 and 1800. Militia camps, concentrated in the south and east of England, were full of soldiers who needed to be fed, which drove prices up even further in those areas. Companies of militia threatened to interfere not just with the free expression of political opinions and the hearts of the local maidens but with people's pockets and stomachs as well. The government, obliged to raise money wherever it could to fund the war, increased tax on almost everything: some peculiar items, like bricks, hair-powder and dogs, and some more everyday ones – coffee, salt, tea and sugar. Contemporary writers complain bitterly about the poor 'wasting' their money on items like this, but in a period before refrigeration and without reliably clean, safe drinking water, tea and salt were less luxuries and more necessities.

Jane's letters speak to a constant low-level anxiety about the cost of food – 'the exorbitant price of fish', 'a rise in tea', questions about the price of 'Butcher's meat' and bread. Guests added considerably to the household expenses at Chawton; it was often a relief when they left. 'You will miss them', wrote Jane to her sister Cassandra, when their youngest brother Charles departed after a rare visit with his family, 'but the comfort of getting back into your own room will be great! — & then, the Tea & Sugar! —'[1]

The dash here speaks volumes. We glimpse the wistful totting up of expense as the teapot is emptied yet again, Cassandra chipping shards off the sugar loaf and pounding them to powder in the kitchen, glowing with secret resentment. And at Chawton, the Austens had a kitchen garden. Their firewood was supplied for free from the Chawton estate. Jane's rich relatives and neighbours shot for sport and sent occasional gifts of meat.

For the poor, matters were far worse.

It was the poor who, spending a higher proportion of their income on food, bore the brunt of inflation. It was the poor who satisfied the inexhaustible appetite of the army and the navy, sometimes voluntarily and sometimes because they were forced to it – kidnapped from the street or the fields by press gangs or unscrupulous recruiting officers, leaving women and children to struggle on without an adult male wage.

And it was the poor, especially the rural poor, who, as the price of living increased and many male wage-earners vanished, were cut off from the resources they had relied on for generations.

England is still overwhelmingly a rural country; only just over 10 per cent of it counts as urban.[2] From the air it's green and pleasant, a patchwork-quilt of fields divided by hedges; tranquil, undisturbed. Go back a few generations, though – say six or seven, to take us to the end of the eighteenth century – and the land would have looked very different.

From the middle ages onwards the country was divided up in two ways: by the parish system, and by manors. These overlapped, so that you might find several parishes in one manor, or a parish that was divided between different manors. Not only did the Church and secular systems sit on top of each other, but by the eighteenth century they were fused together. It was the norm for lay landowners to select the clergymen who were to serve on their properties – as Lady Catherine de Bourgh selects Mr Collins, as Jane's own father was selected by a distant cousin. There were also plenty of lay landowners who had obtained the right to cream off some of the tithes.

Tithes (literally, 'tenths') were essentially a tax levied by the Church on everything produced in a parish, a system that began before the Norman Conquest. It was a widespread practice in medieval and early-modern Europe. Everything really does mean everything – corn, apples, pigs, eggs, bricks. Collecting and selling all of these different types of tithes could take up a lot of a clergyman's time. No one was immune, except the tithe holder. In fact, we learn that Lady Catherine de Bourgh has picked Mr Collins to be the clergyman for Hunsford in part because he's willing *not* to claim his full tithe rights, but instead to reach an 'agreement' that is 'not offensive to his patron'.

The tithe system had been designed to support the Church, both at an individual level and on an institutional one, with a certain proportion going to the local priest and the rest being spirited away into the nearest monastery or bishop's palace. The idea was that the Church was then in a position to support the poor; in practice the Church's charitable exertions were, at best, uneven. When Henry VIII broke with Rome and confiscated the Church's property, much of it was sold, and the right to take tithes was often sold along with it. Local priests still got their portion, but a good deal of the money that had previously ended up in the coffers of the Church ended up in private hands – in the hands of families like the Tilneys and the Knightleys.

Jane surely intended her readers to understand that the wealth of the Northanger Abbey estate, and of the Donwell Abbey estate in *Emma*, was, in part, based on two centuries of collecting tithes – or, rather, of diverting them away from the Church. That's half the point of giving the estates those 'Abbey' names.

Tithes were hated, particularly once war taxation began to bite. And by the end of the eighteenth century they were no longer remotely fit for purpose. Not only did a large proportion of tithes vanish into the pockets of private individuals, but yet another local tax system – poor rates, or parish relief – was required in order to actually provide support to the impoverished inhabitants of a parish. In theory, everyone was entitled to be supported by the parish of their birth, or, in the case of married women, the parish their husband had been born into. In practice, parish officials often tried to evade or minimise their responsibilities. The stories about women in labour being shoved across parish boundaries are probably largely apocryphal, but being reliant on the parish wasn't designed to be an attractive option and people tried very hard to avoid it.

Nevertheless, poor rates were often a considerable expense. They were based, for the most part, on the value of land owned; it was the only real disadvantage to being a landowner. The ownership of land determined the right to vote in elections, to sit on a jury, to hunt. Landowners – men like Mr Darcy or John Dashwood, and, on a smaller scale, Colonel Brandon and Mr Knightley – were incredibly powerful. Minor crime and local judicial matters like licensing were dealt with by magistrates, justices of the peace; men of standing in the community and, crucially, men of property. They were untrained, and often entirely ignorant of the law, but they were in a position to ruin people's lives. Landowners were the major local employers. They usually owned the cottages that workers rented. They were the people who decided who qualified for parish relief.

Indeed, so much of the income of an average cottager, or an average tenant farmer, went straight back into the pockets of the larger landowners, or into their control, that the labouring poor would never have survived if it hadn't been for the existence of a rough and ready safety-net, a primitive form of social security.

This was common land.

∽

Originally all the land in a manor belonged to the lord of that manor, held from the Crown – the manor house, the parkland immediately around it, the woods, the arable land, often still farmed in small strips, and pasture. Then, too, there were the areas that weren't really suitable for farming, that were too boggy, or too steep; scrubby, littered with stones. These were known by all sorts of names: heath, forest, waste.

It was fairly usual for tenants to enjoy 'rights of common'. Some of these rights have strange, beautiful names, drawn from legal Latin and medieval French. There's *piscary*, which is a right to fish, and *pannage*, which permits you to take your pigs to forage for acorns. *Turbary* is the right to cut turf for fuel. *Estovers* is the right to take wood. There was also the right to pasture for animals. These rights still exist in some places – there are commoners in the New Forest in Hampshire, and on Port Meadow in Oxford.

'Common land', technically speaking, is land that is subject to these legally-enforceable common rights. In practice, though, lords of the manor weren't, for a long time, all that concerned with legalities. Use of common land, and of the 'waste', the agriculturally unprofitable areas of the manor, was rarely policed. Only the cruellest landowner would have objected to an old woman picking sticks for her fire in the depths of winter; only the silliest, too, given that the alternative to sacrificing a little firewood was paying higher poor rates.

So people were allowed to wander freely over a vast amount of the countryside, perhaps 8 or 9 million acres at the beginning of the eighteenth century according to some estimates: 25–30 per cent of England.[3]

If you needed firewood, you could send a child to collect some. In season there might be berries and mushrooms. You might set snares for rabbits, if the local landowner was willing to turn a blind eye. And you could keep animals – chickens and geese, pigs, cows and sheep. You could have wool or eggs and butter and cheese to sell at market, meat to exchange with your neighbours, something to vary an unappealing diet of soup and gruel and bread. The historian Ruth Perry suggests that the commons and wastes, efficiently exploited, could effectively double the income of a rural labouring family.* You might build on the common if you needed to, always provided you threw up your dwelling overnight and there was smoke rising in the morning. Even outsiders like gipsies were tolerated as long as they kept to the common or the waste, and didn't stay for too many days together.

For left-wing historians, this is paradise, the garden of Eden – land shared according to need. And, as in every paradise, there was a fall. In the case of common land, it was enclosure.

Enclosure wasn't stealing common land from the people, in spite of what a large number of historians still assert. The commons and wastes *weren't* public land; they were private land that landowners were either legally obliged or simply happy to permit access to. If they weren't happy it was possible to buy all the land back and shut everyone out that way. More complicated, but still achievable, was arranging some financial inducement that would convince common-ers to give up their legal rights, or, instead of paying, portioning out small plots of the land. Most of the time it wasn't worth the trouble, or the expense.

Sometimes, though, it was. And as agricultural engineering and technology improved, and new methods of farming and new breeds were introduced, the sums began to add up differently. Then, too, the population of England began to get larger. In 1750 it was less than 6 million. By 1811, it had reached the 10 million mark. By 1821, it stood at 12 million.[4]

---

* In her book *Novel Relations* (2004), Perry estimates that fuel was worth £4 a year, corn gathered from gleaning about the same, and milk and dairy products from a single cow about £9: £17 or thereabouts, at a time when a labouring man could expect to earn in the region of £20. *A Political Enquiry into the Consequences of Enclosing Waste Lands*, an anti-enclosure pamphlet of 1785, asserts that the women and their children using the full resources of the common land could contribute more to the family than a man in full employment (p. 43ff.).

Population growth had been seen as a positive thing through most of the early modern period, but no longer. Britain struggled to feed herself during the wars with France, really struggled. The prospect of feeding more and more mouths was a sobering one. It wasn't necessary to agree with all the theories of the Reverend Thomas Malthus to be haunted by the spectres he conjured up in his 1798 *Essay on the Principle of Population*: death, doom, and disaster, 'sickly seasons, epidemics, pestilence, and plague', 'gigantic inevitable famine'.

Official census-taking began in 1801, but even without the official data, it was clear that the traditional way of using the land wouldn't work for much longer. Where twenty families had gathered firewood, 40 would shiver through the winter, or else strip the woods entirely, leaving nothing for the next year or the year after. Thirty cows could graze peacefully; 60 would destroy the turf before moving on to crops. And in the age of revolutions, what could be relied on to stand in the way of a starving mob?

The half-trained militia whose ranks were drawn from the poor? A local clergyman? Not if he collected tithes: he was the one taking food out of people's mouths.

Something fundamental had to change.

An increasing number of landowners began to enclose, to shut off access to land. Parliament passed laws to make the process easier and quicker. An Enclosure Act would begin by naming the lord of the manor, rectors and vicars, and other local landowners who claimed common rights or tithe and describing exactly what rights they claimed. It then outlined exactly how the enclosure would benefit them:

[T]he Lands of the respective Proprietors in the said Open Fields ... Meadows, and Pastures, lie dispersed and inconveniently situated ... the other said Commonable Lands and Waste Grounds, are capable of great Improvement by an Inclosure, and it would be very beneficial to the said Owners and Proprietors in general if all the said Fields ... Meadows, Pastures, Commonable Lands, and Waste Grounds, were divided and

inclosed, drained, warped, and embanked, and specific Parts allotted
to the several Persons interested therein, in Proportion …*

The first step, once the enclosure was agreed, was to draw up a map,
almost entirely blank, except for the parish boundary, the village, the
church, houses. Everything else was, potentially, subject to alteration –
rivers and woods, meadows, roads and footpaths. The rest of the land
was parcelled out; the land for the tithe holders, to replace their tithe
entitlement, then the land for everyone else, in proportion.

There would have been digging, ditching, staking, planting; trees
and perhaps old hedgerow boundaries might be grubbed up and new
boundaries laid out, rights of way moved or blocked altogether. If
you had a legally enforceable right, then you would be provided for.
If you didn't, from now onwards the fences and the hedges would bar
your way.

For a while there would be want, that was inevitable, but not once
more intensive, large-scale farming methods had been established; and
once the commons were taken out of the equation, then the market
would do much to control population growth.† Landowners – and their
tenant farmers – could specialise, in sheep, perhaps, or in whatever the
land was particularly good for. Tenant farmers could afford to pay more
rent. Labour would still be needed.

The whole economy of the countryside would be on a more secure
footing, and a more civilised one too – since if you couldn't send your
children to forage on the commons you might as well send them to
school instead. While the land was being reorganised, it made sense to
sort out the unpopular tithe system too, and then people might stop

---

* This passage is from the Enclosure Act for the parishes of 'Gainsburgh', 'Bliton'
and Pilham in Lincolnshire, which was passed in 1796.
† This wasn't what happened. When – as might have been anticipated – the
intensification of agriculture eventually produced a glut of corn, Corn Laws were
introduced to keep the price artificially high.

resenting their clergyman and start listening to him. Modernity was what enclosure offered – order, safety; for how could a country run on lines like this ever descend into the revolutionary anarchy that had engulfed France?

That was the hope. Alongside it, though, was real anxiety about the repercussions of enclosure, not simply among those who suffered from it, and from radicals, but from some quite unexpected quarters. Enclosure Acts didn't require universal agreement and they didn't always get even enough agreement to pass through parliament; 23 per cent of enclosure bills failed between 1760 and 1800.[5] Enclosure could effectively halve the income of labouring families, so that in addition to paying for the enclosure, many landowners would find themselves paying much higher poor rates. Even pro-enclosure writers like Sir Frederick Morton Eden or Nathaniel Kent admitted that, badly managed, enclosure could produce serious harm, increasing poor rates and reducing employment.*

Unspoken was the fear that rather than defeating revolutionary impulses, enclosure would exacerbate them. The poet John Clare, himself a labourer, and briefly a celebrity in the 1820s, explains the alienation that enclosure could produce, the 'men and flocks imprisoned ill at ease'. He also writes of the slow-burning resentment, the sense that the poor had been cheated: 'Inclosure came and trampled on the grave | Of labour's rights and left the poor a slave.'

But for the head of the pro-enclosure Board of Agriculture and Internal Improvement, Sir John Sinclair, enclosure was a patriotic obligation, another way of waging war against the French: 'Let us not be satisfied with the liberation of Egypt, or the subjugation of Malta, but let us subdue Finchley common; let us conquer Hounslow Heath, let us compel Epping Forest to submit to the yoke of improvement.'

---

* Sir Frederick Morton Eden's *The state of the poor*, published in 1797, and Nathaniel Kent's 1775 *Hints to gentlemen of landed property* both discuss the potential harm which might result from badly-handled enclosure.

The war with France, the fear of demographic catastrophe, the desire to control – and also to feed – the country, all of these helped to add to a sense of urgency. Enclosure occurred from the Tudor period into the twentieth century, in a desultory, piecemeal fashion. It grew in popularity throughout the eighteenth century. But it exploded in the twenty years between 1795 and 1815. Of all the Enclosure Acts passed over a 160-year period, around half were passed in these two decades. More than 3 million acres of British wastes, commons and heaths were enclosed during this time – 5,000 square miles.[6] To give you some idea of scale, that's roughly a tenth of the area of England. The ecological historian Professor Oliver Rackham suggested that as much as 200,000 miles of hedgerow may have been planted between 1750 and 1850. It's been calculated that parliament must have been passing Enclosure Acts at 'the rate of one a week'.[7]

These twenty years of intensive enclosure – and intense debate – coincide, almost exactly, with Jane's writing career.

Sinclair wasn't wrong in using the language of warfare: enclosure was an aggressive declaration of power, and it stamped a new system on the countryside, as visible as Roman roads or Norman castles.

In 1807 the poet Robert Southey published a book entitled *Letters from England*. He didn't put his own name to it, but instead that of an imaginary foreigner, a Spanish traveller called Don Espriella. Southey was Poet Laureate from 1813 to his death in 1843 but nowadays he's best known as William Wordsworth's neighbour, as brother-in-law to Samuel Taylor Coleridge, and as Charlotte Brontë's earliest literary critic. In 1808 he also became the nephew by marriage of Jane's old friend Catherine Bigg. He was a prolific and indefatigable writer, and his work ranged widely, from youthful radical poetry to a *Life of Nelson*, via a 'historical' epic about a lost tribe of Welsh Native Americans. *Letters from England* is one of his more peculiar efforts. It's never entirely clear whether we're meant to sneer at 'Espriella' as a foolish and misguided foreigner, or be unnerved by his insights into the oddities of English culture.

Espriella has plenty to say about fashions and food. But he also refers, repeatedly, to enclosure. 'The beauty of the country is much injured by enclosures', he writes in one letter. In another he gloomily explains that 'I had been disposed to think that the English enclosures rather deformed than beautified the landscape, but I now perceived how cheerless and naked the cultivated country appears without them'. Whether on Salisbury Plain or the outskirts of London; in the Midlands or Basingstoke – the town closest to Steventon, where Jane grew up – Espriella makes sure to mention whether or not the land is enclosed. An enclosed landscape was unmistakable – it was formed of straight lines, and squares. 'Lines of enclosure lay below us like a map', writes Espriella, describing elsewhere 'an open country of broken ground with hills at a little distance enclosed in square patches and newly as it appeared brought into cultivation'.

We know that Jane read Southey's book. 'We have got the second volume of Espriella's Letters', she explains to Cassandra in October 1808, 'and I read it aloud by candlelight. The man describes well, but he is horribly anti-English. He deserves to be the foreigner he assumes.'[8]

Jane recognised the descriptions, then; she doesn't argue with their accuracy. The country she lived in really was what 'Espriella' described: a land stripped raw, marked by the lines of enclosure, by new fences and sparse, low, struggling hedges; square shapes and locked gates; a world remade.

Five of her six novels include either explicit reference to enclosure or discussion of its results. The exception is *Pride and Prejudice*, which, as we've seen, is about the dream of escaping society entirely. Even there, we find fences. In *Pride and Prejudice*, though, barriers exist to be overcome; early in the novel we're shown Elizabeth, 'crossing field after field at a quick pace, jumping over stiles and springing over puddles with impatient activity', walking into the breakfast-parlour at Netherfield, and straight into Darcy's heart. Stiles are necessary only where a public right of way cuts across enclosed space; they exist as a reminder of previously free access, a ghost of commoning.

Elsewhere the references are less nebulous. In *Sense and Sensibility*, 'inclosing land' is a topic of general conversation at dinner, together with 'politics' and 'breaking horses'. In *Persuasion* a walk from Uppercross to Winthrop leads 'through large enclosures' and the heroine finds herself an inadvertent eavesdropper on a conversation taking place on the other side of a hedge. Meanwhile the hero's brother is, we learn in a throw-away comment, sympathetic to the anger and confusion that enclosure produces. Jane tends to associate approval of enclosure or active involve-ment in it with her less attractive characters. The monumentally selfish John Dashwood complains about the expense of the 'inclosure of Norland Common ... a most serious drain'. When Catherine Morland is being shown around Northanger Abbey by General Tilney, the word 'enclosure' is repeated again and again: 'the whole building enclosed a large court'; 'the new building ... intended only for offices, and enclosed behind by stable yards'; 'the walls seemed countless in number, endless in length ... a whole parish [was] at work within the inclosure'. We're surely meant to understand that General Tilney is an encloser, and not just at Northanger. He's also been busy at Woodston, where Henry Tilney is vicar. As the General tells Catherine, 'it is a family living [...] and the property in the place being chiefly my own, you may believe I take care that it shall not be a bad one'.

It also seems clear that at one point Jane envisaged *Mansfield Park* as a book about enclosure.

We've already spent some time looking at one of Jane's letters to Cassandra, written in January 1813. The first half of the letter is devoted to *Pride and Prejudice*, which was about to be published, and following on from this are a few odd comments that seem to refer to the novel that would become *Mansfield Park*: 'Now I will try to write of something else; — it shall be a complete change of subject — Ordination. I am glad to find your enquiries have ended so well. — If you c^d discover whether Northamptonshire is a Country of Hedgerows, I sh^d be glad again.'[9] *Mansfield Park* is set, for the most part, in Northamptonshire and among its cast of characters are three clergymen – Mr Norris, Dr Grant, and the 'hero', Edmund Bertram. It's generally agreed, though, that there are no hedgerows in *Mansfield Park*.

Several readers assume that Jane left the hedgerows out because she wanted the novel to be factually accurate. Jane's early twentieth-century editor, R.W. Chapman, suggested that she'd planned an eavesdropping scene like the one in *Persuasion*, but 'scrupulously gave it up on hearing that Northamptonshire was not a country of hedgerows'. The writer Virginia Woolf also approved of what she saw as Jane's fastidiousness; 'when she found out that hedges do not grow in Northamptonshire she eliminated her hedge rather than run the risk of inventing one which could not exist'.[10]

There's just one small problem with this suggestion – it's nonsense. Northamptonshire *was* a 'country of hedgerows', or, rather, a country of hedges – very much so. It was one of the counties most affected by enclosure, and by Enclosure Acts, which stipulated the planting of hedges. It's where John Clare, the poet whose verses mourn the coming of enclosure, lived.

And there *are* hedges in *Mansfield Park*. There's the 'rough hedgerow along the upper side of the field' that has been turned into the parsonage shrubbery, and there's another hedge, unmistakably an enclosure boundary, in Thornton Lacey, Edmund's future living.

During a lull in a card game, Henry Crawford tells how, after his horse 'flung a shoe' while out hunting, obliging him to turn for home, he 'found himself … in Thornton Lacey'. Jane has him describe the place in some detail:

> I was suddenly, upon turning the corner of a steepish downy field, in the midst of a retired little village between gently rising hills; a small stream before me to be forded, a church standing on a sort of knoll to my right—which church was strikingly large and handsome for the place, and not a gentleman or half a gentleman's house to be seen excepting one—to be presumed the Parsonage—within a stone's throw of the said knoll and church.

Henry, who gaily admits that he 'can never bear to ask', declares that 'I told a man mending a hedge that it was Thornton Lacey, and he agreed to it'. For a modern reader, this seems to be a completely irrelevant detail. The man might just as well be herding some cows or walking along the road. But for a reader of 1814, living in a country scored and marked by enclosure, a hedge in need of mending was in all probability a hedge that had been deliberately damaged. The recognised way of objecting to an enclosure had always been to damage the enclosure boundary, if possible, to open up the access again. This is exactly what we're told happens to Mr Wentworth, the clergyman brother of the hero of *Persuasion*. As recalled by the local lawyer: 'he came to consult me once, I remember, about a trespass of one of his neighbours; farmer's man breaking into his orchard; wall torn down; apples stolen; caught in the fact; and afterwards, contrary to my judgement, submitted to an amicable compromise.'

The next likeliest explanation, after a formalised protest, is that the locals have been stripping the hedge for fuel. It is, after all, winter at this point in the novel. It was very usual for this to happen, especially where an enclosure had taken place relatively recently; frequent enough for enclosure literature to specify which hedgerow plants wouldn't burn well. Similarly, enclosers were warned specifically not to plant anything that bore edible fruit. It was 'bad policy', an encouragement to 'theft' and 'depredation'.*

What we ought to be seeing in this scene from *Mansfield Park*, I think, is a compressed version of William Wordsworth's poem *Goody Blake and Harry Gill*, a dramatisation of what enclosure meant to the poor; not

---

*   In his *General View of the Agriculture of the County of Hampshire*, published in 1813, Charles Vancouver pronounced: '[I]t is bad policy to increase temptations to theft; the idle among the poor are already too prone to depredation, and would be still less inclined to work, if every hedge furnished the means of support.' Hampshire is, of course, the county in which Jane lived for almost all of her 41 years; 1813 when she was working on *Mansfield Park*.

simply a bewildered unfamiliarity with the surroundings that had been theirs since childhood, but real suffering, real want ('But when the ice our streams did fetter, | Oh then how her old bones would shake!').

Critics are, of course, perfectly happy to accept that a man like William Wordsworth, what Emma Woodhouse would call 'a man of information' – well-read, well-educated, well-travelled – might choose to confront an issue as politically loaded as enclosure. But if you refuse to believe that Jane ever deals with politically sensitive subjects, then you end up tying yourself in knots to get away from the fact that she actually writes about it.

Some critics dodge the issue entirely. Alistair Duckworth's hugely influential *The Improvement of the Estate*, a book all about landscape in Jane's novels, scarcely mentions enclosure.* Some stubbornly insist that despite Jane using the word enclosure, she doesn't really mean it.†
Because we know (don't we?) that Jane's view of the English country-side is just like Emma Woodhouse's and that everything in the garden is rosy. Looking out across the surrounding fields from Donwell Abbey, Emma famously sees 'a sweet view—sweet to the eye and the mind. English verdure, English culture, English comfort, seen under a sun bright, without being oppressive'.

Emma may be 'spoiled by being the cleverest of her family', but given that neither her father nor her sister Isabella offer any competition, that's not really saying a lot. Emma's wrong about pretty much every-thing. Towards the end of the novel she admits it: 'How to understand

---

*   The second, revised, edition of 1994 drops the word in passing in the preface, in a sentence referring to landscape gardening, but the word 'enclosure' still fails to appear in the book's index.

†   An example is Celia Easton, who claims that 'the enclosed kitchen garden [i.e. in *Northanger Abbey*] may be blissfully viewed with no evocation of the losses enclosure effected in rural villages', and declares that Jane 'left the political argu-ments about the enclosure movement behind the doors of rooms where gentlemen gathered after dinner' ('Jane Austen and the Enclosure Movement: The Sense and Sensibility of Land Reform', in *Persuasions* 24 (2002): 71–89, p. 88.)

the deceptions she had been thus practising on herself, and living under!—The blunders, the blindness of her own head and heart! ... She was proved to have been universally mistaken.' Why, then, assume she's right about the landscape? We would do well to be cautious of the much-quoted claim that Jane described Emma as a 'heroine whom nobody but myself will much like' – it appears only in the Victorian biography written by Jane's nephew. And there's really no reason for us to assume that Jane's own views chime with those of her heroine.

If, at the beginning of 1813, Jane intended the novel she was then about to begin, *Mansfield Park*, to centre on enclosure and the Church, then she got distracted. The Church was a major beneficiary of enclosure – tithe owners automatically got a fifth of any enclosure award, they had the right to choose one of the officials who would carry the enclosure out, and they didn't have to pay any of the expenses. It was an active mover in enclosure, not a disinterested onlooker. But the Church's involvement in enclosing, and in the immediate impoverishment of people who were already close to the breadline, is only one of a raft of accusations that Jane brings against it in *Mansfield Park*. That the Church encloses is all of a piece with its acceptance of pluralism (holding multiple parish livings at once); it neglects the physical well-being of its parishioners in the same way that it neglects their spiritual well-being. It owns slaves, and lends Christian respectability to every other slave-owner by doing so; it is morally bankrupt and in urgent need of reform. The evangelicals are right.

The novel focusing on enclosure – what it had changed, what it had damaged, what it meant for the future – had to wait a little while. It had to wait till Jane started work on *Emma*.

∽

In spite of its rich, self-absorbed heroine, *Emma* is about need. Even Emma's surname, 'Woodhouse', reminds readers of necessities – *wood* for a fire, a *house* to shelter you from the elements. The novel's preoccupation with food fits in with this.

And people aren't just hungry in *Emma*; they're desperate.

The group of gipsies who attempt to rob Harriet Smith and her school friend are on the 'greensward' – the turf – at the side of the 'Richmond road', which means they're committing highway robbery, a crime that carried the death penalty. It's unlikely that any of the 'half a dozen children' in the group would be hanged, but the 'stout woman' and 'great boy' who lead them are running a serious risk.* If caught they are almost certain to be convicted, and even if they don't end up dancing on the end of a rope, they'll be transported to Australia. The series of thefts from hen-houses that closes the novel (and convinces the terminally conservative Mr Woodhouse to consent to Emma and Mr Knightley setting a date for their wedding) is a similarly risky enterprise.

And since the gipsies take themselves off pretty quickly, the hen-house thief is probably not a gipsy, an outsider, but somebody in Highbury. Jane flags up two potential candidates. There may, we understand, be more. Jane also alludes to the direct cause of this financial hardship and desperation – enclosure. It's unmistakable. *Emma* is crammed with references to agricultural improvement, parish boundaries, and hedges; loaded, inevitably politicised references, information that there's absolutely no other reason to include.

The novel is set in Surrey, a county that saw 30 enclosures in the first twenty years of the nineteenth century.[11] No one has ever been able to determine whether Highbury is based on Leatherhead or Dorking or Epsom, or is a combination of all three. We're told that Hartfield, Emma's home, is sixteen miles from Brunswick Square, London, where her sister Isabella lives; Mr Weston, Frank Churchill's father, talks of Richmond being nine miles distant, and Manchester Street, also in London, eighteen. Highbury itself is perhaps a little further from, or a little closer to the capital.

---

* Executions were far less frequent than would be assumed from the enormous number of crimes which carried the death penalty.

Highbury is, not to put too fine a point on it, roughly in the same place as the village of Great Bookham, where Jane's godfather, Samuel Cooke, was vicar. The Reverend Mr Cooke was married to Mrs Austen's cousin, a writer who'd had a novel published in 1799, and they had three children, a little younger than Jane. From time to time Jane expresses something not far off loathing for her Cooke cousins. In 1799 she tells her sister that 'I dread the idea of going to Bookham as much as you can do; but I am not without hopes that something may happen to prevent it'. In summer 1808 she complains that a journey planned by her brother Edward might result in being obliged to visit: 'I shall be nearer to Bookham than I c^d wish, in going from Dorking to Guilford.'[12] Jane's dislike seems to have softened, however – perhaps it stemmed originally from jealousy that Mrs Cooke was a published writer, and dissipated once her own books appeared in print. In the summer of 1814, when she was working on *Emma*, it appears that she did visit them – in the letter I use as inspiration for the scene that opens this chapter we find her preparing for a trip to Surrey.

What this suggests is that, whether Highbury itself is real or imaginary, its enclosure may have been modelled on an actual one. Fetcham, the parish immediately neighbouring Great Bookham, was enclosed in 1813. So at the very time that Jane was working on *Emma*, she was being reminded of exactly what enclosure looked like, and what it did.

The enclosure in *Emma*, too, is of recent date; indeed, it seems that it is still in progress. Mr Knightley talks at some length about his plans to move a right of way:

'But John, as to what I was telling you of my idea of moving the path to Langham, of turning it more to the right that it may not cut through the home meadows, I cannot conceive any difficulty. I should not attempt it, if it were to be the means of inconvenience to the Highbury people, but if you call to mind exactly the present line of the path ... The only way of proving it, however, will be to turn to our maps.'

If moving the path is possible, where could 'difficulty' arise? Who does Mr Knightley have to 'prove' anything to? The officials sent to oversee the enclosure, surely.

When Emma takes Harriet on a 'charitable visit' to a 'poor sick family', who live on 'Vicarage-lane', she fondly imagines the near future when she plans for Harriet to be married to Mr Elton and living in the vicarage: 'I do not often walk this way *now*', said Emma, as they proceeded, 'but *then* there will be an inducement, and I shall gradually get intimately acquainted with all the hedges, gates, pools and pollards of this part of Highbury.'

Why doesn't she know them already? She's lived in Highbury all her life and she's familiar with the vicarage – she's surprised to find that Harriet has 'never in her life been inside' it. Well, clearly, while the vicarage ('an old and not very good house') hasn't changed, the landscape has, out of all recognition.

A 'pollard' is a tree that has been cut back; a sign of closely-managed woodland, woodland that doesn't offer much, if anything, by way of sticks for firewood. Enclosers wanted to break commoning traditions as quickly as possible. Enclosure Acts insisted that physical barriers should be put up – ditches dug, fences erected, hedges planted. Gates are necessary only where the land is divided and emphatically private.

It seems likely that these changes to the vicinity are very recent ones. The Romani – the people Jane calls gipsies – have been in England since the 1500s, if not even longer. Genetic studies indicate they left India around a millennium ago, but when they first appeared in the British Isles, they were thought to be from Egypt, hence the old name 'gypsy' or 'gipsy'. Over the last 200 years there's been an increasing amount of intermarrying and assimilation, both with Irish traveller and circus communities, and with the general population – but quite a number still live a traditional lifestyle. They travel the same routes year after year, setting up camp in the same places. But it's clear that the gipsies in *Emma* are not in their usual campsite.

They're camped on the side of the road, somewhere 'retired', but not somewhere Harriet or her school friend have ever been warned about walking. So far as we can gather, in fact, it's unheard of to encounter gipsies anywhere 'young ladies' are likely to go. 'It was a very extraordinary thing!' thinks Emma to herself. 'Nothing of the sort had ever occurred before to any young ladies in the place, within her memory; no rencontre, no alarm of the kind.' Given the speed with which the news spreads ('Within half an hour it was known all over Highbury'), we can be confident that Emma would have known if such a thing had happened at all recently.

So what might Jane have intended an early reader to gather from this scene? That the gipsies, arriving in the neighbourhood of Highbury, found that they couldn't access their usual campsite – presumably somewhere away from the village, somewhere on the common land adjoining the road. And they couldn't access it because, during the period since they last visited, someone had put barriers up. Jane even particularises the exact nature of the barriers: they're enclosure hedges. Harriet's friend, Miss Bickerton, alarmed by the gipsies, gives 'a great scream, and calling on Harriet to follow her, ran up a steep bank, cleared a slight hedge at the top, and made the best of her way by a short cut back to Highbury'.

The 'bank' may be there to prevent vehicles or heavily laden horses gaining access to the land on the other side, or simply to remove the space from sight of the road. The hedge at the top is 'slight' because it's not very long since it was planted. Miss Bickerton, who as a 'parlour boarder' at the local boarding school can't be much older than about twenty, knows about the 'short cut' because, we gather, it's hardly any time at all since it was a publicly accessible footpath. More athletic than Harriet, who's suffering from a stitch in her side after dancing too much the evening before, Miss Bickerton is able to escape the barriers that the enclosers have tried to place in her way. Harriet isn't. The gipsies aren't really so threatening – they're 'clamorous and impertinent', 'insolent', not violent. They disperse as soon as Frank Churchill appears on the scene. It's enclosure that has made the road dangerous; enclosure that's turning the landscape into a hostile one. And once the hedges have grown higher, will even a strong and fit young man be so happy to wander alone along the Richmond road?

This may be the first encounter between gipsies and townspeople in Highbury; it's unlikely to be the last. Memories linger; they linger longest in groups that make a point of adhering to tradition. I've passed Romani encampments myself, driving through the Hampshire lanes – brightly painted caravans drawn up on the grass by the side of the road, open fires – stubbornly sited by rights of way, the only access that remains to what was once common land.

Who's been driving the enclosure? George Knightley, obviously.

The name George means 'farmer'; it comes from a Greek root word connected to soil. Jane makes it explicit that Mr Knightley is a modernising, improving landowner. He wears 'thick leather gaiters' to protect his shoes and clothing when walking through muddy fields. He consults weekly with William Larkins, his estate manager. We're told that many of his conversations with his brother centre around 'the place of a drain, the change of a fence, the felling of a tree, and the destination of every acre for wheat, turnips, or spring corn'. Towards the end of the novel Emma teases him about his fascination with 'new drills' – seed drills, that is. He can frequently be found discussing 'modes of agriculture, etc.', once with Harriet Smith, more often, we gather, with his tenant Robert Martin – Harriet's first (and final) suitor. It's possible that Robert Martin gets his preferred reading, the 'Agricultural Reports', from Mr Knightley. Mr Knightley's interests are, according to Emma, 'his farm, and his sheep, and his library, and all the parish'.

Actually, Mr Knightley is involved in the business of *two* parishes – Donwell and Highbury. Jane devotes quite a lot of time to describing who lives in which parish. We're informed as early as the third chapter that there's 'Highbury, including Randalls' (where the Westons live) in one parish 'and Donwell Abbey in the parish adjoining, the seat of Mr Knightley'. On our first introduction to Robert Martin, readers learn that he rents 'a large farm of Mr Knightley' and lives 'in the parish of Donwell'. We know from Frank Churchill that Frank's father, Mr Weston, discusses 'parish business' after dinner with Mr Cox ('the lawyer of Highbury'), Mr Cole, rich from 'trade' in town, upwardly mobile, and with Mr Knightley. The parishes of Donwell and Highbury may be nominally separate, but, with the exception of Emma's home, Hartfield, 'all the rest of Highbury' is part of 'the Donwell Abbey estate'. What 'parish business' are these men – three of them landowners, one a lawyer, discussing? A rise in poor rates, resulting from the local enclosures? Or further enclosure?

Mr Knightley has to be the lord of the local manor. There are no other great houses about. And given that his estate is called Donwell Abbey, we must be meant to understand that he's also the tithe holder for the parish of Donwell, and probably for Highbury parish as well. There's not much room for doubt, I think, that Mr Knightley has obtained an Enclosure Act for the parish of Donwell, and that it's in the process of being completed; between his freehold land and his tithe rights, it's likely that he could push the Act through without reference to anyone else who owns land or holds rights of common there. But, though the town of Highbury is largely estate land, matters there aren't so simple. There are presumably a number of townspeople who hold rights of common as well as other reasonably sizeable landowners in the parish – Mr Cole, Mr Weston at Randalls, and, at Hartfield, Mr Woodhouse.

Mr Knightley has, it seems, enclosed as much as he can without obtaining an Act of Parliament (remember those pollards and hedges and fences round Vicarage-lane), but the parish isn't fully enclosed yet. Amid all the descriptions of enclosed land in the novel, Jane mentions one area that is still explicitly unenclosed – the 'common field' that lies between Hartfield and Randalls. Common field can be just another way of saying common land, or it can be another feature of pre-enclosure land use – open fields, farmed in strips, that would often be distributed by an annual lottery. There's really only one conclusion to be arrived at, from all the information Jane gives us – Mr Knightley is trying to get a majority of the other landowners in Highbury to agree to another Enclosure Act. Of course he is, if he's the tithe holder for the parish as well as owning most of the land the town is built on. He'll gain even more land for his modern farming methods at no expense to himself.

As so often in Jane's novels, uncomfortable possibilities start to open up. There's a notable omission from the little group of landowners planning the reshaping of the local landscape over the port – Mr Woodhouse, innately conservative, who hates any and all change. His reluctance to leave the confines of his own property (he 'never' goes 'beyond the shrubbery') may be due to hypochondria or it may be due to real feelings of anxiety and stress caused by the shifting, alien landscape outside. However 'useful' Mr Knightley makes himself to Mr Woodhouse, however 'ready to write his letters', however 'glad to assist him', it's difficult to imagine that the older man could easily be convinced to sign up to an enclosure. But Mr Knightley's younger brother John is married to Emma's sister Isabella. Isabella and Emma will inherit Hartfield jointly, as co-heiresses.*

Can we be certain that there's no hope of gain (all those extra acres, fenced and ditched for free, and the £30,000 besides) mixed in with Mr Knightley's feelings for Emma? Does he move to Hartfield because he loves Emma and wants to be with her, or because he's keen to pursue every opportunity of convincing her father to agree with him? He tells Emma that he has been in love with her 'ever since you were thirteen at least'; a shocking moment for modern readers and not an altogether untroubling one for a reader in 1816. At this point, twelve was deemed marriageable for a girl, and fourteen for a boy, but it was vanishingly rare for either sex to be married so young.†

---

* This is a now-outdated form of inheritance also known as co-parceny; basically an inherited and inheritable joint tenancy.

† Both boys and girls could be married at a younger age, but in those circumstances it was possible to revoke the marriage when they were older. See William Blackstone, *Commentaries on the Laws and Constitution of England* (1765–69).

In *Persuasion*, Jane has Captain Wentworth joke about being willing to accept any woman 'between fifteen and thirty', but he ends by marrying a woman of 27. For Jane, a bride below the age of about eighteen or nineteen is considered very young to be married, and the men who have a taste for excessively youthful women – Willoughby, Wickham – are generally revealed to be cads. Mr Knightley isn't in the best of company. Leaving that aside, however, we know that John Knightley and Isabella Woodhouse married when Emma was twelve. Is it coincidence that George Knightley began to think (even if not entirely consciously) of Emma as a possible marriage partner so soon afterwards? Married to Emma, and with his brother married to Emma's sister, Mr Knightley can be certain of pushing the enclosure through – eventually. It won't, after all, really be the sisters who inherit Hartfield, and its votes in any petition for enclosure, but their husbands.

Mr Knightley's suggestion of moving into Hartfield would be pleasing, if it weren't that his willingness to abandon his own house – his own servants, his parish – recalls his more wide-ranging carelessness, his lack of concern for the poor, for the people he has made poorer. Given his zeal for enclosure, and for improving his land, he's a terrible landlord. We have to assume that the cottage which Emma takes Harriet to visit early in the novel belongs to him. Small cottages were generally rented; Highbury is part of the Donwell Abbey estate, and Jane never tells us that the cottage is owned by anybody else. In the cottage Emma finds 'sickness and poverty together' – poverty worsened by Mr Knightley's enthusiasm for enclosure, sickness exacerbated by his unwillingness to spend money on his buildings rather than his land. Jane describes the garden outside the cottage, 'the low hedge, and tottering footstep' and the 'narrow, slippery path'; she has Emma pause 'to look once more at all the outward wretchedness of the place'. The implication is that the building too is dilapidated, ill-maintained.

Emma is the most selfish heroine that Jane ever produces, but, still, she visits the 'wretched' cottage at least once, and she ensures that the cottagers have warm, nourishing food. Does Mr Knightley? He's happy to send apples to the beautiful and accomplished Jane Fairfax, and even to Miss Fairfax's unbeautiful, unaccomplished relatives, the exhaustingly loquacious Miss Bates and her elderly mother – but they, of course, have the merit of being impoverished gentlewomen. Emma supplements the diet of the Bates women constantly, and it's worth noting that she supplements it with more costly, and more nourishing foodstuffs, with meat, and eggs, and pastry-tarts.

The only other occasion on which Mr Knightley provides food is an occasion that Marie Antoinette would have been proud of. It's the 'sort of gipsy party' to pick strawberries at Donwell. The episode comes almost immediately after Harriet's run-in with the gipsies on the Richmond road – only two chapters intervene. It reads like a deliberate parody of traditional commoning practices. The party – well-fed, for the most part, with every advantage money can buy them – 'collect round the strawberry-beds' and, for half an hour, pick fruit, playing at foraging their food. But it's all pretence, it's all for fun. They can stop when they get tired, and wander around the grounds before going into Donwell Abbey to be 'seated and busy' round a dining-table. The servants have produced a 'cold repast', suitable to the hot weather; they will clear it away again. It's true that the dreadful Mrs Elton has somewhat forced Mr Knightley's hand over the party; but it's also true that he lets her. Mrs Elton has grown up in Bristol. She's the daughter of an indifferently successful 'merchant'. There's some excuse for her. But is Mr Knightley really so blind, really so inconsiderate? Even if he believes that enclosure is a patriotic necessity, the only protection against a ticking demographic time-bomb, against want and revolution, does he really care so little about the immediate repercussions of what he's doing? Does he have no concern at all for the poor cottagers, for Harriet's unpleasant experience with the gipsies?

He would be unlikely to care much about the gipsies themselves; few people did. Specific anti-gipsy legislation had been repealed only in 1783. There remained an engrained cultural belief that gipsies would abduct non-gipsy children, given even half a chance.* Gipsies feature as kidnappers in numerous eighteenth- and early-nineteenth-century novels, from *Joseph Andrews* (1742) to Sir Walter Scott's *Guy Mannering* (1815). They can be reasonable foster parents to the children they steal. They can sometimes even repent and help to put matters right, as happens in *Guy Mannering*. But they're consistently presented as a potential danger to the fabric of ordinary families. When not involved in kidnapping, they can be found telling false fortunes (as in *The Vicar of Wakefield* of 1766, enormously popular), stealing, or peddling 'dream books', 'wicked songs' and quack remedies, like 'Tawny Rachel' does in Hannah More's story *Giles the Poacher*. The widely-read magazine, *The Spectator*, called gipsies 'vermin'. William Wordsworth, in an 1807 poem, 'Gypsies', berates them for laziness, announcing in his concluding lines that 'they are what their birth | And breeding suffer them to be; | Wild outcasts of society!'

And William Cowper, so deeply moved by the plight of African slaves, so lyrical on the subject of their sufferings, writes of gipsies with open – and openly racist – contempt, in his long poem *The Task*. They are 'a vagabond and useless tribe', who eat 'flesh obscene of dog | or vermin, or at best of cock | purloined from his accustomed perch'. They 'pick their fuel out of ev'ry hedge'. The 'flutt'ring rags' they wear reveal their 'tawny skin'. They prefer 'squalid sloth' to 'honourable toil'. They beg, they steal; they disguise themselves and fake injuries to garner sympathy. They are strange, alien, 'self-banished from society'.

Against this background, Jane's presentation of the gipsies in *Emma* has to count as relatively positive – nuanced, at least. Harriet and her friend are frightened, undoubtedly; but Jane indicates that there isn't much – if any – real reason for them to be. A 'child' approaches them 'to beg'; their immediate reaction is to 'scream' and flee. 'How the trampers

---

* A belief which could and did spill over from novels and poems into real life. In 1754 Mary Squires, a gipsy, had been convicted of kidnapping a young woman called Mary Canning in spite of the evidence of numerous witnesses that she had been miles away at the time.

might have behaved, had the young ladies been more courageous, must', we're told, 'be doubtful; but such an invitation for attack could not be resisted'. The 'attack', when it comes, comes in the form of 'half a dozen children, headed by a stout woman and a great boy', 'clamorous, and impertinent in look'. Harriet's reaction, which is to get out her purse, is not the wisest thing to do. The 'whole gang' surround her, demanding more. Harriet's terror and her purse are both 'too tempting'. We're not quite at victim-blaming here, but both the novel and the other characters seem confident that the situation might quite easily have been avoided. Screen adaptations, without exception, exaggerate this scene, making it more threatening than it is in the book. The gipsies scare Harriet, but they never touch her.

The arrival of Frank Churchill turns the tables immediately and completely: 'The terror which the woman and boy had been creating in Harriet was then their own portion.' Frank leaves them 'completely frightened'. The details of the incident – the screaming, Harriet's stitch, the 'amused and delighted' 'sensibility' with which Frank describes Harriet's 'naivete' and 'fervour', Jane's careful excision of any real physical danger, or any fear of sexual violence – ensure that this scene is a complicated one, especially given how short it is. Jane's gipsies are not like other writers' gipsies. For a start, nearly all of them are children, so there are no kidnappers here, no fortune tellers, or peddlers of suspect goods. They're not even very good at begging; certainly they haven't perfected the disguises or the professional beggar's whine that Cowper is so ready to accuse them of.

The Romani were frequent visitors to Steventon and to Chawton throughout Jane's lifetime, but, aside from a fleeting reference in a childhood story, this is the only occasion on which they appear in her writing. They're not even necessary to move the plot along; Jane could easily have come up with an alternative. They're in the novel for a purpose.

∽

A famous piece of Marxist literary criticism compares Jane Austen unfavourably to the pioneering journalist and social campaigner, William Cobbett. The two were roughly of an age; both were born in Hampshire and spent much of their lives there. Cobbett, who though a passionate and outspoken critic of the French Revolution, was a lifelong reformer, was mostly out of favour with the British establishment – so much out of favour at times that he served two years in prison and twice had to remove himself to America until passions had cooled. The government feared his influence. Once he set out to make his long-running periodical, *The Political Register*, widely affordable, its circulation went through the roof (rising at one point to more than 40,000 a month). In the 1820s and 1830s, his interest turned to the dire state of the English rural economy; his *Rural Rides* describes what happened in the generation after the rash of enclosures spread across the face of the countryside.

For the Marxist critic Raymond Williams, Cobbett offers a necessary corrective to Jane's genteel comedy of manners:

> [W]hat Cobbett names, riding past on the road, are classes. Jane Austen, from inside the houses, can never see that, for all the intricacy of her social description. All her discrimination is, understandably, internal and exclusive. She is concerned with the conduct of people who ... are repeatedly trying to make themselves into a class. But where only one class is seen, no classes are seen.[13]

The interlude with the gipsies gives the lie to this claim. For a start, it takes place on the road. Lots of the pivotal scenes in Jane's novels take place outdoors, and even when indoors, we're not invariably 'inside the houses'. Sometimes we're in inns, assembly buildings, hotels, cramped rented rooms. Frank Churchill, gentleman of leisure, is in no way in the same social class as the gipsies. Nor is he in the same social class as the illegitimate Harriet Smith. There may be no difference for a Marxist between Frank and Harriet, but for Jane and her first readers there was. Her willingness to force the landed gentry together with other classes without making broad comedy of it is, as we saw when we looked at *Pride and Prejudice*, enormously innovative. So is her willingness to include in her novels marriages that cross class barriers.

But even accepting the much blunter class distinctions of Marxism, there are actually plenty of characters in Jane's novels who can't sit back and wait for money to appear – who need to earn their living, to make their own way. The clergymen don't quite come under this heading, but the sailors certainly do. Captain Wentworth, in *Persuasion*, hasn't joined the navy to have fun and see the world. When he first proposes to Anne, he's penniless apart from his salary. Fanny Price's brother William is earning his keep before he hits puberty. The attorneys, the estate managers: they work. So do the servants.

In fact over the course of her career, Jane becomes increasingly interested in working people, particularly – and perhaps unsurprisingly – in working women.

In *Northanger Abbey* servants are almost entirely anonymous ('a pattened maidservant', a 'footman'). Eleanor Tilney's companion in Bath has a name, but very little more. In *Sense and Sensibility* one or two servants are individualised – the Dashwoods' manservant is called Thomas, Mrs Jennings has a 'Betty'; Thomas even speaks a few lines. But the outline of personalities doesn't appear until *Pride and Prejudice*, where what might be called 'half-servants' – housekeepers, governesses, companions – begin to take on greater significance. Jane differentiates. There is, she tells us, 'nothing remarkable' in the appearance of Anne de Bourgh's companion, Mrs Jenkinson, while Georgiana Darcy's governess-companion Mrs Annesley is described as 'a genteel, agreeable-looking woman', sensitive to the awkward undercurrents in the drawing room at Pemberley and 'proved to be … truly well-bred' by her attempts to defuse them. Georgiana's previous companion, Mrs Younge, is, of course, a crony of Wickham's. She facilitated his intimacy with Georgiana and, for the right price, reveals his whereabouts – and Lydia's – to Darcy. Mrs Reynolds, Darcy's fond housekeeper, has known him from his childhood upwards. She's closer to a stock character, but we're meant to agree with Lizzy's assessment of her – after all, 'What praise is more valuable than the praise of an intelligent servant?'

In *Mansfield Park* the servants have skills, rheumatism, children, grandchildren. We never encounter Miss Lee, the governess at Mansfield, but she's clearly well-qualified. Christopher Jackson, the estate carpenter, does a 'neat job' on the theatre – it's the only positive thing Sir Thomas finds to say about the entire acting scheme. Jackson has a son, Dick, 'a great lubberly fellow of ten years old'. At Sotherton we glimpse from the corner of our eye a gardener, with a sick grandson, who grows 'a very curious specimen of heath'. The Mansfield coachman is afflicted with 'rheumatism'; menaced by the 'doctoring' of Mrs Norris, he recovers. These characters are vivid, individual – the Prices' maid Rebecca is stroppy, wilfully incompetent; even Baddeley, the perfect butler, permits himself a solitary, smug 'half-smile' to see Mrs Norris discomfited.

For Mrs Norris life is one continual battle against 'encroaching' from the servant class. Any concern she demonstrates for them is specious, aimed at showing herself in the best light. But Mr Woodhouse, for all his 'habits of gentle selfishness', shows a real, if mild, affection for his staff and their families. We've come a long way from the nameless servants in *Northanger Abbey* – in *Emma* only a character like Mrs Elton pretends to forget the names of the people who work for her. Mr Woodhouse recommends Hannah, the daughter of his coachman James, for a position as housemaid at Randalls:

'I am very glad I did think of her. It was very lucky, for I would not have had poor James think himself slighted upon any account; and I am sure she will make a very good servant: she is a civil, pretty-spoken girl; I have a great opinion of her. Whenever I see her, she always curtseys and asks me how I do, in a very pretty manner; and when you have had her here to do needlework, I observe she always turns the lock of the door the right way and never bangs it. I am sure she will be an excellent servant.'

But in *Emma* even excellent servants have their disagreements – we learn of a falling-out between Mrs Elton's housekeeper Mrs Wright and Mr Knightley's Mrs Hodges, over a promised 'receipt' (a recipe). Elsewhere we learn, at third- or fourth-hand, that Mrs Hodges is 'quite displeased' about her master sending apples to the Bateses, learn too that she is not a perfectly good-tempered woman ('Mrs Hodges *would* be cross sometimes'). Then there's Emma's governess, Miss Taylor, who begins the novel by retiring, and becoming Mrs Weston. There's Jane Fairfax, who has been 'brought up for educating others', and only narrowly avoids being employed by one of Mrs Elton's friends. These two characters are (or have been) part of the servant class but they're fully fleshed-out; they make the novel. What would happen to the plot, after all, if Miss Taylor hadn't married, or if Jane Fairfax didn't exist?

Emma is also full of people who work but aren't servants. There's the lawyer Mr Cox, involved in Mr Knightley's attempt to enclose Highbury. There's Mr Knightley's estate manager, William Larkin. There's the apothecary Mr Perry, so busy that the reader is continually just missing him as he races off to see his next patient. The impoverished John Abdy was, we're told, a parish clerk for 'twenty-seven years'. We have the shop-keepers – Mr and Mrs Ford, who own a 'woollen-draper, linen-draper, and haberdasher's shop united'; Mrs Wallis, the baker's wife, thought by some to be 'uncivil' and to 'give a rude answer'. We have Mrs Goddard, 'mistress of a school' who, we're told, 'had worked hard in her youth and now thought herself entitled to the occasional holiday of a tea-visit', and 'the three teachers, Miss Nash, and Miss Prince, and Miss Richardson'.

There's nothing like this in any of Jane's earlier novels. Even *Persuasion*, which takes us from a baronet to a monthly nurse, doesn't feature this sheer number and variety of characters. In part, of course, this is because, unlike any of the other novels, *Emma* stays in one place. Jane has only one canvas to fill. The preoccupation with enclosure necessitates precision – just consider how much more we know about the geography of Highbury than we do about Meryton, in *Pride and Prejudice* – but the range and the detail, the care with which class distinctions are traced out, the touching almost every character with shades and tints of personality, these are also Jane's artistic, deliberate choice.

Many of the characters define themselves by their relationship to others, by their status relative to neighbours and acquaintances. The words 'superior' and 'inferior' appear three times more often in *Emma* than in the other novels. But social definitions are seldom, if ever, stable in Highbury; nor are they universally agreed on.

Emma thinks that Mr Elton would do very nicely for Harriet: 'Mr Elton's situation was most suitable, quite the gentleman himself, and without low connexions; at the same time, not of any family that could fairly object to the doubtful birth of Harriet.' Mr Elton, who rates his claims rather differently, is 'affronted' at the idea:

'*I* think seriously of Miss Smith!—Miss Smith is a very good sort of girl; and I should be happy to see her respectably settled. I wish her extremely well: and, no doubt, there are men who might not object to—Every body has their level: but as for myself, I am not, I think, quite so much at a loss. I need not so totally despair of an equal alliance, as to be addressing myself to Miss Smith!'

Emma, in her turn, is entirely taken aback when Mr Elton proposes to *her*, astonished that he 'should suppose himself her equal', should 'fancy himself shewing no presumption in addressing her'.

Does Mr Elton succeed in making an equal marriage? His wife brings 'no name, no blood, no alliance', only a modest fortune from trade, but she isn't shy about asserting her place in the social hierarchy. Though herself from mercantile, slave-trading Bristol – and defensive about the connection (her brother-in-law, she asserts, 'was always rather a friend to the abolition') – Mrs Elton sneers at northern manufacturing towns: 'One has not great hopes from Birmingham. I always say there is something direful in the sound.' She sees herself as Mrs Weston's superior ('I was rather astonished to find her so very ladylike!'), and as equal to 'Knightley' and to Emma – 'You and I must establish a musical club!'

But then, Mr Knightley keeps 'no horses' for his carriage and seldom hires them. He goes about on foot; he has 'little spare money'; he dresses like a farmer – how is Mrs Elton meant to know that he's her social superior? Emma has as her intimate friend not only Harriet Smith – 'the natural daughter of nobody knows whom, with probably no settled provision at all, and certainly no respectable relations' – but her former governess. Where is Mrs Weston from? What is her family background? Has *she* any relations, respectable or otherwise? We never discover. It's best, we gather, to draw a veil over such questions; the answers might not be what we would like. If it comes to that, what social class was Emma's mother born into? Emma has £30,000, so too, we have to presume, does her older sister; that kind of liquidity, when combined with marriage to the untitled, uninspiring Mr Woodhouse, suggests her mother came from trade – successful trade, to be sure, but trade. North of England industry? The West Indies? The East? Emma's sister is married to a London lawyer. The Woodhouses may be the 'younger branch of a very ancient family', but is Emma really in any position to cavil at Mrs Elton's antecedents?*

Critics like to call Emma a snob – and she does spend a lot of time deciding precisely where in the social order people ought to belong. But if she is a snob then she's a very inclusive, persuadable one, willing to embrace a number of her social inferiors, and to change her mind about others. Harriet Smith, Mrs Weston, Mr Weston – who has spent the past 'eighteen or twenty years' 'engaged in trade' – all are her intimates, her associates. She tells herself that the Coles – 'of low origin,

---

* Jane had already, in *Pride and Prejudice*, encouraged her readers to think that she'd grafted some of her fictional characters onto the family tree of the Earls Fitzwilliam who, by the end of the eighteenth century, had come into possession of the great Yorkshire stately pile of Wentworth Woodhouse. We are, perhaps, meant to imagine that the Woodhouses of Hartfield are distant relations. In *Persuasion* Sir Walter Elliot is disappointed to discover that there are Wentworths who have 'nothing to do' with the family.

in trade, and only moderately genteel' – 'ought to be taught that it was
not for them to arrange the terms on which the superior families would
visit them'; but she easily allows herself to be convinced that, after all,
she will accept their invitation. She asserts that Harriet's suitor Robert
Martin belongs to the 'yeomanry', and 'must be coarse and unrefined',
but the letter in which he proposes to Harriet forces her to re-examine
her own ideas:

> She read, and was surprized. The style of the letter was much above
> her expectation. There were not merely no grammatical errors, but as
> a composition it would not have disgraced a gentleman; the language,
> though plain, was strong and unaffected, and the sentiments it conveyed
> very much to the credit of the writer. It was short, but expressed good
> sense, warm attachment, liberality, propriety, even delicacy of feeling.
> She paused over it.

Jane indicates that her readers should be pausing, too; should refrain
from jumping to conclusions. They won't be the right ones. In Highbury
the old rules and conventions don't work. It's a restless, unsettled sort
of place. The landscape is new and unfamiliar – in all sorts of ways.
Paths have moved; barriers have sprung up; maps have to be redrawn.
Characters are constantly on the move, walking, getting in and out of
carriages, travelling to and from London. Mr Weston, we're told, essentially commuted for years – working in London but keeping a house in
Highbury 'where almost all of his leisure days were spent'. Frank pops
into the capital to have a haircut and order a piano (his real object).
Social class creaks and shifts. The Westons, the Martins and the Coles
are moving up, the Eltons too. But the movement isn't all upwards.
One local family, the Abdys, have gone in one generation from parish
clerk to ostler – from a literate quasi-professional to someone who looks
after horses at a staging inn. The Bates women have moved down too,
the daughter further than the mother. ('She is poor; she has sunk from
the comforts she was born to; and, if she live to old age, must probably

sink more.') Characters shore up their sense of their social position by distributing charity to those they see as less fortunate. Shifting social class is so central a concern that at least three of the characters in the novel embody it within themselves.

Where *Mansfield Park* featured one adopted child, *Emma* has three – Frank Churchill (or, rather, Frank Weston Churchill, as he signs himself), Jane Fairfax, and Harriet Smith.

Frank is the son of Mr Weston, but at the age of two is taken to live with his maternal uncle and his uncle's wife, an informal arrangement at first, which later becomes 'so avowed an adoption as to have him assume the name of Churchill on coming of age'. Jane Fairfax is orphaned 'at three years old'. From the daughter of an army officer, she becomes the 'property' of her impoverished grandmother. Later she undergoes another change; a former colleague of her father undertakes 'the whole charge of her education ... and from that period Jane had belonged to Colonel Campbell's family, and had lived with them entirely, only visiting her grandmother from time to time'. Harriet Smith is almost infinitely socially malleable, adapting first to the society of Mrs Goddard's school, then to the Martins, then to Emma and Hartfield. The novel sees the potential of her marrying anybody from Robert Martin to Mr Knightley (Emma acknowledges that the latter marriage is 'far, very far, from impossible').

Harriet, so readily accepted by all of Highbury, turns out to be a cuckoo in the nest. Though 'her allowance is very liberal', though 'nothing has ever been grudged for her improvement or comfort', Harriet is not in fact the 'gentleman's daughter' Emma assumed. Harriet's father turns out to be a 'tradesman, rich enough to afford her the comfortable maintenance which had ever been hers, and decent enough to have always wished for concealment'. Her illegitimacy is 'unbleached by nobility or wealth'. Surely the schoolteacher Mrs Goddard has done wrong in forcing her on Emma's notice as she does? Emma is oddly complacent about the imposition – and it is an imposition: 'a note was brought from Mrs Goddard, requesting, in most respectful terms, to be allowed to bring Miss Smith with her.' Isn't Mrs Goddard an echo of the 'stout' gipsy woman, each of them in charge of a crowd of children who aren't their own, but who bring them money (by begging, by school fees)? Isn't Mrs Goddard, smuggling Harriet into respectable families under false pretences, almost more like a gipsy than the gipsies are?

Is Harriet, the girl who after all doesn't belong in society, so dissimilar to the gipsy children who surround her on the Richmond road, Cowper's 'wild outcasts of society'? She has no home to call her own. Nor do Frank Churchill and Jane Fairfax. Frank Churchill has a yen for travel; he is seldom in one place for long. Jane Fairfax can be found 'wandering about the meadows', gipsy-like. Are Mr Weston and Mrs Bates, who give up, respectively, son and granddaughter in order for those children to enjoy greater financial security, really any different to storybook gipsies who replace other people's children with their own?

There are others in Highbury who are still more like the gipsies.

We know by now – we always knew, really – that the conclusions of Jane's novels are rarely purely comic, but *Emma* ends on a particularly ominous note. It's autumn. Summer is over, the harvest gathered in. The couples are all paired up. Harriet and Robert Martin marry in September, Jane Fairfax and Frank Churchill are 'only waiting for November' (when the approved mourning period for Mrs Churchill will just about be up). Emma and Mr Knightley have 'fixed … as far as they dared' on 'the intermediate month' – October. Mr Woodhouse, however, is still causing difficulties. Emma 'could not bear to see him suffering … could not proceed'. We're at an impasse, until an unlikely solution presents itself:

> Mrs Weston's poultry-house was robbed one night of all her turkeys—evidently by the ingenuity of man. Other poultry-yards in the neighbourhood also suffered.—Pilfering was *housebreaking* to Mr Woodhouse's fears.—He was very uneasy … The result of this distress was, that, with a much more voluntary, cheerful consent than

his daughter had ever presumed to hope for ... she was able to fix her wedding-day.

Readers already have reason to mistrust the purity of Mr Knightley's motives in wanting to marry Emma. That the marriage itself is made possible only by criminal acts and an elderly man's terror doesn't do anything to dispel that lingering sense of unease.

There may – perhaps – be 'perfect happiness' waiting for Emma and Knightley, but for Mr Woodhouse, the presence of a new son-in-law is only the lesser of two evils. And what about everybody else; what about all those people Jane has spent time making real for us? What does the future hold for Highbury and Donwell?

Who does rob the local poultry-yards? The obvious answer is the gipsies. Cowper's gipsies do it ('cock | purloined from his accustomed perch'). It's what happens in literature. But in *Emma* the gipsies are long gone by the time we get to the autumn. They go the same day that Harriet is accosted – 'the gipsies did not wait for the operations of justice; they took themselves off in a hurry'. And Jane has told us about at least two households in Highbury who might very well be reduced to stealing.

One is the poor cottagers Emma and Harriet visit early in the novel. The other is the Abdys, fast declining through the social ranks; the younger Abdy, we learn, 'came to talk to Mr Elton about relief from the parish; he is very well to do himself, you know, being head man at the Crown, ostler, and every thing of that sort, but still he cannot keep his father without some help'. Is any help forthcoming? We never discover. What we do discover is that Mr Elton has a great deal of parish business – 'the magistrates, and overseers, and church wardens, are always wanting his opinion'. What do they want his opinion on? Well, on crime, on dispensing parish relief, and on organising employment for the poor. Mr Elton is busy because there's more than one set of poor cottagers out there, more than one family like the Abdys. This is what Mr Knightley's enclosure has done; and this is what will happen more and more, if he succeeds in his plan to obtain an Enclosure Act for Highbury. There are more people who are going to be forced to turn to crime, to become like the gipsies – thieves, beggars, outcasts from a society that no longer has a place for them.

Emma, a novel riddled with word games and anagrams, issues a challenge to its readers – just like the challenge Jane had issued to Crosby six years earlier. Are we paying sufficient attention? Have we noticed that this novel, dedicated to the Prince Regent, places its heroine's sister in Brunswick Square, a road named in tribute to the Prince's estranged wife, Caroline of Brunswick? That Mr Elton's contribution to Emma and Harriet's riddle book could refer to the Prince of W(h)ales almost as easily as it does to courtship?* Are we taking our authoress seriously enough?

Nothing in the book remains a mystery if we read it carefully. Who robs the poultry-houses? The younger Abdy – or one of many others like him. Has Frank really dreamt, during his absence, about the little-known fact that the busy apothecary Mr Perry thought briefly of buying a carriage? Of course not. Jane Fairfax has passed on this snippet of local news in one of her letters; they are writing to each other. We know a little of Harriet Smith's father, but who is her mother? Someone not altogether unconnected with the Bates family, perhaps. Miss Bates twice refers to her mother calling her Hetty, which can be short for Harriet. Where other characters speak of 'Harriet Smith', Miss Bates makes a point of never using Harriet's first name. Harriet is seventeen to Jane Fairfax's twenty, and Jane Fairfax's mother died, we're told, when Jane was three. It's not proof, but the indications seem to nudge us in the direction of concluding that Harriet and Jane Fairfax may well be half-sisters.

---

*   For an exhaustive take on the riddle, see Colleen Sheehan's two articles for *Persuasions On-Line* (www.jasna.org/persuasions/on-line/) – 'Jane Austen's "Tribute" to the Prince Regent: A Gentleman Riddled with Difficulty', and 'Lampooning the Prince: A Second Solution to the Second Charade in *Emma*', both V.27, No. 1 (Winter 2006).

The answers to a great number – nearly all – of these questions appear hidden in plain sight, in the long, convoluted monologues that Jane gives to Miss Bates. Miss Bates – a middle-aged spinster, one of two daughters of a dead clergyman, living in straitened circumstances with her widowed mother – is the closest to a self-portrait that Jane comes in her novels. Hardly anyone listens to her. A careless reader will skip over half of her speeches. Emma, poor, continually misguided Emma, declares at one point that 'You will get nothing to the purpose from Miss Bates'. She's wrong, of course.

Jane, frustrated, perhaps, by the refusal of the critics to acknowledge what she's trying to do in her novels, is making a point here – you should listen to me; what I have to say is worth hearing.

And in spite of family catastrophes and growing ill-health, this particular middle-aged spinster and clergyman's daughter was getting ready to grapple with some of the most fundamental questions of the age. *Persuasion*, set during the false peace of 1814–15 – between Napoleon's exile to Elba and his return to the French throne, only to be defeated at the Battle of Waterloo – is concerned with world events, with the collapse of dynasties, and with the upending of religious certainties. Poised (perhaps) between epochs, the novel both looks back to the past and forward to a perilous future.

Engraving of 'Proteo-saurus', an ichthyosaur from Lyme Regis,
by James Basire after a drawing by William Clift, 1819.
Mary Anning's 'crocodile', discovered in 1811–12.
© The Geological Society of London

CHAPTER 7

Decline and Fall

Persuasion

Lyme Regis, September 1804. *

She could stand and watch the sea for ever. There are no dirty lodgings here, no cook needing to be physicked. There is only air and dazzling light, white foam, the sloping surface of the Cobb beneath her feet, the gulls swooping, the sea rushing and retreating, never gaining, or so it seems, on this shallow coast, until all at once the tide is in. She has been warned against the tides.

She has been warned against the cliffs, too. The cliffs look as solid as anything, but they are apt – suddenly, without warning – to collapse. They have been doing it forever. There are fragments of rocks scattered all over the beaches, too large by far for the sea to have moved them. Beyond the headland, at Pinny, there is a great landslide, the rocks having tumbled where they fell, now covered with thick vegetation, trees even. It must have happened generations ago.

Running footsteps, a thud. Then gasping sobs and, on a gulp of air, a piercing scream, totally unlike a gull. Looking down on to the lower part of the Cobb, she sees that a young girl has tripped and fallen. No one else is attending. Gathering her skirts in her hand, Jane picks her way down the steps which jut out from the wall, takes the child on to her lap, scolds, cajoles. There is no serious injury, only scraped knees and skinned hands. A handkerchief, dipped in the sea water, to wipe

---

* Based on a letter from Jane Austen to Cassandra Austen (14th September 1804).

away the blood which beads the grubby palms and goose-pimpled legs, the pinafore set to rights, and the girl, still whimpering a little, and growing suspicious of a stranger, now ready to be set on her feet again.

Her feet are bare, and exceedingly dirty.

The girl crouches to gather up some pebbles, and, with great solemnity, presses one of them into Jane's hand.

Only it isn't a pebble, Jane realises, when she looks at it and sees the intricate whorls of an animal embedded in the stone. It is what they call a curiosity, here at Lyme. A snakestone. A fossil. An animal from before the Flood, or perhaps from earlier still—

Readers glancing through a newspaper or magazine towards the end of 1812 might, amid the reports of battles and bankruptcies, have come across this paragraph, widely reproduced in the press:

> PETRIFACTION OF A CROCODILE. – Immediately after the late high tide, there was discovered under the cliffs between Lyme-Regis and Charmouth, the complete petrifaction of a crocodile, seventeen feet in length, in an imperfect state. It was dug out of the cliffs nearly on a level with the sea, at the depth of one hundred feet below the summit of the cliff.

The 'crocodile' was not in fact a crocodile at all but what we call an ichthyosaur, a name coined for it in 1817. The skull of this first specimen had been discovered in 1811. Two local fossil hunters had spent months labouring together with the storms and the autumn tides to reveal the rest of the skeleton; difficult and dangerous work, the more so since one was a boy in his early teens, and the other a girl even younger.

The boy was Joseph Anning, the girl his sister Mary. They'd both been bred to the business of fossils. Before his death in 1810 their father Richard had run a stall selling fossils to tourists, a sideline to his main business, which was cabinet-making. Mary Anning would go on to excavate a vast collection of fossil remains, including the first complete plesiosaur, and the first British example of a pterodactyl. An 1830 engraving, *Duria Antiquior* (A more ancient Dorset), shows the variety of her finds. She corresponded with men of science from all over Europe. Georges Cuvier, the pre-eminent anatomist of the day, thought her plesiosaur must be a fake; he was convinced otherwise. She was recognised as a leading authority, and her expertise was eventually rewarded with small annuities collected by the British Association for the Advancement of Science, the Geological Society, and a donation organised by the prime minister.

Such recognition, for a woman almost entirely self-educated, who came from a non-conformist background, and had been reliant on parish relief, is extraordinary. It's more extraordinary than the legend that Mary Anning survived being struck by lightning as a baby, perhaps in some ways even more extraordinary than her discoveries. It's not all that hard to find fossils in Lyme. The town lies in the south-west of England, on the 'Jurassic coast' – nearly a hundred miles of Devon and Dorset coastline which was once prehistoric sea-bed. The cliffs around Lyme are composed for the most part of a rock called blue lias; clayey, soft, crumbling, prone to collapse. Blue lias is rich in fossils – abundantly, exuberantly rich. Stepping off the Cobb, the stone harbour, onto the beach, you can find yourself almost tripping over them. Ammonites and belemnites lie in the open, undisguised, or waiting only for a few gentle taps from one of the geological hammers you can buy in every shop to reveal themselves; the twists and coils of ancient sea-creatures, relics of another world entirely.

At first glance Jane Austen and dinosaurs make for strange bedfellows, rather like the 'mash-ups' (*Pride and Prejudice and Zombies; Mansfield Park and Mummies*) which were popular a few years ago.

But Jane spent at least one long holiday in Lyme, and probably two. It seems that both Jane and Cassandra were somewhere very close by in 1803, since one of Jane's letters mentions witnessing a serious fire in Lyme and the only one which fits happened in November of that year.[1] And we know that in the late summer of 1804 half the Austen family went there, Jane staying on at Lyme with her elderly parents while Cassandra travelled to Weymouth with their brother Henry and his wife, cousin Eliza. A letter from Jane to her sister describes sea-bathing, dancing at the Assembly Rooms, and walking on the harbour wall, the Cobb. She seems cheerful; there's energy, vibrancy in her writing. Her frustrations are petty ones – a bad cold, a broken piece of furniture which she has to arrange to have fixed.

Did Jane ever pass Mary Anning, then aged five, in the streets of Lyme? According to the census, the town's population in 1811 was only around 2,000 people – the size of a largish secondary school perhaps. It would have been even smaller in 1804. Jane mentions 'Anning', Mary's father Richard, by name in her letter to Cassandra – snobbishly, perhaps unconsciously so, she doesn't do him the compliment of attaching a 'Mr' to his surname. In his capacity as a cabinet-maker he 'valued' a 'broken lid' – some item of the lodging house furniture which had been damaged. Did he come to the rooms the Austens had rented, or did they take the piece to him? It would have depended on what the item was. The price he asked – for repairing it, presumably – was five shillings, which the Austens thought too steep.

But still, if we imagine Jane in Richard Anning's workshop, her fingers hovering over the trays of fossils set out for the tourists, we're no distance at all from the truth. If not in Richard Anning's shop, then she would have seen fossils in other shops in Lyme, or on the beach. She could hardly have avoided it. The cliffs were no more stable then than they are now. John Feltham's 1813 *A Guide to all the Watering and Sea-Bathing Places*, a sort of Regency *Lonely Planet*, makes a point of mentioning the geological instability of Lyme: 'the violence of the tide [...] has made great encroachments, the cliffs being composed of a kind of marl and blue clay incorporated with lime, that easily give way.' Landslides, on the Jurassic coast, mean fossils. The town was already famous for them before the 'crocodile' was discovered. A *History of Lyme-Regis*, published in 1823, describes how 'for many years the first visitors, in their rambles upon the beach, attentively sought after small shells, cornua ammonis [ammonites], &c., which they distinguished by the general term of "curiosities"'.

Did the 'curiosities' of Lyme, the sea-lilies and snakestones, ever set Jane to wondering? She wouldn't have been alone if they did. The newspaper report of 1812 detailing the discovery of the Lyme 'crocodile' ends on an almost audible gulp. The 'petrifaction' was dug out 'at the depth of one hundred feet below the summit of the cliff'. The question, unspoken, but present nevertheless, is – what was it doing there?

The writer Charlotte Smith composed a poem, *Beachy Head* – left unfinished on her death but published in 1807 – which asks almost exactly this question:

> Does Nature then
> Mimic, in wanton mood, fantastic shapes
> Of bivalves, and inwreathed volutes, that cling
> To the dark sea-rock of the wat'ry world?
> Or did this range of chalky mountains, once
> Form a vast bason, where the Ocean waves
> Swell'd fathomless?

As a young woman, Jane had devoured Smith's novels. Her favourite, as a teenager, was the first, *Emmeline or The Orphan of the Castle*, published in 1788 – she adored the anti-hero, Delamere.* Set partly in Bath, *Emmeline* features a much-courted heroine faced with choosing between two men, one almost the first marriageable man she encounters, the other unknown to her until she meets him by chance halfway through the novel; one her cousin, one a naval captain; one named Frederick, one

---

*   Jane refers to Delamere in her *History of England*, dated 1791.

named William. Jane clearly had Smith in mind when writing *Persuasion*, then.* From Jane Austen to fossils is, really, just a step.

∽

We tend to think of the war between science and religion as being a mid-Victorian affair, but the battle lines were drawn up earlier. Over the course of the eighteenth century an increasing number of scientists had begun to question whether the biblical creation story could possibly be literal truth. By the time Oxford's first professor of geology, the Reverend William Buckland, a frequent visitor to Lyme, gave his inaugural lecture in 1819, he had to admit that it was 'impossible' to cram geological change into the time-spans given in Genesis. If geology showed that 'the present system of this planet is built on the wreck and ruins of one more ancient', that didn't mean the Bible was wrong, just that it had left that bit out. The Good Book didn't, after all, ever actually 'deny the prior existence of another system of things'. Perhaps units of time lasted longer in the beginning; perhaps 'in the beginning' was better understood as stretching out to countless aeons.

The twenty or thirty years before Buckland's lecture – Jane's teenage years, her adulthood – were twenty or thirty years of creeping, growing doubt. In the 1780s James Hutton made the first steps towards the theory of plate tectonics. Erasmus Darwin, grandfather of the more famous Charles, was a doctor and writer who published the first description of evolution in 1794, in his *Zoonomia*: 'Would it be too bold to imagine, that in the great length of time, since the earth began to exist … that all warm-blooded animals have arisen from one living filament, which the great first cause endued with animality?'

Did Jane read *Zoonomia*? We don't know – but it's probable that she read Erasmus Darwin's later poem *The Temple of Nature*. A copy of the book showed up in 2014 in the United States, with what looks to

---

* There are other borrowings from Charlotte Smith in Jane's novels; Professor Jacqueline Labbe, of Sheffield, has written extensively about them.

be the Reverend George Austen's book-plate glued into the front. It's tempting to think that its purchase may have been inspired by the fossils of Lyme. Certainly, if it did belong to Jane's father, it must have been bought around the time of the family's holidays on the south coast; the book (a second edition of the poem) was published in 1803. By the end of January 1805, George Austen was dead.

Erasmus Darwin had a restless, brilliant mind. The extensive footnotes to *The Temple of Nature* touch on subjects as diverse as submarine design, language acquisition, classical literature, geology, and evolution. What was a hesitant suggestion in *Zoonomia* is, by the time of the publication of *The Temple of Nature*, very much closer to an assertion:

[N]ew microscopic animalcules would immediately commence wherever there was warmth and moisture, and some organic matter ... Those situated on dry land, and immersed in dry air, may gradually acquire new powers to preserve their existence; and by innumerable successive reproductions for some thousands, or perhaps millions of ages, may at length have produced many of the vegetable and animal inhabitants which now people the earth.

Or, as Darwin puts it in the poem:

Organic Life beneath the shoreless waves
Was born and nurs'd in Ocean's pearly caves;
First forms minute, unseen by spheric glass,
Move on the mud, or pierce the watery mass;
These, as successive generations bloom,
New powers acquire, and larger limbs assume;
Whence countless groups of vegetation spring,
And breathing realms of fin, and feet, and wing.

'Thus', we're told, 'the tall Oak, the giant of the wood'; the 'Whale'; the 'lordly Lion'; the 'Eagle' – and us, 'Imperious man, who rules the bestial crowd, | Of language, reason, and reflection proud' – all, according to Darwin, 'arose from rudiments of form and sense', from an 'embryon point', from 'microscopic' entities.

Forget the American, French, agricultural, even industrial revolutions; this was the ultimate one – not just a revolution, but a bulldozing of the most deeply-rooted certainties of Western culture. The 'organic remains of a former world' (to borrow the title of a series published between 1804 and 1811) made this world foreign, unfamiliar; English rocks disgorging 'skeletons and bones of various fish unknown ... on our shores', as a correspondent to the *Gentleman's Magazine* described them in a letter dated May 1817. What of religion, if what was now England had clearly been underwater for far longer than the handful of months described in the book of Genesis, if the 6,000-odd years of biblical time was beginning to look absurdly, impossibly too short? What else is unreliable or fictionalised? What on earth can you be sure of, when you can't be sure of the ground beneath your feet?

∞

Persuasion itself is, in some ways, not unlike a fossil. We have the scaffolding of a story, but not the complete fleshing out. There are roughnesses – detail which is missing, or where the connections aren't altogether clear. Revelations appear with startling abruptness; characters fall in love, or run off to live together, out of the blue. At times we're left to guess at motivations, to theorise, to jump gaps. The title may not even be Jane's own, though the frequency with which the words 'persuasion' and 'persuade' appear in the text suggest that it must have been meant as a central theme.

Is it fair to view *Persuasion* as an unfinished novel? Uniquely among Jane's adult work, a portion survives in manuscript – the chapter which closes the book, and a variation on the second-to-last chapter. It's dated July 1816 – a full year before Jane died. The novel didn't appear, though, until five months after her death, so there seems to have been a delay of some sort. *Persuasion* probably is the work Jane describes in a letter which appears to belong to early 1817 as 'a something ready for Publication, which may perhaps appear about a twelvemonth hence', 'short, about the length of Catherine [*Northanger Abbey*]'. She warns her correspondent – her niece Fanny – that the information 'is for yourself alone'.[2] We can do no more than speculate on whether there were second, or third thoughts; on whether Jane hesitated, or was too ill, or not quite convinced, on whether she intended to publish the book exactly as it stands.

Perhaps we'd do better to view the abrupt shifts, the gaps which open up in the text, as thematic. *Persuasion* features a lot of sudden drops and breaks. The words 'fall' and 'fell' appear more often in this short book than they do in Jane's longer novels. The heroine Anne's nephew falls from a tree and breaks his collarbone. Her headstrong rival in love, Louisa Musgrove, falls and cracks her skull on the Cobb at Lyme. Sir Walter and his eldest daughter Elizabeth, scrambling to maintain their social position, take a house on a street in Bath where planned building work had been halted because of landslides.

For half a century or more after Jane's death, critics agreed (broadly) on what her best novels were. *Pride and Prejudice* was ranked first, then *Emma* and *Mansfield Park* more or less together. Those who strongly preferred one tended to think less of the other; as time went on, *Emma* gradually edged ahead and *Mansfield Park* fell behind. The other three novels, among them *Persuasion*, were also-rans – with *Persuasion*, for some, hardly making it out of the starting gates. The *British Critic* pronounced that *Persuasion* was 'in every respect a much less fortunate performance' than *Northanger Abbey*, which was published alongside it. Under the ownership of the Reverend Norris, self-appointed guardian of the Anglican Church, editorial policy would naturally have disapproved of the obviously evangelical Anne, who is 'no card player' and strongly disapproves of 'Sunday travelling'. A critic of 1859 judged the novel to be the 'weakest' of the six – not a view which many modern readers share.[3]

Rather than find artistic merit in the novel, critics were keener to view it as an autobiographical work, and to see in Anne Elliot a self-portrait – Jane herself. Anne is a far more desirable portrait of the authoress than poor, snubbed, middle-aged Miss Bates the vicar's daughter, particularly for male critics.

'Into one particular character, indeed', claims an alarmingly enthusiastic reviewer of 1823, 'she has breathed her whole soul and being; and in this we please ourselves with thinking, we see and know herself. And what is this character? – A mind beautifully framed, graceful, imaginative and feminine, but penetrating, sagacious, profound.' Anne / Jane is 'pure in morals, sublime in religion', 'sweet soother of others' affliction, – most resigned and patient bearer of her own', with 'smiles, that would arrest an angel on his winged way'. The review goes on and on in the same vein.[4]

A century later, the writer Rudyard Kipling, author of *The Jungle Book*, of muscular, imperialist tales of India, and of the short story called *The Janeites*, wrote a poem about Jane – and *Persuasion*.* It's called *Jane's Marriage*. In it Kipling sends Jane 'to Paradise', as is 'only fair'. The paradise is, naturally, marriage. He insists that there must have been a real 'Captain Wentworth | The man Jane loved!' and that *Persuasion* tells 'the plain | Story of the love between | Him and Jane'.

Now, I've been working quite hard in this book to convince you that Jane is an artist, that her work is carefully considered, structured, themed, that she uses her writing to examine the great issues of her day. But there's a grain of truth in Kipling's poem, and even in the 1823 review.

It isn't often that we can put Jane in precisely the same place as her heroines; in *Persuasion*, which uses largely real-life locations, we can. We know that Jane walked on the Cobb at Lyme in 1804 when she was 28 years old – almost exactly the age Anne Elliot is, when she retraces

---

* I mentioned *The Janeites* briefly in Chapter 4. It deals with the experiences of an ordinary British soldier in the trenches and his belief that his superior officers – admirers of Jane's novels – belong to a secret society called the Janeites, a belief which begins as broad comedy and ends by saving his life.

her creator's footsteps. Anne, like Jane, visits Lyme in the autumn; like Jane, she goes on to spend the winter in Bath. Anne's visit to Lyme ends abruptly with Louisa's fall; not long after Jane left Lyme, in December 1804, her close friend (and distant cousin) Anne Lefroy fell when her horse bolted with her, sustaining fatal injuries. It was the second time Jane had lost someone she'd been close to in a violent accident. In 1798 her cousin and namesake Jane Cooper, who'd been at school with her and Cassandra, was killed when her carriage overturned. Only one of Jane's heroines, it's worth noting, is ever actually shown venturing out on horseback. Oddly, this one is timid Fanny Price – whether we can draw any conclusions about her creator's attitude to her from this is another question.*

Anne Elliot, we're told, associates Bath with the loss of her mother; Jane, too, associated the city with the loss of a parent. It was in Bath, in January 1805, only a few weeks after Anne Lefroy's violent death, that Jane's father died. He was well into his seventies, but, apart from occasional bouts of fever, enjoyed good health. His death was a shock. 'It has been very sudden!' lamented Jane, in a letter breaking the sad news to her brother Frank, '— within twenty four hours of his death he was walking with only the help of a stick, was even reading!'[5]

Persuasion, for Jane, exposed the kind of feelings which never really stop being raw. Might she, nevertheless, have been tempted to put her name to it, if she'd lived? She'd published four novels already, she'd received favourable reviews for *Emma*; the dedication to the Prince Regent was a compliment, even an endorsement. As early as 1813 she'd acknowledged that her anonymity was unlikely to last for ever, especially since Henry, 'in the warmth of his Brotherly vanity & Love', was fond of informing total strangers that his little sister had written *Pride and*

---

* Willoughby gives Marianne a horse, but we never see her ride it. Lizzy Bennet is 'no horsewoman', though her sister Jane is. We're never shown Catherine Morland, Elinor Dashwood, or Anne Elliot on horseback. Frank Churchill asks whether Emma is 'a horsewoman' – we're not given an answer, but presumably not.

Prejudice. 'He, dear creature, has set it going so much more than once', sighs Jane. 'The Secret has spread so far as to be scarcely the Shadow of a secret now'; she must try 'to harden myself'.[6]

And by 1816, when she was writing *Persuasion*, she must have begun to harden. She puts her own birthday in it. It's right there, in the third paragraph of the novel – 'December 16th'.

We find hardly any dates in Jane's other novels. Very little is fixed, as to time. The weeks and months slip by, Christmas comes, Easter goes, the workings of the plot dovetail smoothly together, but references to a particular day in a particular month are vanishingly rare, and there's no very obvious relevance attached to them when they do appear. We're informed that Mr Collins arrives at Longbourn on Monday 18th November, which tells us nothing we couldn't work out from elsewhere. The fact that Harriet Smith's birthday is 24th June ought to be important given the mystery which surrounds her birth, but having brought it up Jane never mentions it again. Letters are seldom dated with anything other than the month.* Nor is it possible, despite the best efforts of quite a number of eminent critics, including Chapman, Jane's early-twentieth-century editor, to determine a timeframe with the assistance of almanacs and perpetual calendars; the dates mentioned simply aren't sufficiently consistent.

Some of this may be deliberate. In her teenage *History of England*, Jane announces that she has included the dates 'which it is most necessary for the Reader to know'; there are only four, one of which is teasingly vague, one wrong, and another the date she finished writing it. Dates aren't actually necessary to understanding or enjoying the early novels. They may not have been there; if they were, publishers may have suggested they be removed. Jane, remember, refers to having 'lop't and crop't' *Pride and Prejudice*, a process which might easily have included

---

* Compare this to novels-in-letters of the period – Fanny Burney's *Evelina*, for example, where, though the year may be left vague, almost every single letter is exactly and consistently dated as to day and month.

erasing date markers from the text in an attempt to make the novel feel fresher. *Mansfield Park* must be set around the time of the abolition of the slave trade, but, as we saw in Chapter 5, Jane goes to quite a lot of trouble to direct the attention of readers to that period without making the temporal references any more precise. To be honest, the novel courted quite enough trouble without opening itself up to claims that the Bertrams, with their gambling son and adulterous daughter, were based on a real slave-owning family.

And the timeframe for *Emma*, published at the end of 1815, actually makes no sense at all. There's one scene indicating that travel to Europe is possible for the characters – Frank Churchill expresses a desire to 'go abroad' and to see some of the places in 'Swisserland'. These, for almost a whole generation, were accessible only through books. With the exception of the short period of armistice in 1802–3, leisure travel in Europe was out of the question for two decades. And since European tourism seems to be a possibility for Frank, there are three options. One option is that the novel is set in what was, for Jane, the near future. Another is that the novel is set during the 1802–3 armistice. This would make sense of Miss Bates' possible reference to the 1801 union between Britain and Ireland ('different kingdoms, I was going to say, but however different countries'), but complete nonsense of Mrs Elton's defensiveness about an 'abolition' which wouldn't yet have happened. A third possibility is that *Emma* may be set contemporaneously with its composition – 1814 into 1815. But there were some earth-shattering historical events in 1814 and 1815 – the restoration of the French monarchy, Napoleon's confinement to the island of Elba in summer 1814, his escape in February 1815, his final defeat at Waterloo – and not one is referred to by any of the characters. The effect is oddly disturbing; despite its painstakingly realistic world-drawing, the novel as it stands is impossible, uncoupled from history. It can't have happened like that.

Persuasion, by contrast, is tied tightly to historical fact. We're never allowed to forget exactly when these fictional events are taking place, and against what backdrop. The temporal setting isn't just clear – it's precise, almost to the week. The novel begins in the summer of 1814, when the characters are still adjusting to 'this peace' – the abdication of Napoleon and the (in fact only temporary) cessation of the war which had dominated everything in Britain for the past twenty years. Anne and Wentworth are reunited in the last week of February 1815; the very same week, in fact, that Napoleon escaped from Elba and, landing in France, began to gather an army about him again. Jane chooses to place the entire action of the novel during the 'false peace' of 1814–15. Time matters in *Persuasion*.

Jane chooses, too, to open the novel in a way unprecedented in her writing, with not just dates, but almost a whole page of them. Having produced for her readers the figure of 'Sir Walter Elliot, of Kellynch-Hall in Somersetshire', she reproduces an extract from his favourite book, the *Baronetage*:

'ELLIOT OF KELLYNCH-HALL.

'Walter Elliot, born March 1 1760, married, July 15 1784, Elizabeth, daughter of James Stevenson Esq. of South Park, in the county of Gloucester; by which lady (who died 1800) he has issue Elizabeth, born June 1 1785; Anne, born August 9 1787; a still-born son, Nov. 5 1789; Mary, born Nov. 20 1791.'

Precisely such had the paragraph originally stood from the printer's hands; but Sir Walter had improved it by adding, for the information of himself and his family, these words, after the date of Mary's birth — 'married, Dec. 16 1810, Charles, son and heir of Charles Musgrove Esq. of Uppercross, in the county of Somerset,' — and by inserting most accurately the day of the month on which he had lost his wife.

Some of this is satire. Sir Walter, penning in the dates of deaths and marriages, is treating the book like a family Bible; this is his bible – the book he turns to not only for 'occupation' but also 'consolation' – but, like the multitude of mirrors in his dressing room, it offers him a delightful sense of his own superiority rather than any spiritual sustenance. There's also something more complicated at work here.

The *Baronetage* is almost certainly Debrett's *Baronetage of England*, first published in 1808. It was popular, and quickly became a standard work of reference. Each entry begins with information on the current holder of the title before going on to trace, as Jane says, 'the history and rise' of the family. What it doesn't have, or certainly not in such profusion as this fictional entry, is dates. There are only years of birth for children, particularly those who aren't in line to inherit, and there's certainly no reference to still-born offspring. So why does Jane claim that the paragraph had stood 'precisely such … from the printer's hands'? Why put dates – and so many dates – here?

Well, we know that one date at least is significant – 16th December, the wedding anniversary of Mary and Charles Musgrove, is Jane's birthday. It's also the anniversary of the death of Anne Lefroy.

The coincidence preyed on Jane's mind for years. In 1808, she even wrote a poem about it, entitled *To the Memory of Mrs Lefroy who died Dec:r 16 — my Birthday*. It's not all that good, but then heartfelt poetry seldom is. It begins:

> The day returns again, my natal day;
> What mixed emotions with the Thought arise!
> Beloved friend, four years have pass'd away
> Since thou wert snatch'd forever from our eyes. —
>
> The day, commemorative of my birth
> Bestowing Life and Light and Hope on me,
> Brings back the hour which was thy last on Earth.
> Oh! bitter pang of torturing Memory! —

The poem ends:

Fain would I feel an union in thy fate,*
Fain would I seek to draw an Omen fair
From this connection in our Earthly date.
Indulge the harmless weakness—Reason, spare.—

The day that Jane picks for Anne Elliot's birthday is 9th August, the day, in 1798, that her cousin Jane Cooper had been killed.† Unless this is a wild coincidence, then in the first paragraphs of *Persuasion* we find Jane hiding references to the sudden, violent deaths of two of her relations. Why commemorate them here? Surely because *Persuasion*, set at a turning point in history, located partly in Lyme, is a novel about instability, about things being overturned, about loss, destruction, and change.

Those dates were for Jane herself, perhaps, too, for her family and close associates. But there's another date which she deliberately puts into the text to bring the same topics to the forefront of her readers' minds; the date on which the Elliot son is still-born – 5th November 1789. 1789 was the year in which the French Revolution began. 5th November, as British readers will know, is Bonfire Night. All over the country, people let off fireworks, munch on toffee apples, burgers and sausages, and watch as a 'guy' is burned to ashes on top of a bonfire. A guy is an effigy, a rough figure stuffed with straw or newspaper, and usually dressed up as an unpopular figure of the moment (Tony Blair and George W. Bush were both favourites during the early 2000s). It used to represent a man, Guy Fawkes, one of the conspirators who, in 1605, attempted to blow up the Houses of Parliament, together with the king, James I. They intended to place one of the young princesses on the throne, educating

---

* 'Fain would I' is equivalent to 'I wish I could'.

† Deirdre Le Faye's *A Chronology of Jane Austen and Her Family* gives 7th August, which seems to be an error. The *Reading Mercury* of Monday 20th August 1798 describes the accident as taking place 'Thursday se'nnight', that is, 'a week last Thursday', so the 9th. The *Newcastle Courant* and the *Ipswich Journal* both give the date as the 9th, in differently worded reports.

her as a Catholic and marrying her to a Catholic prince. The conspiracy was discovered on 5th November, and the conspirators tortured and executed in the usual gory fashion. The following year, an Act of Parliament was passed, requiring that clergymen preach a thanksgiving sermon on 5th November.* That Act wasn't repealed until 1859.

In 1688 James II, grandson to James I, was deposed, in what used to be called the 'Glorious Revolution'. He was replaced by his daughter and son-in-law, who took the throne as joint monarchs – William and Mary. James II had made a series of mistakes, chief among which were his attempts to reintroduce Catholicism to Britain. So badly had he mishandled matters that parliament decided to get rid of him, and of his son and rightful heir, and invite James's eldest daughter and her husband to seize the throne instead. William and Mary deliberately delayed their invasion in order that they could land in Britain on 5th November, and present an act of dynastic overthrow as rescuing the nation from the 'Popish' threat. 5th November 1789 is a very loaded date indeed.

Let's turn back to the Elliot entry in the *Baronetage*, looking this time at names. The Elliots are not an imaginative lot when it comes to naming. There have been at least three Sir Walters, and the heir presumptive, 'William Walter Elliot Esquire', also has it as a middle name. The current Sir Walter has three daughters – Elizabeth, Anne, and Mary. Of these, our heroine Anne appears to be the odd one out, since a feature of the 'history and rise of the ancient and respectable family' is 'all the Marys and Elizabeths they had married' along the way. Anne may perhaps be named for her godmother Lady Russell, a practice which was very common. Only the youngest of the daughters, Mary, is married, to 'Charles, son and heir of Charles Musgrove Esq. of Uppercross'. We're also given the name of Anne's maternal grandfather – James Stevenson.

Jane, as we've seen, is conservative in christening her characters. She's far more restrained than either her own family or other novelists

---

*   An Act for a Public Thanksgiving to Almighty God every Year on the Fifth Day of November, also known as the Thanksgiving Act.

of the period. Her heroines in particular are given plain names – just like her: Catherine, Elinor, Elizabeth, Anne. Fanny, Marianne, and Emma are as exotic as it gets. This is a far cry from the kind of names other novel heroines had – Camilla, Belinda, Evelina, Ethelinde, Celestina, Monimia.

Often Jane seems to select names almost at random, and she doesn't hesitate to re-use them. The heroine of *Northanger Abbey*, remember, was presumably once called Susan rather than Catherine, since the work was sold to Crosby under that title; Susan Price is Fanny's younger sister in *Mansfield Park*. John and Isabella Thorpe and John and Isabella Knightley have little or nothing in common; nor do Mary Bennet and Mary Crawford.

But in *Persuasion* there's a definite trend – these are names which belonged to the Stuarts, the dynasty that ruled first Scotland, and later the whole island of Britain. The Stuart dynasty takes its name from Sir Walter Stewart – son-in-law to one king and father of another. After two and a half centuries ruling Scotland, the Stuarts succeeded to the English throne as well when Elizabeth I died childless. The names of the Stuart monarchs of Britain? James, Charles, Charles, James, Mary, William, and Anne. After Anne's death, and in defiance of even the vaguest adherence to dynastic succession, the crown ended up with the House of Hanover – the Georges, who give their name to the 'Georgian' era.*

Reminders of the Stuarts – of Stuart history – crop up quite a lot in *Persuasion*. The Elliots were evidently Royalists during the English Civil War. The title – 'dignity of baronet' – was, we're told, a reward granted by Charles II for their 'exertions of loyalty'.† The 'first year of Charles II'

---

* There were dozens of people with a better claim to the British throne than George I.

† We're told that the Elliot family had been 'first settled in Cheshire', but not when they relocated to Somerset. The reference to their 'exertions of loyalty' during the Civil War possibly suggests we should imagine the first baronet aiding Charles II during the period that the king was hiding from parliamentary troops in the west country.

is probably meant to be 1660, the year of the Restoration, but of course he became king the moment his father, Charles I, was beheaded by parliament in 1649. 'Exertions of loyalty' indicates the earlier date, 'dignity of baronet' points to the later. The double reference, the deliberate uncertainty Jane creates here, glosses over the years of parliamentary rule, but it leaves the gap visible.

This is far from being the novel's only reference to the instability which marked the later years of the Stuart dynasty. In 1685 the Duke of Monmouth, an illegitimate son of Charles II, attempted to seize power. He landed his invasion forces on the Cobb at Lyme – that fact, and the fossils, were the two things that everyone knew about the town.*

One of the earliest casualties of the English Civil War, illegally tried for treason by parliament and sacrificed by Charles I, was the Earl of Strafford, whose family name was Wentworth. Jane means us not to miss this. She makes Sir Walter comment explicitly on the coincidence of names, when he affects to have forgotten all about his former neighbour, Captain Wentworth's brother:

'Wentworth? Oh! ay, – Mr Wentworth, the curate of Monkford. You misled me by the term gentleman. I thought you were speaking of some man of property: Mr Wentworth was nobody, I remember; quite unconnected; nothing to do with the Strafford family. One wonders how the names of many of our nobility become so common.'

---

* See, for example, *England delineated, or, a geographical description of every county in England and Wales*, published in 1788 by John Aikins: 'At Lyme landed in 1685 the Duke of Monmouth, for the execution of his ill-judged design against James II which terminated in his own destruction and that of many others' (pp. 309–10). Similarly, Philip Luckombe's 1791 *The beauties of England* describes 'Lyme-Regis, or King's Lyme' as 'a sea-port of good trade, and remarkable for a pier, called the Cobb, situated about a quarter of a mile from the town, and which forms a harbor that perhaps has not its equal in Europe', before immediately afterwards explaining that 'The Duke of Monmouth landed here 1685, when he came against James II' (pp. 32–3).

And the novel's insistent reminders of dynastic instability – of dynastic failure – stretch further back. Mary, Elizabeth, and Anne are the names of the only English queens who'd ruled in their own right by the time Jane was writing. Mary I and Elizabeth were half-sisters, the two daughters of Henry VIII. Mary II – who deposed her own father – was succeeded first by her husband, William, and then by her sister Anne. Every one of these queens also failed, and failed personally, being female, in the first duty of any monarch – to secure the succession by producing healthy, legitimate heirs.* The Tudor dynasty ended with Elizabeth, and the Stuart dynasty with Anne.

Jane knew this. Her own *History of England* which, incidentally, mentions Thomas Wentworth, the Earl of Strafford, reads as Stuart hagiography. It's a mocking imitation of history books with political agendas, and it's never entirely clear quite how serious her love of the Stuarts is. Nevertheless, she does claim to love them, especially Mary, Queen of Scots, the mother of James I of England. She professes herself shocked that the people 'dared to think differently from their Sovereign, to forget the Adoration which as *Stuarts* it was their Duty to pay them', and claims that the 'one argument' which will convince 'every sensible & well disposed person' about the rightness of Charles I's conduct, 'is that he was a Stuart'.

The names Jane gives the characters in *Persuasion* really aren't random; nor is the preoccupation with succession.

∽

There were plenty in Britain who'd objected to the House of Hanover as foreign, as not understanding the country and the people, as favouring their German dominions. The second Jacobite rebellion in 1745, which

---

* Mary I had no children. Elizabeth I never married. Mary II suffered two miscarriages, while her sister Anne, who experienced seventeen pregnancies in seventeen years, endured miscarriages, multiple still-births, and the eventual loss to disease of the children born living.

aimed to return the Stuarts to the throne in the person of Bonnie Prince Charlie, swept from Scotland through England as far south as Derby, only just over a hundred miles from London. The way Jane knits the Elliots into recent British history might make us wonder what the family's politics were during 1745. Sir Walter's 'contempt' for 'the almost endless creations of the last century' suggests snobbery, but perhaps also a lingering family tradition of disliking Hanoverian rule. It might even be an additional factor in his original disapproval of Frederick Wentworth as a prospective son-in-law. Frederick is a German Christian name; Frederick's sister, Mrs Croft, is called Sophy – a name she shares with Sophia, Electress of Hanover, the woman through whom the House of Hanover traced its dubious claim to the British throne. These names, too, are undoubtedly done for effect. It isn't just that we know Mrs Croft's first name – this happens with a handful of Jane's other married women – it's that we read it over and over again, because Admiral Croft invariably (and unusually) calls her by it.

The Elliots' removal from Kellynch, the arrival of the Crofts and Sophia Croft's brother, Frederick Wentworth, replays the dynastic break, the replacement of the Stuarts with the Hanoverians. But the adult Jane isn't starry-eyed or romantic about Britain's disinherited kings. Anne experiences 'pain', 'severe' pain, in seeing her home occupied by 'strangers', but the pain comes from the conviction that 'they were gone who deserved not to stay, and that Kellynch Hall had passed into better hands than its owners'.

And besides, dislike of the House of Hanover, doubts over its real legitimacy, were one thing; the prospect of it ending was another. And the dynasty wasn't in great shape at the time Jane was writing *Persuasion*. George III had descended again into one of his periodic bouts of madness. Though he'd fathered fifteen children by his wife, he had only one legitimate grandchild, Princess Charlotte. The succession was hanging by the slenderest of threads – the life of a young woman who might easily die in childbirth (and who in fact was fated to do so, though Jane didn't live to know it).

Modern republicans love to point out that it would be more accurate to refer to the current British royal dynasty, the House of Windsor, by its pre-First World War name, the House of Saxe-Coburg-Gotha. In fact modern royals have a far lower proportion of foreign blood than some of their predecessors did. Princess Charlotte's mother was from Brunswick, in Germany. Her father, the Prince Regent, later George IV, came from almost exclusively German stock.

'Remember that we are English', scolds Henry Tilney in *Northanger Abbey*. Emma, too, eulogises her own country, its 'English verdure, English culture, English comfort'. Readers sometimes perceive Jane's 'Englishness' as equally unthinking; robust and straightforward, self-explanatory. But it's nothing of the kind. Jane's two naval brothers sailed all over the world. She had a French cousin, born in India; she had a sister-in-law from the West Indies, an aunt too. In the early, absurd *Love and Freindship*, a Spanish-born, French-educated heroine with Irish-Scottish-Italian heritage bounces around Britain. In *Lesley Castle*, a more serious early effort, the castle itself lies 'two miles from Perth', in Scotland. Another of the characters Jane created as a teenager is on the verge of embarking for India, just as one of her aunts had done in real life. In the last novel Jane ever worked on – the fragment known as *Sanditon* – she was about to introduce a mixed-race character.

Mr Darcy, son of Lady Anne Fitzwilliam, nephew to Lady Catherine de Bourgh, isn't English in any straightforward way. In *Emma*, Jane Fairfax's foster-sister marries and goes to live in Ireland. Crawford is a Scottish name. So is Elliot. And since the name Walter is also markedly Scottish, 'Sir Walter Elliot of Kellynch Hall' is designed to seem almost aggressively un-English, long before we arrive at his Irish cousins, the Dowager Viscountess Dalrymple and the Honourable Miss Carteret. At Kellynch Hall, even the gardener isn't English. He's Scottish; his name is 'Mackenzie'.

'The Dalrymples', we're told, 'were cousins of the Elliots', sufficiently close to send 'letters of ceremony' until the accidental omission of a condolence letter put an end to the correspondence. Sir Walter has 'once been in company with the late viscount but had never seen any of the rest of the family'; recall that he is 54. What is the relationship, exactly? How far does it go back? Are we to imagine an Elliot daughter, Sir Walter's aunt, or great-aunt, marrying an Irish viscount? Was one of the 'Marys and Elizabeths' born in Ireland, making Sir Walter (and his daughters) partly Irish as well as Scottish? How Irish are the Carterets, anyway? Dalrymple is another Scottish name, but Carteret sounds French. Jane's Carterets may be a deliberate reference to the real-life Channel Island family of the same name, or we may be meant to read them more generally as descendants of the Norman invaders of the twelfth century, as some members of the Irish nobility were. On the solitary occasion Jane allows us to hear Lady Dalrymple speak, she is as mindlessly patriotic as Henry Tilney or Emma Woodhouse, but for Ireland, not England, or even Britain.

The Elliots, and their cousins, are at a concert in the Assembly Rooms in Bath. Captain Wentworth is there too; Anne – and the reader – overhear Sir Walter and Lady Dalrymple talking about him:

'A well-looking man,' said Sir Walter, 'a very well-looking man.'

'A very fine young man indeed!' said Lady Dalrymple. 'More air than one often sees in Bath. — Irish, I dare say.'

'No, I just know his name. A bowing acquaintance. Wentworth — Captain Wentworth of the navy. His sister married my tenant in Somersetshire, — the Croft, who rents Kellynch.'

Whatever the truth of Lady Dalrymple's ancestry, she clearly identifies herself with the Irish. For her, Wentworth, a 'very fine young man' with an 'air', must be Irish. He isn't – or so we gather. Sir Walter is of course in a position to be reasonably certain about Wentworth's background; a man seeking to be welcomed as a prospective son-in-law would be expected to provide plentiful information about his family and prospects. Sir Walter knows what Wentworth *isn't* – he isn't Irish, he's 'nothing to do with the Strafford family'. But this is all we ever learn.

We discover where Wentworth has been – 'St Domingo', Gibraltar, the Mediterranean, the West Indies – we meet his sister, we're told about his brother, but where he's from, his background, his parentage, remains a closed book.

The wider point Jane seems to be developing with the Elliots and their cousins, the larger question, is where national identity comes from, and to what extent it matters. If an Irish aristocrat can have a Scottish title and a French name; if it isn't necessary for English monarchs to be born in England, have English parents, or even speak English; if you can be in the *Baronetage of England* when your ancestry is Scottish and Irish – what does being English mean? Does it mean anything at all?

In *Emma*, Jane showed us, in exquisite detail, one small corner of England being altered. With *Persuasion*, the royal names, the repeated references to Ireland and to Scotland, the reminders of disruptive historical events, make it clear that she was working on a broader canvas – broad, but consistent. Change, continual, continuing change, is the universal theme. Nothing in *Persuasion*, absolutely nothing, is fixed.

∽

The novel begins with a removal, as the Elliots abandon Kellynch for Bath, and Anne hardly stops moving afterwards, from Kellynch to Uppercross, from Uppercross to Lyme and back again, to Kellynch Lodge to stay with her godmother, then to Bath. In Bath, she's constantly ranging around the city. At the end of the novel, she gets, not a home, but a carriage – 'a very pretty landaulette'. It's a lot of movement to fit into such a short novel, short both in terms of pages and of narrative time.

The real-life locations Jane selects for the novel very probably did have personal significance to her, but they're thematically significant as well – all the locations are, in different ways, intrinsically unstable. The fictional Uppercross, home to the Musgroves – the family Anne's sister has married into, the family Anne could have married into herself, if she'd chosen – is being made modern and unlike itself, changed from order into disarray. The area around Lyme was subject to landslides; so too, to a lesser extent, was Bath. There are layers of history and prehistory waiting to be exposed in these places – the ruins of a Roman city, the skull of an ancient crocodile.

Everywhere the novel turns, we see certainties being eroded.

Jane picked Lyme quite deliberately. She wants us to think about ichthyosaurs and ammonites. She takes some pains to set those crumbling cliffs – and what they contain – centre stage.

The party from Uppercross visit Lyme in November, 'too late in the year', Jane tells us, 'for any amusement or variety which Lyme, as a public place, might offer'. There is no sea-bathing or dancing for Anne, Wentworth, and the Musgroves: 'the rooms were shut up, the lodgers almost all gone, scarcely any family but of the residents left.'

But whereas, in one of Jane's earlier novels, this might have been almost all the description offered, here we're suddenly launched into a lengthy and lyrical paragraph which, bar a brief reference to the Cobb, is all about the landscape, the surroundings – both man-made and natural:

[T]he next thing to be done was unquestionably to walk directly down to the sea. — and, as there is nothing to admire in the buildings themselves, the remarkable situation of the town, the principal street almost hurrying into the water, the walk to the Cobb, skirting round the pleasant little bay, which in the season is animated with bathing machines and company, the Cobb itself, its old wonders and new improvements, with the very beautiful line of cliffs stretching out to the east of the town, are what the stranger's eye will seek; and a very strange stranger it must be, who does not see charms in the immediate environs of Lyme, to make him wish to know it better. The scenes in its neighbourhood, Charmouth, with its high grounds and extensive sweeps of country, and still more its sweet retired bay, backed by dark cliffs, where fragments of low rock among the sands make it the happiest spot for watching the flow of the tide, for sitting in unwearied contemplation; — the woody varieties of the cheerful village of Up Lyme, and, above all, Pinny, with its green chasms between romantic rocks, where the scattered forest trees and orchards of luxuriant growth declare that many a generation must have passed away since the first partial falling of the cliff prepared the ground for such a state, where a scene so wonderful and so lovely is exhibited, as may more than equal any of the resembling scenes of the far-famed Isle of Wight: these places must be visited, and visited again, to make the worth of Lyme understood.

Jane's description of Lyme's surroundings is unusually detailed and poetical (just think how different it is to the description of Pemberley), but the effect, in spite of the 'extensive sweeps', the 'sweet retired bay', and 'romantic rocks' – is unsettling. The 'partial falling of the cliff' may have created a 'wonderful', 'lovely' scene, but the 'dark cliffs' are a looming presence, their menace made visible in the 'chasms' and in the 'fragments of low rock' which litter the beach below.

And what, exactly, is lurking among the 'fragments'? Relics of the past, reminders of the vastness of time, of its relentless onward rush, of 'many a generation' which has 'passed away'; relics of the past – fossils. Readers who had been to Lyme themselves might almost have been able to see them.★

The trip to Lyme ends, of course, with the terrible accident on the Cobb. Louisa's fall mirrors the falling cliffs; her catastrophic head injury signals the damage that Lyme can wreak – the lasting 'shock' it can inflict on people, and on their beliefs. The party are scattered; Anne goes first to stay at Lady Russell's house, and then accompanies her to Bath.

★ Jane makes a point of telling us that Captain Harville has gathered 'something curious and valuable from all the distant countries' he's visited; he displays them in his rented house in Lyme. Are we meant to imagine that he has added, or will add, some of the Lyme 'curiosities' – fossils – to his collection? There is, too, a faintly reptilian flavour to two of the ships Captain Wentworth has sailed on – the *Asp* and the *Laconia*. 'Asp' is a poetic term for a snake. Sparta, in Laconia, was associated with serpents. There were dozens of other, non-reptilian ship names Jane could have used, or invented – she doesn't.

Anne, we're told – told twice – dislikes Bath. She went to school there, grieving for her mother; she was taken there by Lady Russell when she was mourning the broken engagement with Captain Wentworth. It has never been a place of solace for her; it isn't one now. She finds no order there, no beauty. The city is full of 'the dash of other carriages, the heavy rumble of carts and drays, the bawling of newspapermen, muffin-men and milkmen, and the ceaseless clink of pattens [over-shoes]'. The 'extensive buildings' appear 'smoking in rain'.

And the street that Jane sends Anne to is not one to make her feel any more settled, or secure.

Sir Walter, Elizabeth, and Elizabeth's friend Mrs Clay are living in 'Camden Place'. Upper Camden Place, now Camden Crescent, was developed in the 1780s, but only two-thirds of the proposed development was ever completed. During construction, a series of landslides took place on the north side of the crescent and a number of houses had to be demolished. The land there seems to be particularly unstable – there have been at least two further landslides, one as recently as 2012. It's possible that the unstable houses were demolished while Jane was living in Bath – the Crescent looks larger on a map of 1800 than it does on one drawn up ten years later.*

These days the centre of Bath is a UNESCO World Heritage Site. It feels like walking through history; it's one of those places you can imagine you're really getting close to Jane. The city centre didn't suffer much bomb damage during the Second World War, though the Upper Assembly Rooms was all but destroyed, what you see nowadays being little more than a facsimile rebuilt, lovingly, on the same footprint. But for Jane, Bath wouldn't have looked romantically historical. The buildings were new, few of them built before the mid-eighteenth century. Some of them were very new. Where we see warm, golden walls, Jane would have seen blindingly white ones – Bath stone changes colour as

---

* Camden Crescent Viaduct Historic Building Report, 2006.

it weathers. Anne, at the beginning of the novel, 'dreads' the prospect of 'the white glare' of Bath.

It must actually have been quite an odd experience, seeing architecture inspired by the classical world – the Circus, modelled on the Colosseum; the Royal Crescent; the Pump Room with its Greek lettering, picked out in gold, above the door – recreated in bright, dazzlingly new materials. And it must have been made odder by the fact that Bath had looked a lot like this before. The modern baths were built directly on top of the Roman ones. Almost everywhere workmen dug in Bath, they found the ruins of the Roman city which had once occupied the same space. It happened all the time. A local newspaper, the *Bath Chronicle* of 26th August 1813, reported the discovery of 'several ancient relics (most probably of Roman origin)' in 'the Crescent fields' – the open space in front of the Royal Crescent. These relics were particularly grisly ones – a stone coffin and skulls. Others were more appealing. So many remnants of the Romans were discovered that the city created a museum, the Repository of Bath Antiquities, specially to house them.

As the *Bath Chronicle* proudly opined in 1815, the city 'might justly lay claim, 1700 years ago, to the same character of elegance and taste by which it is at present distinguished'.[7] But some classically educated visitors to Bath – perhaps even a fairly uneducated visitor, who had grown up in a boys' school, as Jane had done – might have found in this replaying of the past a source of apprehension rather than pride. A very famous, and unsettling, passage in Book 8 of Virgil's *Aeneid* describes a visit to a site which is covered in ruins but which will later become Rome. The poet conjures up the buildings he and his readers know, ghosts of the future. Weren't the gleaming modern elegancies of Bath (the Corinthian columns, the classically-inspired pediments) equally haunted by the fallen pillars and fractured inscriptions continually being dug up? If Bath had looked like this before, and slid into ruins, what was to stop it happening again?

Was Bath a city that England could be proud of, in any meaningful sense, when the architecture was almost entirely foreign? Earlier in the novel, Jane posed the same question pretty explicitly – what is English? Is anything? She tells us that Uppercross 'a few years back had been completely in the old English style', that the family live in a 'substantial and unmodernized' house, set about with 'old trees'. But changes are creeping in – a 'farm-house' in the village has been 'elevated into a cottage' for the oldest Musgrove son to live in with his own family. It has a 'veranda, French windows, and other prettiness'. We do find another 'window cut down to the ground' in *Mansfield Park*, but these are the only 'French windows' in Jane's novels, and the only 'veranda', a word which comes probably from the Portuguese, via India, and was understood during Jane's lifetime to be Indian. New names, foreign influences, alien architecture – Uppercross is no longer in the old English style.

The old is giving way to the new. The 'old-fashioned square parlour' of the 'Great House' is 'gradually' being given what Jane calls 'the proper air of confusion' with 'a grand piano-forte and a harp, flower-stands and little tables placed in every direction'. We're invited to imagine 'the originals of the portraits against the wainscot, the gentlemen in brown velvet and the ladies in blue satin' coming alive again to gaze in horror at 'such an overthrow of all order and neatness!' The Musgroves themselves, 'like their houses', Jane mischievously informs us, 'were in a state of alteration, perhaps of improvement'. The parents were in the 'old style', the 'young people in the new'.

The 'old style' is connected to 'order and neatness', the 'new style' is confused, chaotic. The younger generation are – almost without exception – quite remarkably fickle. The eldest Musgrove daughter, Henrietta, vacillates between her attraction to Captain Wentworth and her affection for her cousin, with whom she has long had an understanding. The eldest Musgrove son, Charles, switched his affections from Anne to her younger sister Mary; it wasn't done quite as speedily as Mr Collins manages it in *Pride and Prejudice*, but it happened 'not long afterwards'. Louisa Musgrove is set on Captain Wentworth; by the time he has been absent from her for two months, she's engaged to another man. And it isn't just the Musgroves whose hearts are changeable.

Captain Wentworth flirts with Henrietta and Louisa; he marries Anne. Anne shows flickers of interest in Captain Benwick and in her cousin, William Elliot; we have to presume that at one point she showed at least a little interest in Charles Musgrove, since he doesn't seem the sort of man to propose without perceiving any encouragement. Captain Benwick is in mourning for his dead betrothed. She dies in June 1814, and Benwick doesn't hear of her death until the August. But he recovers apace. By November he is attracted to Anne; by February he's engaged to Louisa. It would seem, as Mary Musgrove says, that 'Such a heart is very little worth having'.

Just as with poor Harriet Smith, and her infinitely changeable affections, it's easy to be scornful about Benwick – and perhaps a little about the other characters too – but this isn't necessarily the response Jane is urging us towards. Of the younger generation, it's only Elizabeth Elliot who shows interest in just the one potential marriage partner; her loyalty – or her resistance to change – reaps no reward.

At the end of the novel, in the chapter which we know was reworked almost completely, and which I think we're justified in seeing as a deliberate reinforcement of the book's themes, Jane has Anne and Captain Harville embark on a lengthy discussion of whether men or women are more faithful. Both characters are intelligent – too intelligent to insist, in the end, that fidelity is innate to either 'man's nature' or 'woman's'. Captain Harville proffers an analogy between men's physical strength and the strength of their emotions, and brings forward the evidence of 'books'; Anne tops his analogy ('man is more robust than woman, but he is not longer lived'), and the pair agree that a woman might reasonably object that the books were 'all written by men'.

What Anne really argues for all the way through this conversation, what Jane is arguing, is that women are socialised into 'loving longest when existence or when hope is gone'. It's a 'privilege', but 'not a very enviable one'; 'our fate rather than our merit'. 'We cannot help ourselves', Anne says, 'We live at home, quiet, confined, and our feelings prey upon us. You … have always a profession, pursuits, business of some sort or other, to take you back into the world immediately, and continual occupation and change soon weaken impressions.' Society expects men to remarry, but it disapproves of women who do the same; as Jane remarks early on in the novel, 'That Lady Russell ... should have no thought of a second marriage, needs no apology to the public, which is rather apt to be unreasonably discontented when a woman does marry again, than when she does not', while 'Sir Walter's continuing in singleness requires explanation'.

Is a second attachment (or even a third) really wrong? Should it be seen as some sort of moral failure to fall in love again?

Jane had been quite as grateful as she needed to be for the long essay on her work which appeared in the *Critical Review* in 1816. Though the tone was generally positive, the 'total omission' of *Mansfield Park* had rightly irked her. And among the praise had been criticism, that Jane's novels (and others) were not romantic enough, that they 'taught the doctrine of selfishness', linking love – 'Cupid' – 'with calculating prudence'. *Persuasion* is Jane's answer – and, like all her novels, it twines pragmatism ('prudence') and romance together. Jane even borrows the language of gardening to describe how Anne, like a plant, was 'forced into prudence in her youth', learning 'romance as she grew older', 'the natural sequence of an unnatural beginning' – beautiful flowers on a stem made stronger by interference.

Anne may insist that women love 'longest' but we, as readers, know that at the beginning of the novel she wasn't really 'in love' with Wentworth any more. Look at what Jane writes: 'time had softened down much, perhaps nearly all, of peculiar attachment to him.' A 'second attachment' would, we're told, have been 'the only thoroughly natural, happy, and sufficient cure'. 'Natural' and 'happy'; not faithless, not selfish, not to be scorned in either men or women. Romance is natural, nostalgia is natural, but so is moving on.

There's an element of moral judgement, of course – the fact that Anne has the potential to respond to more than one man isn't to be compared with the duplicity of William Elliot, who marries for money, and later manages to carry on with Mrs Clay while courting Anne and stringing Anne's older sister Elizabeth along. But we should note that Mrs Clay comes in for very little disapproval from her creator, even though she's a flatterer, even though she deceives her friends, and becomes William Elliot's mistress. Jane holds out the possibility that Mrs Clay's 'cunning … may finally carry the day', and that, having failed in her earlier object of marrying Sir Walter, she may succeed in becoming 'the wife of Sir William'. Jane punishes women who have sex outside marriage relatively gently – far more gently than was usual in the literature of the period – but she usually does punish them. Eliza, in *Sense and Sensibility*, is sent away into decent obscurity. Maria Rushworth is condemned to live with her aunt Mrs Norris. Lydia winds up married to Wickham, which is punishment enough in itself. What happens to Mrs Clay looks much more like a partial endorsement of her behaviour.

Mrs Clay is, as her name suggests, malleable, adaptable, and in *Persuasion* there are advantages to malleability. Those who don't bend will break.

∽

Persuasion is the book in which Jane confronts the reality of sudden and untimely death, memorialising the falls which had killed her cousin Jane Cooper and her friend Anne Lefroy. It features the bad colds and wasting diseases usual in one of Jane's novels, but the characters are also menaced with violent accidents and fractures – little Charles Musgrove's broken collarbone, the accompanying fears that he might have damaged his spine; Louisa Musgrove's severe, mind-altering concussion. Elsewhere in Jane's adult writing accidents are usually averted – Jane Fairfax isn't dashed overboard, someone grabs her in time – and if they aren't averted they're minor, resulting in no more than a sprained ankle. It isn't Tom Bertram's fall which makes him ill towards the end of *Mansfield Park*, but the excessive drinking which accompanies it. In *Persuasion*, accidents threaten death or paralysis.

There's also a thematic significance to them. Jane makes the point quite explicit.

Shortly before the main characters set off on their visit to Lyme, Anne accidentally eavesdrops on a conversation between Louisa and Captain Wentworth. Louisa has cleared the field by forcing a reconciliation between her sister Henrietta and Henrietta's intended; she has Captain Wentworth to herself. Captain Wentworth – imprudently, we might think – begins to praise Louisa's firmness. Half-jokingly, he uses a nut, a hazelnut, as a sort of visual aid, as a symbol for Louisa herself:

'Let those who would be happy be firm. Here is a nut,' said he, catching one down from an upper bough, 'to exemplify: a beautiful glossy nut, which, blessed with original strength, has outlived all the storms of autumn. Not a puncture, not a weak spot anywhere. This nut,' he continued, with playful solemnity, 'while so many of his brethren have fallen and been trodden under foot, is still in possession of all the happiness that a hazel nut can be supposed capable of.' Then returning to his former earnest tone—'My first wish for all whom I am interested in, is that they should be firm. If Louisa Musgrove would be beautiful and happy in her November of life, she will cherish all her present powers of mind.'

This passage was written about fifteen years before the first record of the use of 'nut' as slang for 'head'; but slang commonly enters spoken language some time before it appears in writing and 'nut' seems to have originated among sailors. Jane may quite possibly have intended an ironic allusion here, because after all, when Louisa, refusing to listen to caution, jumps off the upper part of the Cobb, it's her skull, and only her skull ('there was no injury except to the head') which gets smashed on the stones below.* The result, translated into modern medical thinking, is a massive concussion and probable minor brain damage. Louisa's

---

* It may just be a coincidence that, among several other meanings, 'cob' is another name for hazelnut. By the later nineteenth century, a 'cobb' had also come to mean a blow to the head.

'health, her nerves, her courage, her character' are, it appears, permanently changed; as her brother says, 'she is altered; there is no running or jumping about, no laughing or dancing; it is quite different'.

After her accident Louisa remains painfully sensitive to external stimuli, jumping at sudden noises – 'if one happens only to shut the door a little hard', complains Charles, 'she starts and wriggles like a young dab-chick in the water'. Louisa, who prided herself on being someone who had 'no idea of being so easily persuaded', is reshaped. She is 'turned' into a different person, 'a person of literary taste, and sentimental reflection' like Captain Benwick, her betrothed. Anne is amused by the idea, but also indulgent; so too is Jane. There is 'nothing in the engagement to excite lasting wonder … nothing to be regretted', 'no reason against their being happy'.

The outcome isn't so very terrible. Firmness, total immunity to outside influence, isn't sustainable. Captain Wentworth didn't get his nut metaphor quite right. The 'firm' nut which has 'outlived all the storms of autumn', which is 'glossy' and 'in possession of all the happiness that a hazel nut can be supposed capable of' won't stay glossy for long – it will dry and wither, while its 'brethren', 'trodden underfoot', exposed to the sun and the rain, flourish and grow.

You have to open your mind – at least a little. Change can't be evaded; it's a law of nature, there's no use in arguing with it.

It's only Sir Walter – vain, 'half a fool', clinging to outdated loyalties – who thinks that he's immune to the processes of time, who believes that he and his favourite daughter Elizabeth are 'as blooming as ever, amidst the wreck of the good looks of everybody else'. He fondly imagines that he is untouched and unaltered in spite of the fact that he can 'plainly see how old all the rest of his family and acquaintance were growing. Anne haggard, Mary coarse, every face in the neighbourhood worsting.' Even Elizabeth, nearly as vain as her father, can't quite convince herself that time has stood still for her, that she is 'the same handsome Miss Elliot that she had begun to be thirteen years ago'. Feeling 'her approach to the years of danger', she doesn't read the *Baronetage* any more. She dislikes being reminded of 'the date of her own birth'.

'To my eye you could never alter', declares Captain Wentworth to Anne, in the first flush of love renewed. But however 'pleasing a blunder', this is patently untrue – when they first met again, after nearly eight years apart, he found her 'wretchedly altered'. And Anne has changed – Jane doesn't allow us to ignore the fact, or to rush over it in a flood of romantic feeling. 'Time', as Wentworth remarks, 'makes many changes'. For Anne, time not only changes, it destroys, it obliterates: 'What might not eight years do? Events of every description, changes, alienations, removals—all, all must be comprised in it, and oblivion of the past—how natural, how certain too!'

When Anne visits her old school-friend Mrs Smith, the 'first ten minutes' are full of 'awkwardness' and 'emotion':

> Twelve years were gone since they had parted, and each presented a somewhat different person from what the other had imagined. Twelve years had changed Anne from the blooming, silent, unformed girl of fifteen, to the elegant little woman of seven-and-twenty ... and twelve years had transformed the fine-looking, well-grown Miss Hamilton, in all the glow of health and confidence of superiority, into a poor, infirm, helpless widow.

Wentworth has changed as well. It's surely only Anne's romantic partiality which leads her to see, on their first meeting at Uppercross, 'the same Frederick Wentworth'. If nothing else, he's spent the intervening eight years on board ship, on active service. His sister, we're told, looks older than she is, 'the consequence of her having been almost as much at sea as her husband'. The sea, as Mrs Clay observes, 'is no beautifier'. Neither Anne nor Wentworth is the same person.

Nor is their love really the same love. What was it based on, when they were young? Good looks – he was 'a remarkably fine young man', she was 'a very pretty girl' – and generally desirable character traits – his 'intelligence, spirit, and brilliancy', her 'gentleness, modesty, taste, and feeling'. But, Jane tells us, 'half the sum of attraction ... might have been enough, for he had nothing to do, and she had hardly anybody to love'. The pair fall in love 'rapidly and deeply', seeing in each other 'highest perfection'. And at the first test, the first trial, the relationship crumbles. Their second love, their fully mature love, is a different creature. They are 'more tender, more tried, more fixed in a knowledge of each other's character, truth, and attachment; more equal to act, more justified in acting'.

Attachment revived, interest re-kindled, acquaintance re-established – none of them are the same. Re-union isn't the same as union. The original typesetting of the novel, which hyphenates a large proportion of these kinds of words, makes the break explicit.* Restoration, return; they're fictions. The past is out of reach.

Jane has Anne articulate this same idea. Anne is tempted, terribly tempted, just for a few moments, by the prospect of marrying her cousin Mr Elliot, not so much for the man himself, but for other reasons:

> For a few moments her imagination and her heart were bewitched. The idea of becoming what her mother had been; of having the precious name of 'Lady Elliot' first revived in herself; of being restored to Kellynch, calling it her home again, her home for ever, was a charm which she could not immediately resist. Lady Russell said not another word, willing to leave the matter to its own operation; and believing that, could Mr Elliot at that moment with propriety have spoken for himself! – she believed, in short, what Anne did not believe. The same image of Mr Elliot speaking for himself brought Anne to composure again. The charm of Kellynch and of 'Lady Elliot' all faded away. She never could accept him.

---

* In the surviving manuscript chapters quite a number (though not all) of these kinds of words are hyphenated.

It takes magic to create the illusion that paradise can be regained, or that time can stand still – 'charm', bewitchment. It takes wilful stupidity to believe it. William Elliot's claim that Anne's name 'has long possessed a charm over my fancy', his expressed wish that it 'might never change' – that she remain an Elliot by marrying him – both are unreal. His feelings are only pretend. Spells fade, mirages vanish; they're no good in the real world.

But Anne acknowledges that she might have been 'induced' to marry her cousin. She acknowledges – just as Jane acknowledges – the potent draw of the past, the fantasy that by going back, you will find what is perfectly safe and familiar. The past, her family, have a hold on her. Quite early on in the novel, we find Anne trapped by yet another Walter, her two-year-old nephew. She's kneeling next to the sofa in the drawing room in her sister's house, trying to settle her other nephew – Charles, the one with the injured collarbone. Walter, in the manner of two-year-olds, climbs on her back. 'She could not shake him off. She spoke to him, ordered, entreated, and insisted in vain. Once she did contrive to push him away, but the boy had the greater pleasure in getting upon her back again directly.' One of the other two adults present tries to coax the child into behaving, but Walter is having none of it. What happens next? Captain Wentworth strides across and plucks the child off her:

> In another moment, however, she found herself in the state of being released from him; some one was taking him from her, though he had bent down her head so much, that his little sturdy hands were unfastened from around her neck, and he was resolutely borne away, before she knew that Captain Wentworth had done it.

That's what Wentworth represents for Anne: separation from what she knows, from the weight of her own history. When she chooses Wentworth, she rejects the title and the big house, family and tradition – all the things that novel heroines had wanted since the novel began.

They have little to offer her. Her father can afford to give her 'only a small part' of the dowry to which she is legally entitled under his own marriage settlement. What she chooses is a life which is fundamentally unsettled, uncertain – even dangerous.

At the end of the novel she is restored, not to her childhood home or to her mother's title, but only to 'the rights of seniority and the enjoyment of a very pretty landaulette' – a dashing carriage. When, earlier in the book, the Crofts drive Anne back to Uppercross in their gig, they narrowly avoid, in turn, a 'post', a 'rut', and a 'dung-cart'. Captain Wentworth claims that they are 'upset' – overturned – 'very often'. Anne – who shares a name with Anne Lefroy, whose birthday is the anniversary of Jane Cooper's death in a carriage accident – is taking a terrible risk in that 'pretty landaulette'. Jane Cooper was married to a naval captain, too.

Prudent though she was as a young woman, Anne, in the end, embraces risk. It's the price she has to pay, the price that she is willing to pay. The novel ends with Napoleon's escape from Elba; its first readers knew how that would be resolved, but still they would have shared Anne's 'dread of a future war' – another war – and 'the tax of quick alarm', the ever-present threat that the 'sunshine' may be dimmed – perhaps permanently.

Jane begins the final chapter of *Persuasion* by asserting that 'When any two young people take it into their heads to marry, they are pretty sure by perseverance to carry their point'. 'This may', she acknowledges, 'be bad morality to conclude with, but I believe it to be the truth'. The *British Critic* thought this was the whole point of the work.* It's difficult to believe that Jane wasn't playing with the critics here. For a start, the whole plot has been driven by the fact that Wentworth and Anne

---

*   '[I]ts *moral* ... seems to be, that young people should always marry according to their own inclinations.'

couldn't 'carry their point', that they were separated. And there are other elements, in this final chapter, which could be objected to, for various reasons. There's the indulgent treatment of Mrs Clay; Lady Russell (an older woman, Anne's godmother, in a position of moral authority) having to 'admit that she had been pretty completely wrong'; the improvement in Mrs Smith's financial circumstances when she recovers her husband's property 'in the West Indies'.

But all the way through Jane has been working her readers towards one very particular moral, one revolutionary conclusion.

Persuasion, from the very beginning, challenges us to think about history not as a smooth, orderly progression, but as disrupted, random, chaotic, filled with death and destruction, invasion and revolution. It seeks to make us aware, in Lady Russell's words, of 'the uncertainty of all human events and calculations'. And further than that, it asks how, if the past is filled with uncertainty and violent change, if the land you're standing on was once under the sea, you can be sure of anything? How can you rely on tradition or order or identity when the whole world is mutable, when dynasties crumble and all your deepest beliefs might be based on fiction? All the accumulated wisdom of the past – 'all histories, all stories, prose and verse' – is partial, biased. It isn't enough.

History can't be divided into neat chapters, it doesn't come to conclusions, it doesn't keep moving in the same direction. The characters in the novel think that the war is over, that Napoleon is defeated; but as Jane shows us the Elliots, and the Dalrymples, and the Musgroves, and the Crofts, all drifting towards Bath to drink the waters and attend concerts and card parties, she's taking us closer and closer to the resumption of hostilities. She takes some pains to provide us with the details which enable us to work out that the reconciliation between Anne and Wentworth takes place during the last week of February 1815, the very same week, in fact, that Napoleon escaped from Elba.

You can't escape the tide of history, you can't stay firm against that kind of pressure; you have to give way and let yourself be carried, if you want any hope of surviving.

In Lyme, Jane confronts her readers with the unimaginable scale of geological time, and their own insignificance. In Bath, one gleaming white city built on the ruins of another, she shows us a hero and heroine learning to accept and let go of the past and walk together into the unknown.

And it is – it always will be – unknown. Advice, in the end, is 'good or bad only as the event decides'. There's no way of knowing whether 'cheerful confidence in futurity' or 'over-anxious caution' is the right course. There is no right course. Early on, Anne thinks that 'exertion' and 'Providence' should be trusted. But for Wentworth, Providence is very little more than a joke. In the inn at Lyme, bored by Mary Musgrove's flood of talk about how peculiar it is that they should be in the very same inn with 'the heir to Kellynch' and not know, he remarks, faintly derisive, that 'we must consider it to be the arrangement of Providence'. And by the end of the novel, 'Providence' is consigned to the history books, connected to the vanishing past and the atrophying Sir Walter. In the chaotic world of *Persuasion*, you can't trust that even God has a plan; if he does, it must be beyond human understanding.

Anne, in addition to being the most mature of Jane's heroines, is the most modern. Like other naval wives, Anne will have to learn how to live by herself when her husband is at sea, perhaps for years at a time, how to exist independently of anyone, to manage business. Alone of all Jane's heroines, there will be times when Anne is her own woman. We can imagine her – if she weathers the dangers of that carriage, and of childbearing – living on into the nineteenth century, as Jane's brothers and sisters did, watching the railways and the factories arrive, seeing the British Empire rise.

Jane feels confident enough, in the chapter she revised, to boast, indirectly, of what her novels are doing. Up till now, the 'pen' has been, as Anne and Harville agree, in the hands of men; only a few lines earlier, Jane makes Wentworth drop his. It's time – at last – for women to start telling their own stories.

But by the time Jane finished writing *Persuasion*, her own end was already in sight.

In Memory of
JANE AUSTEN,
youngest daughter of the late
Revd GEORGE AUSTEN,
formerly Rector of Steventon in this County,
she departed this Life on the 18th of July 1817,
aged 41, after a long illness supported with
the patience and the hopes of a Christian.

The benevolence of her heart,
the sweetness of her temper, and
the extraordinary endowments of her mind
obtained the regard of all who knew her, and
the warmest love of her intimate connections.

Their grief is in proportion to their affection
they know their loss to be irreparable,
but in their deepest affliction they are consoled
by a firm though humble hope that her charity,
devotion, faith and purity, have rendered
her soul acceptable in the sight of her
REDEEMER.

Jane Austen's gravestone in Winchester Cathedral, Hampshire.
© Courtesy of Dean and Chapter of Winchester Cathedral

CHAPTER 8

The End

Winchester, July 1817.[*]

College Street is at present very quiet, very genteel, very suitable for an invalid such as herself. And there is really very little to be seen from her bedroom window, nothing of note, so that it hardly signifies that she cannot drag herself there. Hardly at all.

Instead she conjures up the view from her own bedroom at Chawton or, before that, the garden in Castle Square in Southampton, remembers the tang of salt, the promise of spring. There is little else to do. She can listen to the bells tolling. She can compose comic verse in her head. She can lie staring at the ceiling, contemplating eternity.

It is raining again, she's told. Saint Swithin's curse for moving his shrine, *July in showers.* As if one ever needed a curse to explain away the rain in England.

Cassandra wishes her to rest, and Dr Lyford agrees, so at least someone is happy with her.

Cassandra nurses her so devotedly. She only wishes that she felt she deserved it.

She wishes she had been better, or braver. All through April and the first weeks of May, as she lay in her bed in her own room waiting for the end, she thought about what was left undone, unfinished. Such long confinements she has had, so much longer than her sisters-in-law with their babies.

---

[*] Based on Jane Austen's letters to various correspondents and her will (April and May 1817), and Cassandra Austen's letter to Fanny Knight (July 1817).

So many delays, so much time wasted.

She has done them justice, to the best of her poor ability, her books, her children. She's done all she could for them. Susan was always unlucky. Miss Lambe will never be born now, but she can see her, oh so clearly —

What will become of them all, after she's gone?

I, Jane Austen, of the Parish of Chawton do by this my last Will & Testament give and bequeath ... Well, it is written.

She remembers driving through Winchester in the spring of 1809. She had thought she had another 30 or 40 years left to her then. But no. Eight years. She has had eight years.

She should have liked to have seen Switzerland. The Alps. Beyond ...

She is so tired. Sleep – is that all – now – if she closes her eyes – to sleep —

Pray for me, oh pray for me.

Jane was only 41 when she died. She was ill, we know, but we have no idea what her final illness was.

It may have been any one of the long list of ailments that have been suggested over the years; Addison's disease, perhaps, or tuberculosis, or lymphoma, or breast or ovarian cancer. The most recent candidate is something called Brill-Zinsser disease, a rare recurrence of typhus. Equally, it may have been ulcerative colitis, or some other serious bowel issue. Several of Jane's brothers tended to stomach disorders, and her hypochondriac mother claimed to as well; the condition often runs in families. Stomachs were, however, rather a preoccupation in the period, in part because one of the few effective medications, freely available over the counter and taken for anything and everything, was laudanum – alcoholic tincture of opium – which causes chronic constipation. The symptoms Jane mentions include 'bile' (digestive problems) and also backache, fever, fatigue, and oddities in her complexion (she refers to having been 'black & white & every wrong colour'). Together, these don't really point to any one diagnosis over another.*

She seems to have dated the beginning of her illness to around the middle of 1816, when she was finishing *Persuasion*. Whatever it was, the symptoms came and went, periods of better health alternating with weeks or months when she was very ill indeed.

Her response appears to have been to start writing another novel. We have it, in manuscript. We know it as *Sanditon*, though Jane herself may have had a different title in mind. It's very much a draft, a work in progress; there are dashes, abbreviations, moments of clumsiness – it breaks off abruptly, in what looks to be the middle of a scene. Set after the Battle of Waterloo (it's mentioned), in a brand-new seaside resort, it features a brace of entrepreneurs, a family of hypochondriacs, a would-be seducer, an impoverished companion, and some schoolgirls, one of whom is Jane's first mixed-race character, a Miss Lambe, 'about seventeen, half mulatto, chilly and tender'.

So is this a new departure? Not entirely. *Sanditon* is a slightly uneasy combination of the old and the bracingly fresh. It begins with a carriage accident, a plot device which was already hackneyed when Jane was a teenager, and which she mocked in her early, exuberant novel-in-letters, *Love and Freindship*. The literary references are old, out of date; Fanny Burney's *Camilla*, published in 1796, is briefly mentioned, while the active sexual fantasies of the self-styled seducer Sir Edward Denham were, Jane writes, first inspired by 'all the impassioned, & most exceptionable [i.e. objectionable] parts' of the novels of Samuel Richardson, written 60 or 70 years before. Towards the end of the manuscript, though, comes what is, for Jane, a highly unusual passage of landscape description – unusual not simply in that it's there, but in its depiction of a scene glimpsed through mist, reminiscent, we might think, of the

---

* Though we can, I think, probably discount the theory that Jane was murdered by one of her sisters-in-law, floated – half-seriously – in Lindsay Ashford's 2011 novel *The Mysterious Death of Miss Austen*.

idiosyncratic (and fiercely criticised) work of the artist J.M.W. Turner, whose pictures Jane may very plausibly have seen in some of her visits to London art galleries.*

Jane may still have been keen to innovate, even on her sickbed. The presence of what was presumably to be a fairly prominent mixed-race character could easily have attracted adverse publicity, particularly if Jane meant to marry her off. Maria Edgeworth, recall, had been obliged to cut any references to interracial relationships from the second edition of her novel *Belinda*. We saw, when we looked at *Mansfield Park*, that Jane was alive to the hypocrisy and self-deception which surrounded Britain's overseas slave-holdings. In Chapters 6 and 7, on *Emma* and *Persuasion*, we saw that she wasn't afraid to court controversy. What might she have intended to do with *Sanditon*, if she'd lived? How much of the plot did she work out in her head and never get down onto paper? We have no way of knowing. We're already, I think, on slightly shaky ground with *Northanger Abbey* and *Persuasion* – novels which, so far as we can tell, Jane herself was still hesitating over letting anyone else read. If we're going to draw any conclusions at all from *Sanditon*, we have to tread carefully.

Jane began *Sanditon* thinking – hoping – that her condition would prove manageable. The abrasive attitude she takes in it to sickness and medicine feels like tough-minded positive thinking, determinedly adhered to. Certainly she seems to have been correct in her own belief that her condition was affected by her mental state.† As we'll see in a minute, a number of stressful situations arose for the Austen family around the time that Jane fell ill. In the early spring of 1817 she suffered a particularly serious relapse after learning the terms of her uncle's will – serious enough to inspire her to write her own.‡ By the middle of May,

---

*   A letter of May 1813 refers to visiting exhibitions of paintings.

†   'I have an idea that agitation does [...] as much harm as fatigue'; letter to Cassandra Austen, 8th–9th September 1816.

‡   See letter to Charles Austen, 6th April 1817. Her will wasn't witnessed, possibly an indication that she didn't discuss it with anybody else.

however, she was feeling somewhat recovered, and it was to promote her recovery that she went to stay in Winchester, a Dr Lyford at the hospital there having proved, she thought, helpful to her.

So towards the end of May, Jane and Cassandra borrowed their brother James's carriage, and, accompanied by Henry, travelled the sixteen miles from Chawton to Winchester, the old English capital which was once home to King Alfred the Great. They settled themselves in 'comfortable Lodgings engaged for us by our kind friend Mrs Heathcote', on College Street, in the shadow of Winchester cathedral.[1]

Jane stood the journey very well, 'with very little fatigue' she assured her nephew and future biographer James-Edward, now a student at Exeter College Oxford. Indeed, she was 'gaining strength very fast' and no longer had to spend all day in bed. She was well enough to 'sit upon the Sopha', she wrote, with cautious cheerfulness; 'I [...] can employ myself, & walk from one room to another'. From the 'Bow-window' of their 'neat little Drawg-room', she could even look down into the garden of the headmaster of Winchester College, the great public school which James-Edward had attended, as did a number of his cousins. They would not be lonely. Another of Jane's nephews, Charles, was a current pupil; he was to be invited to take breakfast with his aunts. Mrs Heathcote called every day.*

Depression often accompanies severe illness, and Jane goes on to say that she cannot feel she is worthy of all the 'Love', of all her 'anxious simpathizing friends'. But, though lamenting that neither her 'handwriting' nor her 'face have yet recovered their proper beauty', this

---

* Mrs Heathcote was a long-standing friend of the Austens, and for many years a near neighbour. Before her marriage she had been Elizabeth Bigg. Her brother had, according to much later family rumour, once been engaged to Jane, for one night only, but the engagement, if it really had ever happened, was now long forgotten. Her younger sister was also a friend, but she was at this point travelling on the Continent, as Jane noted: 'we shall not have Miss Bigg, she being frisked off like half England, into Switzerland.'

letter of Jane's is – faintly – optimistic about her prospects for recovery. 'Mr Lyford says he will cure me', she writes, and if he fails, well then, she jokes, she will seek redress from the 'Dean & Chapter', the cathedral officials.

There was to be no cure, however. This letter to James-Edward, dated 27th May 1817, is the last of Jane's we possess.*

The final weeks of Jane's life, from the end of May through June into July, are vague. Various family members visited. From what they wrote and remembered afterwards, we can identify a serious recurrence of Jane's illness around the middle of June and a growing doubt that she would ever recover. What Jane was feeling, what she was thinking, we can only speculate. With regard to her death, we have little more than Cassandra's record to rely on – a letter she wrote a few days afterwards to their niece Fanny. This kind of text is always suspect; lies cluster to death like flies. Suffering is always mercifully short, when it happens at all. The dead always look peaceful. But we can reconstruct the following timeline with a fair degree of confidence.

On the evening of Tuesday 15th July Jane's 'complaint returnd', and for the next 'eight & forty hours she was more asleep than awake'. Jane's 'looks altered', she 'fell away' – became gaunt – but, says Cassandra, 'tho' I was then hopeless of a recovery I had no suspicion how rapidly my loss was approaching'.

15th July is the feast day of Saint Swithin, a ninth-century bishop of Winchester. According to tradition, the weather on his feast day will continue uninterrupted for the next 40 days – the saint's punishment for the people of Winchester transferring his remains from the burial site he'd chosen. There is, in fact, a tendency for weather systems to sit over the British Isles for weeks at this time of year. It's very possible that

---

* The 'final' letter which Henry Austen quotes snippets from in his *Biographical Notice of the Author* doesn't survive; given the fibs he tells elsewhere in the *Notice*, I think we have to be suspicious of whether the quotations are even genuine, certainly of whether they were taken out of context, or from earlier correspondence.

the comic poem about Saint Swithin and the Winchester races, usually attributed to Jane, was written on this Tuesday. In his *Notice*, Henry claims that Jane was well enough to write some verses shortly before she died, and these would certainly fit. Jane's mastery of prose didn't, as we've seen before, extend to poetry. The verses are fun, frivolous and, in their obsession with the weather, somehow uniquely English. There's only one discordant note. At the end of one line the word 'gone' appears instead of what would fit the rhyme – 'dead'.

So do we have Jane's final composition here? Well, perhaps. And perhaps a declaration of her belief in her own greatness, too. The story of Swithin's curse, remembered by a dying writer, surely calls to mind the curse carved on the tomb of William Shakespeare ('Good friend for Jesus sake forbear | To dig the dust enclosed here. | Blest be the man that spares these stones, | And cursed be he that moves my bones.').

On the Thursday, the 17th, Cassandra explained, she went out after dinner, 'to do an errand which your dear aunt' – Jane – 'was anxious about'. She 'returnd about a quarter before six' to find her sister 'recovering from faintness & oppression'. Jane was 'able to give me a minute account of her seisure & when the clock struck 6 she was talking quietly to me'. The respite was brief. The 'same faintness' returned, followed this time 'by the sufferings' which left Jane struggling to find the words to express herself:

> She felt herself to be dying about half an hour before she became tranquil & aparently [*sic*] unconscious. During that half hour was her struggle, poor Soul! she said she could not tell us what she sufferd, tho she complaind of little fixed pain. When I asked her if there was any thing she wanted, her answer was she wanted nothing but death & some of her words were 'God grant me patience, Pray for me Oh Pray for me'.

Dr Lyford was sent for. He 'applied something to give her ease' – almost certainly a substantial dose of laudanum – '& she was in a state of quiet insensibility by seven oclock at the latest'.

From then on, according to Cassandra, Jane said nothing, and 'scarcely moved a limb'. Let's share Cassandra's pious belief that 'we have every reason to think, with gratitude to the Almighty, that her sufferings were over', and that Jane couldn't feel anything, that she didn't dream. She was lying at what sounds to have been an incredibly awkward angle, with her head 'almost off the bed', for nine and a half hours. Cassandra and their sister-in-law Mary – James Austen's wife – had to take turns to support Jane on a pillow on their laps. There was no movement at all, save 'a slight motion of the head with every breath'. For those last hours, then, Jane was drugged, sprawled out without any attempt at decorum, her eyes shut, her breath hesitating every time, hesitating and, at length, stopping altogether.

At half past four in the morning of Friday 18th July, she died.

She was, it's fairly clear, killed with kindness. A dose of opiates strong enough to knock her out completely for nine hours has to have at least hastened her death. Most people who die from a heroin overdose die because their breathing stops; a number of physiological responses to heroin and other opiates work to depress respiration. We may have to consider the – frankly horrifying – possibility that Jane's illness wouldn't, on its own, have proved fatal, or not so soon; that it may have been the drugs, and only the drugs, which killed her.

Her father had been well into his seventies when he died. Her mother was to live to the age of 87. Cassandra didn't die until 1845. Frank, the closest of the siblings in age to Jane, survived to the 1860s, to be 91. Thirty, forty, even fifty years more wouldn't have been far-fetched. Think – there could have been no uncertainty about what Jane looked like, no scope for the idealised portrait that's going to be simpering up at us from the new £10 notes; we'd have photographs. Jane could have travelled to Europe, to America. She could have gone on trains, on steamships, met Charles Dickens, the Brontë sisters, George Eliot. She could have written another dozen novels.

But instead, Cassandra closed Jane's eyes. Then, from what she says, she went about the other 'last services', by which she seems to mean the business of laying Jane out – tidying her hair, straightening her limbs and her nightdress – and prepared to break the news to the rest of the Austens.

∽

The past couple of years had been hard for the wider Austen family. Edward was embroiled in a costly legal case over the Chawton estate. Early in 1816 Charles's ship had been wrecked, and though the subsequent hearing cleared him of any blame, and no lives were lost, his career fell into the doldrums, as was the case with so many naval officers after the end of the wars with France. There had been Jane's illness. The eldest of the eight siblings, James, had also been suffering from ill-health. He was too ill to attend Jane's funeral and died two and a half years later. Charles's daughter Harriet – Jane's god-daughter – had been suffering from 'water on the brain', treated with mercury.* Then there was Henry. Henry, too, had been afflicted by bad luck, or perhaps the consequences of bad management, which spiralled out to affect half the people he knew, among them his servants, his mother, his siblings, and his nieces and nephews.

From his early militia career, Henry had shifted into banking. In March 1816, his bank collapsed. The rich members of the family, Edward, and Mrs Austen's brother, James Leigh-Perrot, had been Henry's guarantors. They lost £30,000 between them. James and Frank Austen lost money, so too did Cassandra and Jane – smaller sums, but significant to them. The whole clan had to tighten their belts. The death of Uncle Leigh-Perrot, in March 1817, could have mended matters. Years before, he'd inherited from his Perrot connections; his wife was a West Indian heiress, though not on a grand scale; in 1808 he waived any rights to the Leigh family estate of Stoneleigh in return for a lump sum of £24,000

---

* This is the old term for hydrocephalus; Harriet lived for another five decades, so if the diagnosis was correct she seems to have escaped any life-threatening complications.

and a substantial annuity which would continue to be paid to his widow. He had no children of his own. But he made no immediate provision for his nieces and nephews, and none at all for his sister.* It's the old, familiar story of primogeniture, but it was no less painful for all that, and, since even James Austen's inheritance waited on another death, it meant that financial anxiety continued for the entire family.

Given all this, what they did after Jane's death is rather odd.

They arranged for her to be buried in Winchester, in the cathedral, beneath the soaring roof where Mary I married Philip of Spain, alongside the carved bone boxes containing the jumbled remains of Anglo-Saxon kings and queens. And they selected a vast tombstone for her – larger than any other member of the family has.

Why? There was a trend during the early nineteenth century for lavish, showy funerals, among the upper classes, at least. But a country clergyman's daughter, an unmarried spinster, didn't require a lavish funeral – no one would have been expecting one. It wasn't something that the wider family tended to do, even for its richer and more important members. Take Uncle Leigh-Perrot, who died in the same year as Jane – his will stipulates that he should be buried in a private and inexpensive manner.

It wasn't common, at this point, for unmarried women to be buried away from their families, or even to have their own gravestones; by far the most usual thing, in such a situation, was for a daughter's name to be added to her parents' tombstone. This may have been part of the problem for the Austens, of course. Jane's father had died, and been buried,

---

*   Uncle Leigh-Perrot divided his estate unequally between his wife, his eldest nephew James, and six of Mrs Austen's other children, should they survive his widow. Two nephews are left out entirely – one is Edward Cooper, the other is George Austen Junior, who is almost always missing from the family record. The will's structured in such a way that, though James was left the quite onerous task of acting as a trustee to his aunt, there was no financial benefit to the Austen family at all until Mrs Leigh-Perrot died.

in Bath, and her mother was still living. Jane may have spent most of her life in Hampshire, but her father's family had come from Kent, her mother's from Gloucestershire and Warwickshire. They weren't really long-settled anywhere.

The obvious choice would have been to bury Jane at Chawton. Even allowing for the practicalities of removing the body, it could easily have been made into the more economical option, too. Winchester cathedral was a high-status burial place, with proportionately higher burial fees. There was, too, greater social pressure involved, the – perceived – requirement for a larger, grander gravestone than would be necessary in a small rural churchyard.

It was July when Jane died, but the journey to Chawton, where she had been living and worshipping, or to Steventon, where she had grown up and where her brother James was vicar, was, even by the standards of 1817, hardly any distance at all, only a matter of, at the very most, three or four hours. And it would have been more natural, somehow. When Cassandra died, three decades later, her body was transported twice as far, from Portsmouth back to her home. There were, of course, trains by then; maybe travel had come to be seen as less difficult. Perhaps there were concerns about how Jane's body would appear after being jolted about in a cart, but no corpse is improved from lying in a coffin for days in summer, in a city, which is what ended up happening. The funeral, though it seems to have been arranged quite quickly, didn't take place until Thursday 24th July, almost a full week after Jane had died. It was an early-morning affair, before the daily round of services began.

Jane's will, written in April of the year she died, left everything to her sister, except for two individual legacies – £50 to her brother Henry, and the same sum to his old French servant, Madame Bigeon. The widespread financial disaster resulting from Henry's bankruptcy was still, we can see, very much on her mind. The will also instructed, as was standard, that her funeral should be paid for from her own money. So every penny of the funeral expenses, over and above what was necessary or decent, was, effectively, a decision to reduce Cassandra's inheritance.

We know that Jane's funeral costs amounted to £92. This sum presumably included the piece of mourning jewellery that Jane had wanted to arrange for her niece Fanny, which would have been likely to cost something in the region of five guineas (a little over £5). But there appear to have been very few of the pricey extras which undertakers so delighted in adding. It seems that Cassandra laid her sister out herself; it's unlikely that watchers were paid to sit with the corpse or mourners hired. There was no funeral carriage, no plumed horses; the cathedral was, after all, only the shortest of walks away. Cassandra anticipated that there 'would be nothing to keep us here afterwards', suggesting that we shouldn't imagine anything resembling a wake, no drinks or distribution of special funeral biscuits, as sometimes happened in the period. 'Everything', wrote Cassandra, 'was conducted with the greatest tranquility' – such tranquillity, in fact, that she almost missed seeing the 'little mournful procession' leave; middle-class women generally didn't attend funerals. It was a quiet affair.

The lion's share of that £92, then, went on the cathedral burial fees and the tombstone. This is at a time when £50 would keep you for a year. Quiet Jane's funeral may have been; it wasn't cheap. Was it really sensible, or necessary, to spend so much money on burying Jane in a prominent position, with an expensive gravestone?

Only a handful of people were buried in Winchester cathedral in 1817, indicating, we might think, that you would need to make an argument for burying a visitor, a stranger, there, and that you might have to look for a sympathetic ear. The second requirement wouldn't have been particularly problematic: the Austen family had personal connections to more than one member of the 'chapter', the senior cathedral clergy. The late husband of Jane's old friend Mrs Heathcote had belonged to the chapter; another chapter member had married a cousin of James Austen's first wife. And Henry Austen was personally acquainted with the Bishop of Winchester, Brownlow North. After his catastrophic failure as a banker, Henry had decided that perhaps he would, after all, reconsider the career his father had wanted for him – that of a clergyman. He wrote to Brownlow North, and went to be examined by him; by the end of 1816 he was already serving as a curate at Chawton. Still, requesting the burial would have used up a fair amount of the good-will available towards the Austens, and they weren't, in 1817, in any position to squander good-will recklessly.

So why do it? Why bury Jane in Winchester cathedral, when there were cheaper and easier options readily available? Why spend so much money on the grave of an unmarried sister, a spinster aunt, at a time when money was tight? Did someone, or several someones, in the family view it as an investment? Did they anticipate, perhaps, that Jane's books would help to repair the family fortunes or at least provide a nest-egg for Cassandra? Jane was – at last – flying pretty high in her career when she died. She'd recently moved to John Murray who was a dynamic, successful publisher. She'd been invited to dedicate a novel to the Prince Regent, who had professed himself, through his librarian, a fan of her work. The influential literary magazine, the *Critical Review*, had published the long and altogether very positive essay on *Emma*, mentioning both *Sense and Sensibility* and *Pride and Prejudice* with approval, and comparing Jane's work to that of the most-admired – and best-paid – writers of the day.

If part of the reason for choosing Winchester was as an investment, though, it looks very much as if there were those in the family who didn't agree. The inscription on Jane's tombstone is long, abnormally so, especially for an unmarried woman, but it doesn't include any indication as to *why* it's so long. It never identifies Jane as a writer, still less does it name her novels. Instead the inscription talks at length about Jane's family, her 'intimate connections', about *their* 'warmest love', 'their grief', 'their loss', 'their deepest affliction', their consolation. Jane herself is barely present, obscured beneath a thick varnish of the acceptable womanly virtues ('patience', 'benevolence', 'sweetness', 'charity, devotion, faith and purity'). There's only one solitary phrase which suggests that the woman whose memorial this is was in any way remarkable – a reference to 'the extraordinary endowments of her mind'.

We don't know who composed the inscription. For me, though, it has the flavour of a text written by committee, an attempt at combining two very different ideas about how Jane should be remembered. It's an inevitably infelicitous compromise between publicity-seeking and decent obscurity.

There are strong indications that there was disagreement within the family as to whether Jane's identity as a writer ought to be acknowledged.

The fact that Jane was an author was, by the time she died, an increasingly open secret. As early as 1813, remember, we found her sighing over Henry's tendency to boast about his little sister's literary achievements. Locally, in Hampshire, there were so many routes for the gossip to have taken that it must have been close to becoming common knowledge.

But the obituaries that appeared in the local newspapers on Monday 21st July make no reference to her novels.* They're short and uninformative. They're also all worded slightly differently – one mentions Jane's father, another where she lived, though not her Christian name, which, given the prevailing naming conventions, could well have led acquaintances to think that it was Cassandra who'd died rather than Jane. Yet another varies the spelling of 'Austen' and 'Chawton'.† Perhaps they were penned by different writers. Perhaps they were written hurriedly, or dictated, by one person. But they're all of them conventional.

The obituary that appeared in the *London Courier and Evening Gazette*, on Tuesday 22nd July, on the other hand, is rather remarkable:

On the 18th inst. at Winchester, Miss Jane Austen, youngest daughter of the late Rev. George Austen, rector of Steventon, in Hampshire, and the Authoress of Emma, Mansfield Park, Pride and Prejudice, and Sense

---

* See *Hampshire Telegraph*, *Hampshire Chronicle*, and *Salisbury and Winchester Journal*, all Monday 21st July 1817.

† 'Yesterday morning died in College-street, Miss Jane Austin, of Chalton near Alton, in this county.'

and Sensibility. Her manners were most gentle; her affections ardent;
her candor was not to be surpassed, and she lived and died as became
a humble Christian.*

It mentions Jane's novels; it talks about her as a person, kindly, proudly.
It looks, on the surface, like the perfect text to have used on Jane's
gravestone.

And the first line and a half is very similar to what actually does
appear on the gravestone. The last couple of lines, though, contain
some potentially problematic phrases. Harmless enough, to talk about
Jane's 'most gentle' manners, but there's a quality of fierceness to the
word 'ardent' – it means, after all, burning, flammable, fiery. It can be
dangerous. Among the characters in Jane's novels who are described
as behaving in 'ardent' ways are the unstable Marianne Dashwood,
the sexual predators Willoughby and Henry Crawford, and Mr Elton,
in his unwelcome proposal to Emma Woodhouse. 'Candor', too, has
troubling elements. The word meant either freedom from malice or
'impartiality, open-mindedness', frankness, outspokenness, even. Jane
Bennet, in *Pride and Prejudice*, is praised at one point for the first sort
of candour, her 'candour without ostentation or design — to take the
good of every body's character, and make it still better, and say nothing
of the bad'.

Jane Austen's candour, though, was the other sort, less Pollyannaish,
more incisive. We've seen her rising to outspokenness, to a most ungen-
tle frankness – in her foolhardy letter to Crosby in April 1809; when she
attacked the hypocrisy of the clergy in *Mansfield Park*. We've seen her
criticise primogeniture and suggest that change, voluntarily undertaken,
may be the only safeguard against revolution. We've seen her mention to
her readers the drug that could stop childbed becoming a deathbed. In
Emma she exposed the damage wrought by enclosure. In *Persuasion* she
confronted the possibility that there was no orderly progress to history,

---

*   This was picked up and reprinted, with varying changes, by other newspapers.

no grand plan. It wasn't in Jane's nature to 'say nothing of the bad' or to ignore what was difficult, or unwelcome.

And as for those three final words in the obituary, which look so neutral to most modern readers, they may well have been the most problematic of all. Throughout Jane's life, the phrase 'a humble Christian' had been strongly associated with writers who questioned Church of England orthodoxy, with Methodists, Quakers, Baptists, and evangelicals of all persuasions. It appeared in texts with titles like *The Evangelical Preacher* and *Practical Discourses on Regeneration* – spiritual rebirth, that is – and in the work of theologians such as the Baptist John Fawcett and William Dalgliesh, a (to some heretical) minister of the Church of Scotland.* It wasn't neutral at all.

Do we have, here, the explanation for Henry Austen's peculiar insistence, in his *Biographical Notice*, on stating that Jane's 'opinions accorded strictly with those of our Established Church'?

And who wrote this obituary, with its lightly-veiled suggestions of religious unorthodoxy, its hints at fiery outspokenness? Who sent it to a publication based in London, which would have a wider readership? Henry would be the likeliest candidate, if it weren't for his protests in the *Biographical Notice*. Cassandra?

We do have a copy of the text of the obituary, probably written in Cassandra's handwriting; that doesn't of course mean that she composed it. Who else? Did Jane perhaps write it herself? Was sending off the obituary perhaps the 'errand' that she was so 'anxious about', the errand which took Cassandra away from her sister the day before Jane died, that she didn't want to specify, even in a letter to her own niece?

Well, as with so much of Jane's life, we have no way of knowing.

What we can say, with confidence, is that Jane's opinions really didn't accord anything like as strictly with 'those of our Established Church' as Henry claimed. Her novels offer ample proof of her reservations.

---

* The conservative writer Hannah More uses it too, but she moved in evangelical circles.

And even in her final sickness, living next to Winchester cathedral, she remained scornful about the failings of the Church she'd been raised in, and the Anglican clergy whose ranks had included her own father and – now – two of her brothers.

I mentioned before that in the last letter we have of Jane's she jokes about applying to the 'Dean and chapter' of the cathedral if Dr Lyford failed to cure her. She talks about 'drawing up a Memorial', and laying it before them. She had, she remarked, 'no doubt of redress from that Pious, Learned & disinterested Body'.

Some biographers have tried to read this as an expression of orthodox Anglican piety, in line with what Jane's family wanted everyone to believe. This doesn't work, not if you spend any time at all delving into the identities of the men who made up the cathedral chapter in 1817 – information which Jane herself would surely have known, given her friendship with Mrs Heathcote.

The Dean of Winchester, who had earlier been rector of Alton, the market town nearest to Chawton, was Thomas Rennell. His son, also Thomas, worked closely with Henry Handley Norris, helping to edit the *British Critic*, the literary magazine that reviewed every one of Jane's novels save for the one which urged its readers towards thinking about slavery and featured a character who shared Norris' name, his facile philanthropy, and his hypocrisy: *Mansfield Park*. Not so 'disinterested', then. And the cathedral clergy were not particularly 'pious' or 'learned', either.

In fact, the Winchester cathedral chapter in 1817 is a telling illustration of how nepotistic the Church of England was, and of how closely, how intimately, its interests were allied to the interests of Britain's political and economic elite.

The Bishop of Winchester was Brownlow North. North's father had been a senior courtier, his half-brother had been prime minister. North progressed rapidly in his career, and was appointed to a number of lucrative positions in the Church. He married a West Indian heiress and preached before the Society for the Propagation of the

Gospel, which, as we saw in Chapter 5, was the slave-owning arm of the Church of England. Among the twelve members of the chapter were men who had married into West Indian slaving families, men who had connections to the royal household, and, as well, two of the bishop's sons, his nephew, two of his sons-in-law, his niece's husband, and his wife's brother-in-law.*

These are the men that Jane is talking about, men born with silver spoons in their mouths, men who've been given jobs not because they've earned them but because of who they are, men who own slaves. She's being sarcastic.

Thinking back to Jane's letter to Crosby, in which she adopted the identity of 'Mrs Ashton Dennis' purely to declare herself 'M.A.D.', remembering the recklessness which peeks out time and again in her writing, it's not impossible to imagine her 'drawing up a Memorial', similar to the text of the obituary, and having it sent to the cathedral officials. Jane, in her wilder moments, could have delighted in getting the title of her anti-Church, anti-slavery novel into a cathedral run by slave-owners. Maybe Jane was buried in Winchester cathedral because she wished to be. Maybe it was intended as a private joke; a joke which failed, because the text on her tombstone carefully avoids ever mentioning her writing.

It would be ironic if, in death, Jane finally found readers who understood exactly the point she was trying to make.

The gravestone inscription is, undoubtedly, odd. It was thought odd as early as 1817, the year Jane died, when the author of a book about Winchester cathedral felt the need to include a paragraph explaining who on earth Jane was:

Amongst the interments in this pile, is one of a lady whose virtues, talents, and accomplishments entitle her not only to distinguished

---

* One of North's grandsons was appointed to the (paid) role of registrar of the diocese as a child.

notice, but to the admiration of every person who has a heart to feel and a mind to appreciate female work and merit. The lady alluded to, Miss Jane Austen, who was buried here, July 1817, was author of four novels of considerable interest and value. In the last, a posthumous publication, entitled 'Northanger Abbey,' is a sketch of a memoir of the amiable author.[2]

The story about the cathedral verger who, in the 1850s, was so terribly bemused that visitors should want to see Jane's grave probably isn't true. There was, at any rate, no excuse for the verger's ignorance, since the grave of 'Miss Jane Austen, the authoress' is included in the short list of 'Chief Monuments' in the 1854 *Cathedral Handbook*.[3]

The visitors came, and they keep coming.

They come to see Jane. They hurry past the war memorials, and the tombs of dead bishops. They scuff the painted floor tiles, centuries old. They glance at the place where Saint Swithin's shrine used to stand, peer at the small statue of the diver who shored up the cathedral's watery foundations, perhaps descend briefly into the dankness of the crypt. And then they go to stand in front of Jane's gravestone and pay homage.

From the moment her first novel was published, Jane's readers have been unable to ignore her. They've been drawn to compare themselves to her characters, or to fall in love with them. They've read her over and over again. Some of them have rejected her, angrily, confusedly. Some of them have suggested she should be used as a form of medication. Her novels are powerful. Even if they haven't understood everything that she wrote, readers have always been able to sense that. It's why she's still being read now, when Maria Edgeworth, Fanny Burney and Sir Walter Scott are only footnotes in literary history.

I began this book with Jane's letter to the publisher Richard Crosby, and it's him I come back to. Because in the end, Jane was perfectly right to have been 'mad' with Crosby & Co. It was their fault that *Susan – Northanger Abbey* – wasn't ever read by the audience it had been intended for. And that first failure may well have been responsible for what looks like a substantial delay in sending out the books we know as *Sense and Sensibility* and *Pride and Prejudice*, with the result that they, too, were never read in the context their author had intended. They were mis-read, by most, at least, as light and delightful, not as anything more substantial. And by then, the damage was done. Critics, convinced that they understood the kind of novels Jane was writing, ignored the less comfortable, more challenging ideas in *Emma* and *Persuasion*, or, where a pretence of ignorance was impossible, as with *Mansfield Park*, pretended that the novel didn't exist.

If Jane's first novels had appeared earlier, when they were meant to, they could never have been so thoroughly, so almost universally, misun-derstood. The family could have concealed and equivocated as much as they liked; it wouldn't have been as successful. All the presumptions and preconceptions – they wouldn't have been able to take root in the way that they did. From the very beginning, we would all have approached Jane differently, we would have read her differently. We'd have seen her more for what she was.

Because in the end it doesn't matter whether Jane wrote her own obituary, or whether or not she wanted to be buried in Winchester cathedral. It doesn't matter how she died, who she loved, or what she looked like.

In the last chapter I mocked the enthusiasm of the 1823 reviewer who believed that Anne Elliot was an authorial self-portrait, but it's that anonymous review which, in the end, contains one of the most insightful judgements about Jane, and her work:

– a scanty and insufficient memoir […] is all the history of her life, that we or the world have before us; but, perhaps, that history is not wanted, – her own works furnish that history. Those imaginary people, to whom she gave their most beautiful ideal existence, survive to speak for her, now that she herself is gone.

Forget the Jane Austen you think you know. Forget the biographies, forget the pretty adaptations. Ignore the banknote. Read Jane's novels. They're there to speak for her; love stories, yes, though not always happy ones, but also the productions of an extraordinary mind, in an extraordinary age.

Read them again.

FURTHER READING

Henry Austen, *A Biographical Notice of the Author* (published with *Northanger Abbey* and *Persuasion*, 1817/1818)

James-Edward Austen-Leigh, *A Memoir of Jane Austen* (1870 [dated thus, though published December 1869], 1871)

∽

Fanny Burney, *Evelina, or The History of a Young Lady's Entrance into the World* (1778)

Edmund Burke, *Reflections on the Revolution in France* (1790)

John Clare, *Poems Descriptive of Rural Life and Scenery* (1820)

Thomas Clarkson, *The History of the Rise, Progress, and Accomplishment of the Abolition of the African Slave-Trade* (1808)

William Cobbett, *Rural Rides* (1830)

William Cowper, *The Task* (1785)

Erasmus Darwin, *The Temple of Nature, or The Origin of Society* (1802)

Maria Edgeworth, *Belinda* (1801)

William Godwin, *Caleb Williams, or Things as they Are* (1794)

Anne Radcliffe, *The Mysteries of Udolpho* (1794)

Samuel Richardson, *Pamela, or Virtue Rewarded* (1740–41)

Walter Scott, *Marmion, A Tale of Flodden Field* (1808)

Charlotte Smith, *Emmeline, or The Orphan of the Castle* (1788)

— *The Emigrants* (1793)

— *Beachy Head* (1807)

Robert Southey, *Espriella's letters, translated from the Spanish* (1807)

Mary Wollstonecraft, *A Vindication of the Rights of Woman* (1792)

∽

Paula Byrne, *Belle: The Slave Daughter and the Lord Chief Justice* (HarperCollins, 2014)

Lenore Davidoff and Catherine Hall, *Family Fortunes: Men and Women of the English Middle-Class 1780–1850* (Routledge, 1987, 2002)

Alistair Duckworth, *The Improvement of the Estate: A Study of Jane Austen's Novels* (Johns Hopkins UP, 1971, 1994)

Celia Easton, 'Jane Austen and the Enclosure Movement: The Sense and Sensibility of Land Reform', in *Persuasions* 24 (2002): 71–89, p. 88.

Adam Hochschild, *Bury the Chains: The British Struggle to Abolish Slavery* (Macmillan, 2005; also subtitled *'Prophets and Rebels in the Fight to Free an Empire's Slaves'*)

Ruth Perry, *Novel Relations: The Transformation of Kinship in English Literature and Culture, 1748–1818* (Cambridge UP, 2004)

Simon Schama, *Rough Crossings: Britain, the Slaves, and the American Revolution* (BBC Books, 2006)

Colleen Sheehan, 'Jane Austen's "Tribute" to the Prince Regent: A Gentleman Riddled with Difficulty', and 'Lampooning the Prince: A Second Solution to the Second Charade in *Emma*', both in *Persuasions On-Line* V.27, No. 1 (Winter 2006), www.jasna.org/persuasions/on-line/

Raymond Williams, 'Three around Farnham', in *The Country and the City* (Hogarth Press, 1973, Oxford UP, 1975)

NOTES

Chapter 2: *Northanger Abbey*

1. Letter to Cassandra Austen, 17th May 1799.
2. Letter to Cassandra Austen, 2nd June 1799.
3. It's advertised in the *Bath Chronicle* for that week.
4. Letter to Fanny Knight, probably spring 1817.
5. Letter to Cassandra Austen, Thursday 20th–Friday 21st November 1800.
6. Letter to Cassandra Austen, 27th–28th October 1798.
7. Letter to Cassandra Austen, probably Tuesday 12th–Wednesday 13th May 1801.
8. *Chester Courant*, 26th March 1805, p. 4.
9. Letter to Fanny Knight, Sunday 23rd–Tuesday 25th March 1817.
10. *The Guardian*, review of Val McDermid's 'updating' of *Northanger Abbey*, 2014.

Chapter 3: *Sense and Sensibility*

1. Letter to Francis Austen, 22nd January 1805.
2. *British Critic*, May 1812.
3. Letter to Fanny Knight, 30th November 1814.
4. William Blackstone, *Commentaries on the Laws and Constitution of England* (1765–69).
5. Lenore Davidoff and Catherine Hall, *Family Fortunes: Men and Women of the English Middle-Class 1780–1850* (Routledge, 1987, 2002), p. 323.

Chapter 4: *Pride and Prejudice*

1. *Hampshire Chronicle*, Saturday 30th June 1798, p. 1.
2. *Hampshire Chronicle*, Saturday 9th September 1797.
3. *Gloucester Journal*, Monday 7th November 1796, p. 4.
4. *Edinburgh Review*, July 1830.
5. *Gentleman's Magazine*, September 1816.

Chapter 5: *Mansfield Park*

1. Letter to Cassandra Austen, 17th–18th October 1815.
2. Simon Schama, *Rough Crossings: Britain, the Slaves, and the American Revolution* (BBC Books, 2006), p. 37.
3. Albert P. Blaustein and Robert L. Zangrando, eds, *Civil Rights and African Americans: A Documentary History* (Northwestern UP, 1991), p. 38.
4. Edward Long, *Candid Reflections upon the Judgement Lately Awarded by the Court of King's Bench in Westminster-Hall on What is Commonly Called the Negroe-Cause, by a Planter* (London, 1772), p. 34.
5. Letter to Cassandra Austen, 24th January 1813.
6. *Chester Chronicle*, 2nd December 1791, p. 3.
7. *A catalogue of forest trees, flowering shrubs, plants, flower-roots, and seeds: sold by Gordon, Dermer, and Co. Seedsmen, In Fenchurch-Street*, p. 110.
8. Beilby Porteus, Bishop of Chester, *A sermon preached before the Incorporated Society for the Propagation of the Gospel in Foreign Parts; at their anniversary meeting* (London, 1783), pp. 18–29.
9. Bryan Edwards, *The history, civil and commercial, of the British colonies in the West Indies. In two volumes* (Dublin, 1793), Vol. 2, pp. 34–5.
10. Robert Norris, *A short account of the African slave trade, collected from local knowledge, from the evidence given at the bar of both Houses of Parliament* (Liverpool, 1788), pp. 11–12.
11. Gilbert Francklyn, *An answer to the Rev. Mr. Clarkson's essay on the slavery and commerce of the human species, particularly the African; in a series of letters* (London, 1789), pp. 88–9.
12. *The Christian Instructor, or Congregational Magazine*, March 1823, p. 136.
13. Letter to Cassandra Austen, Tuesday 24th January 1809.
14. Letter to Fanny Knight, Friday 18th–Sunday 20th November 1814.
15. Letter to Cassandra Austen, Sunday 8th–Monday 9th September 1816.
16. Letter from James Stanier Clark to Jane Austen, 16th November 1815.

Chapter 6: *Emma*

1. Letter to Cassandra Austen, 27th–28th October 1798.
2. UK National Ecosystem Assessment (2011).
3. Alan Everitt, 'Common Land', in *The English Rural Landscape,* ed. Joan Thirsk (Oxford UP, 2000), pp. 210–35, p. 210.
4. See Julie Jeffries, *The UK population, past, present and future*, part of the Office for National Statistics series, *Focus on people and migration* (2005).

5. S.J. Thompson, 'Parliamentary enclosure, property, population, and the decline of classical republicanism in eighteenth-century Britain', *The Historical Journal*, 51, 3 (2008), pp. 621–42, p. 624.

6. A.H. John, 'Farming in Wartime: 1793–1815', In *Land, Labour and Population in the Industrial Revolution: Essays Presented to J.D. Chambers*, ed. E.L. Jones and G.E. Mingay (London: Edward Arnold Ltd, 1967), pp. 28–47, p. 30.

7. Simon Winchester, *The Map that Changed the World* (Viking, 2001/Penguin, 2002), p. 23.

8. Letter to Cassandra Austen, 2nd October 1808.

9. Letter to Cassandra Austen, 29th January 1813.

10. Virginia Woolf, unsigned review in the *Times Literary Supplement*, 8th May 1913.

11. According to *The Enclosure Maps of England and Wales, 1595–1918: A Cartographic Analysis and Electronic Catalogue*, ed. Roger Kain et al. (Cambridge UP, 2004).

12. Letter to Cassandra Austen, 8th–9th January 1799; letter to Cassandra Austen, 26th June 1808.

13. Raymond Williams, 'Three around Farnham', in *The Country and the City* (Hogarth Press, 1973, Oxford UP, 1975).

Chapter 7: *Persuasion*

1. Letter to Cassandra Austen, 7th–9th October 1808.

2. Letter to Fanny Knight, 13th March 1817.

3. George Lewes, unsigned article, 'The Novels of Jane Austen', in *Blackwood's Edinburgh Magazine* (July 1859).

4. *Retrospective Review*, 1823, vii, pp. 131–5.

5. Letter to Francis Austen, 22nd January 1805.

6. Letter to Francis Austen, 25th September 1813.

7. The *Bath Chronicle*, 25th May 1815, p. 3.

Chapter 8: The End

1. Letter to Anne Sharp, 22nd May 1817.

2. John Britton, *The history and antiquities of the see and cathedral church of Winchester* (1817), p. 109.

3. M.E.C. Walcott, *A Handbook for Winchester Cathedral* (1854), p. 8.

INDEX

Note: Literary characters are listed under their surnames

A

Abdy, John (father) 248, 251
Abdy, John (son) 251, 255
abortion 49–50
accidents 290–2, 296
adopted children 252–3
Alexander, Emperor of All Russia 215
Allen, Mrs 43
Andrews, Miss 56
Anne, Queen 278
Annesley, Mrs 146
Anning, Joseph 260
Anning, Mary 260–1, 262
Anning, Richard 261, 262
Antigua 183, 185, 186, 198
anxiety 134
apricots 194–5
Ashford, Lindsay 303
Auden, W.H. 91
Austen, Anna 52, 80, 176, 207
Austen, Cassandra (mother of Jane) 43,
    119–20, 121, 308
Austen, Cassandra (sister of Jane) 2, 9, 10,
    13, 217, 261–2, 309
    after Jane's death 311–12, 316
    as confidante of Jane 27
    death 311
    fiancé 81, 85
    and Jane's final illness 301, 306, 307–9
    Jane's letters to
        from Bath (1799) 37

from Chawton/London (1813–15)
    122, 123–4, 169, 172, 196, 215,
    229
from Lyme Regis (1804) 259, 262
from Steventon (1798–1801) 48–9,
    75, 119–20
Austen, Charles (brother of Jane) 13,
    119–20, 129, 171, 183, 219, 304, 309
Austen, Charles (nephew of Jane) 305
Austen, Edward 4–5, 10, 13, 170–1, 309
    adoption 79, 198
    in Bath 37–8, 43–4
    and Chawton 84, 215–17
Austen, Eliza 5, 9–10, 13, 120, 137, 177, 262
Austen, Elizabeth (Lizzie, niece of Jane)
    170
Austen, Elizabeth (wife of Edward) 37–8,
    43, 54, 84
Austen, Fanny *see* Knight, Fanny
Austen, Frances 54
Austen, Francis (Frank) 13, 14, 17–18, 26,
    269, 308, 309
    in navy 79, 119–20, 194
Austen, George (brother of Jane) 13, 80,
    310
Austen, George (father of Jane) 12, 16,
    79–80, 183, 198, 265
    death 80–1, 84, 269, 308
Austen, Harriet 309
Austen, Henry 5, 170–1, 177, 262, 305
    Biographical Notice of the Author 19–21,
        306, 307, 316
    career 13, 129, 198, 312–13
    childless 80

Austen, Henry (*continued*)
  financial problems 309, 311
  on Jane's writing 269–70, 314
  and publishers 18, 172
Austen, James 13, 76, 183, 309–10
  at Steventon 76, 80, 198
Austen, Jane
  as artist 33
  on banknote 11
  in Bath 12, 15, 37–8, 43–4
  biographical details 12
  candour 315–16
  at Chawton 5, 14, 84, 125, 215–17
  Cobbett compared with 245
  critics on 24–6, 267–8, 320
  death 302, 307–9
  final illness 301–3, 304–6
  funeral and burial 310–14, 318–19
  as never married 70
  novels
    editing 29
    publication 12
    speaking for Jane 320–1
    see also individual works
  obituaries 314–16
  poetry 18, 307
  religious beliefs 206–7, 316–17
  romantic stories about 27–8
  in Southampton (Castle Square) 1–9,
    14–15, 301
  at Steventon 14, 75–6, 119–21
  will 311
Austen-Leigh, Caroline 28
Austen-Leigh, James-Edward 119,
    305–6
  A Memoir of Jane Austen 26–7, 79
Austen, Marianne 170
Austen, Mary (wife of Frank) 17
Austen, Mary (wife of James) 28, 76, 80,
    85, 119, 308
Austen, Mary-Jane 8, 9
Austen, Philadelphia 6, 13, 110
Austen, Rebecca 52
Austen, William (nephew of Jane) 38

B

baronets 141
Bates, Miss 142, 242, 251–2, 255–6
Bates, Mrs 77, 242, 251, 253
Bath 285–6
  Austens in 12, 15, 37–8, 43–4
  in *Persuasion* 282–3, 284–5, 298
Beckford, Margaret 194
Beckford, William 194
Becoming Jane 28, 122
bedrooms 47–8
The Beggar's Petition 64–5
Belinda 21, 42, 45, 304
Belle, Dido Elizabeth 179–80
Bennet, Elizabeth 81
  and Darcy 143, 144–6, 149–51, 155, 156,
    157–62, 163–5
  and Lady Catherine 145
  and militia 132, 133
  as radical 161–2
  unconventionality 160, 164
  walking alone 134
  and Wickham 144, 147
Bennet, Jane 142, 147, 153, 159
Bennet, Kitty 132
Bennet, Lydia 131–3, 146–7, 160, 161, 166
Bennet, Mary 136
Bennet, Mr 81–2, 147, 152–3, 158, 161
Bennet, Mrs 132, 151–3, 156, 158, 161, 165
Benwick, Captain 288, 292
Bertram, Edmund 187, 195, 197–8, 208–10,
    213
Bertram, Julia 191, 196
Bertram, Lady 175, 185
Bertram, Maria 175, 177, 187, 189–90, 191,
    193–4
Bertram, Sir Thomas 175, 183, 185–6, 192,
    195, 210, 213
Bertram, Tom 183
Bible Society 202, 203–4, 206–7
Bickerton, Miss 237
Bigeon, Madame 311
Bigg, Catherine 227
Bigg-Wither, Harris 27–8, 29

Bingley, Miss (and sister) 135, 148, 149, 155

Bingley, Mr 142, 146, 149, 151–3, 155–6, 159, 164

The Birthday 44, 46

Blackstone, William 96, 240

Blue Beard 44

Brabourne, Lord 29

Brandon, Colonel 92, 102, 107–8, 110–16, 127

'brass' 91

Bride and Prejudice 122

Brighton 128, 132–3, 135

British Critic 171–2, 211–12

Brontë, Charlotte 25–6, 51, 227

Buckland, Reverend William 264

Burke, Edmund 109, 137–40, 142, 150, 161

Burney, Fanny 30, 45, 140, 319
    see also Camilla; *Evelina*

Byrne, Paula 180, 197

Byron, Lord 172

C

Cadell, Thomas 82

Caesarean section 52

Caleb Williams 46

Camilla 42, 45, 59, 154, 303

Campbell, Colonel 252

Caroline of Brunswick 255

Catherine, or the Bower 109

Cecilia 42, 136

census-taking 224

chain and the cross 201–2

chains 196, 201

Chandos, Dukes of 79

Chapman, R.W. 230

Chapone, Hester 164

Charles I, King 277

Charles II, King 276–7

Charlotte, Princess 52, 279–80

Chatham 128

Chawton Cottage 5, 14, 84, 125, 215–17

Chester, Bishop of 199–200

childbirth 48–9, 50–2, 54
    in fiction 53

Church of England
    challenges as institution 202–3
    failings 208–12, 317–18
    and slavery 198–202, 207, 210, 318
    and tithes 220–1, 233

Churchill, Frank 234, 237–9, 244, 245, 252–3, 255, 271

Churchill, Winston 125, 126–7

Clare, John 226, 230

Clarkson, Thomas 183–5, 193, 200–1, 207

Clay, Mrs 285, 290, 293, 297

clergy 143

Cobbett, William 245

Codrington, Christopher 198

Cole, Mr 239, 250–1

Cole, Mrs 250–1

Coleridge, Samuel Taylor 19, 227

Collins, Charlotte (*née* Lucas) 143, 145, 148, 157

Collins, Mr 143–4, 161, 220

common land 221–3, 227

consumption 54

Cooke, Samuel 235

Cooper, Edward 206, 310

Cooper, Jane 2, 129, 269, 274, 290, 296

co-parceny 240

Corn Laws 225

Cornwallis, Admiral 194

cousins, marriage between 177

Cowper, William 83, 186, 187–8, 243

Cox, Mr 239, 248

Crawford, Henry 176, 177, 189, 205, 208–9

Crawford, Mary 79, 189, 193, 194–5, 208–9

Critical Review 171, 313

Croft, Admiral 129, 279, 296

Croft, Mrs 129, 279, 296

Crosby, Benjamin 4, 6

Crosby, Richard 7–8, 17, 319–20

Crosby (publishing firm) 42–3

cross and the chain 201–2

Cumberland, Richard 192

Cuvier, Georges 261

D

Dalrymple, Lady 280–1
Darcy, Fitzwilliam 141, 142–3, 146, 163–7
    and Elizabeth 143, 144–6, 149–51, 155,
        156, 157–62, 165–7
    snobbery 148–51, 155–7, 163, 167
Darcy, Georgiana 42, 166
Darwin, Erasmus 264–6
Dashwood, Elinor 85, 92, 96–8, 100, 106–7
    and Edward Ferrars 96, 98, 100, 104,
        106, 116
    and wealth 101–2
Dashwood, Fanny 85, 95, 97–8
Dashwood, Harry 87, 94
Dashwood, John 87, 92, 94–5, 97, 114
Dashwood, Margaret 85
Dashwood, Marianne 83, 85, 89, 96–7
    and Brandon 115–16
    and wealth 101–2
    and Willoughby 93, 99, 100, 104, 107, 115
Dashwood, Mrs 95, 97, 102, 107
dates, in Jane's novels 270–5
Davinier, John 180
De Bourgh, Anne 95
De Bourgh, Lady Catherine 95, 127, 141,
    143–6, 161, 166–7, 220
death penalty 234
Denham, Sir Edward 303
Dixon, Mr 129
Donwell 238–9
Duckworth, Alistair 232

E

earls 141
East India Company 108–9, 110, 174
Easton, Celia 232
eclampsia 51–2
ectopic pregnancy 51
Eden, Sir Frederick Morton 226
Edgeworth, Maria 21, 45, 47, 129, 140, 217,
    304, 319
Edwards, Bryan 200
Egerton 172
Elegant Extracts 190

Elegy to the Memory of an Unfortunate Lady 65
Elford, Sir William 163
Elinor and Marianne 9, 82–3
Elizabeth I, Queen 278
Elliot, Anne 40, 126, 129, 206, 267–9,
    288–96, 298
    and Bath 282, 285–6
    as self-portrait of Jane 267–9, 320
    and Wentworth 272, 281, 285, 288, 289,
        293–7
Elliot, Elizabeth 267, 275, 285, 288, 290, 292–3
Elliot, Sir Walter 267, 272–3, 275, 279–81,
    285, 289–90, 292, 298
Elliot, William 288, 289–90, 294–5
Elton, Mr 236, 249, 251, 254
Elton, Mrs 195, 196, 242, 249–50, 251
Emma 217–56
    as about need 233
    on enclosure 234–41, 254–5
    introductions in 154
    reviews 172–3
    servants in 247–8
    timeframe 271
Emmeline 148, 263–4
enclosure 210, 223–8, 234–6
    in Jane's novels 228–33, 234–41, 254–5
entails 86–8
Evelina 44–5, 93, 136, 148, 159
Evelyn, Mr 44

F

Fairfax, Jane 77, 242, 248, 252, 253, 255
The Fatal Secret 66
Fawkes, Guy 274
Feltham, John 262
feme covert 95
Ferrars, Edward 92, 93, 96–8, 102–6, 116
Ferrars, Mrs 96–8, 102–3
Ferrars, Robert 92, 97–8, 103
fidelity 288–9
Fielding, Henry 122
firewood 222, 224
First Impressions 9, 16, 82, 119, 135
Fishguard 128

Fitzgerald, Lord Edward 130
Fitzwilliam, Colonel 141, 142–3, 146
Fitzwilliam, Earl 142
food 217, 233, 241–2
  cost of 218–19
Foote, Samuel 108
Fordyce, James 164
Forster, Colonel 134
fossils 260–1, 262–3, 265, 284
Fox, Charles James 23
France, war with 21–2
Francklyn, Gilbert 200–1
Frank (slave) 183
French Revolution 136–9, 186

G

Gambier, Admiral 120
Gardiner, Mr 146–8, 150–1, 166, 181
Gardiner, Mrs 146–7, 150–1, 166
Garson, Greer 126
George III, King 279
George, Prince Regent 211, 255, 280, 313
Gifford, William 172–3
gipsies 216, 223, 234, 236–8, 242–5, 253–5
Goddard, Mrs 252–3
Godwin, William 46, 66, 91, 140
'Gordon Riots' 137
gossip 142–3
Gothic novels 41, 42, 55–7, 59, 63, 70
Gould, Mr 44–5
grandparents 77
Grant, Dr 174, 194–5
Great Bookham 235
Grey, Sophia 93–5
gruel 217

H

habeas corpus 22, 136
hair 104
hairstyles 176
The Hare and Many Friends 64
Harville, Captain 284, 288–9, 298
Hastings, Warren 103, 109–10, 137, 138
Hawkins Browne, Isaac 193

Hays, Mary 21
Heathcote, Mrs 305, 317
hedgerows 197
Highbury 24, 234–40, 248–9, 251, 254
history, tide of 297
History of England 9, 27, 270, 278
Hochschild, Adam 181, 187, 199
Hodges, Mrs 248
Hutton, James 264
hyperemesis 51

I

incest 177
India 92, 107–10
ingenuity 124
inheritance 78–80, 86, 88–91
interracial relationships 45
intestacy 78
introductions 151–8
invasion, threat of 128–9
Ireland 128–30, 137

J

Jacobite rebellions 278–9
James I, King 274
James II, King 275
Jane Austen House Museum 14, 84, 125
The Janeites 125, 268
Jane's Marriage 268
Jennings, Mrs 94, 95, 98, 102, 107, 145
The Jewel in the Crown 126
jewellery 92
jointure 78, 95

K

Kent, Nathaniel 226
Kipling, Rudyard 125, 268
Kirby Hall 180
Knight, Fanny (*née* Austen) 169–71, 206,
    215–16, 312
  letters to 46, 52, 91, 206, 267, 301, 306
Knightley, George 235–6, 238–42, 249–50,
    252, 254–5
  and Emma 234, 238, 240, 253–4

Knightley, Isabella (*née* Woodhouse) 234, 240–1
Knightley, John 240–1
Knightley, Keira 122
knowledge, classes of 32
Kotzebue, August von 44, 46, 192

L

Labbe, Professor Jacqueline 264
Lady Susan 16, 38
Lambe, Miss 302, 303
land, importance of 77–8
Larkin, William 238, 248
Lascelles, Lady 194
Latin 80
Le Faye, Deirdre 29, 274
Lefroy, Anne 269, 273, 290, 296
Lefroy, Ben 207
Lefroy, Tom 27, 28–9, 32, 129
Leigh, Jane 76, 77
Leigh, Thomas 77, 79
Leigh-Perrot, James 183, 309–10
Leinster, Duchess of 47
Letters 28–9
Lewes, George Henry 25, 26
Lindsay, John 179
Liverpool, Lord 203, 211
livings 198
Lloyd, Martha 85, 119
Lodge, David 67
Long, Edward 182
Longfellow, Henry 25
Lord Ellenborough's Act 50
Love and Freindship 9, 280, 303
Lovers' Vows 44
Lucas, Sir William 141, 148, 156, 157–8
Lyford, Dr 301, 305, 306, 307
Lyme Regis 259–65, 277, 282–4, 298

M

Macaulay, Thomas 25
magistrates 221
malleability 290
Malthus, Reverend Thomas 224

manors 219–20, 222
Mansfield, Lord 179, 181–2, 186
Mansfield Park 171–213
    as about enclosure 229–33
    as about ordination 196–7
    as about slavery 180, 182–3, 185–6, 187–8, 190–6
    film 180
    introductions in 154
    lack of reviews 171, 173–4, 211–12
    as political novel 30
    publication 171
    servants in 247
    as sober novel 174
    timespan 185–6
Mapleton, Marianne 71
Marmion 123, 124, 166
marriage
    in Jane's time 31, 240–1
    proposals 149
    settlements 94–5
Martin, Robert 238–9, 251, 252, 253
Mary I, Queen 278
Mary II, Queen 275, 278
Mary, Queen of Scots 278
Masters of Ceremonies 153, 154
masturbation 49, 68–9
Meryton 131, 133–4, 151, 153, 155
Middleton, Annamaria 93, 114
Middleton, Sir John 107
Middleton, John (son of Sir John) 114
Middleton, William 114
militia 131–4, 218, 224
'Miss Catherine' 38–9, 46
Mitford, Mary Russell 162–3
Monmouth, Duke of 277
More, Hannah 243
Morland, Catherine
    and 'alarms of romance' 72
    in bedrooms 46, 48, 67–9
    character 39–40
    and chest in bedroom 60–1
    Henry Tilney and 39, 41, 58–60, 62–3, 68, 70
    reading 41, 55–66, 72

Index

Morland, James 57–8
Morland, Mrs 54
Morton, Miss 98
Munro, Henry 130
Murray, Anne 179
Murray, Elizabeth 179–80
Murray, John 172–3, 313
Musgrove, Charles 273, 275, 287–8, 290, 292
Musgrove, Henrietta 287–8, 291
Musgrove, Louisa 267, 269, 284, 287–8, 290–2
Musgrove, Mary 53, 273, 275, 287–8, 292, 298
The Mysteries of Udolpho 55–7, 58–64, 65, 66, 100–1

N
The Nabob 108–9
Napoleon Bonaparte 271–2, 296, 297
national identity 282
Nibbs, James 183
nobility, in Jane's novels 140–1
Norris, Henry Handley 203–5, 207, 211–12, 267, 317
Norris, Mrs 175, 177, 183–4, 189, 194–5, 204–5, 247
Norris, Reverend Mr (Mansfield Park) 174
Norris, Robert (of Liverpool) 184–5, 200, 203–4
North, Brownlow 312–13, 317–18
Northamptonshire 229–30
Northanger Abbey 16, 17, 38–72, 123
    bedroom scenes 67–9
    as comic 55
    on history 34
    introductions in 154
    publication 38
    review 66
    see also Susan
novels
    as genre 122–3
    Jane on 41–2

O
Olivier, Laurence 126
ordination 196–7

P
Paine, Thomas 130
Palmer, Frances 183
Palmer, Harriet 183
Palmer, Mrs 53
Palmer, Thomas 114
Pamela 114, 165
Papillon, Mr 206
parable of the talents 81
parish system 219–21
Perry, Mr 248, 255
Perry, Ruth 222–3
Persuasion 266–98
    change as theme 282–8, 292–6
    conclusion 19, 126, 296–8
    dates in 270–5
    introductions in 154–5
    names in 275–8
    temporal setting 270, 271–2
    as unfinished 266–7
    war in 126
Phillips, Mrs 165
Pitt, William 123
'plate' 92
Plumptre, John 170, 206, 207
pluralism 198, 210, 233
politics, Jane on 123–4
pollards 236
poor rates 221, 222, 226
population growth 223–4, 225
pregnancy 48–52
    in Jane's novels 52–4, 70–2
prejudice 136, 139–40, 167
The Prelude 139
Price, Betsey 205
Price, Fanny 174–8, 185, 191, 201, 205–6, 213, 269
    and Edmund Bertram 195, 208–9, 213
    as reader 186–7
Price, Mary 205

Price, Mr 175–6
Price, William 174, 175, 208
pride 136, 167
Pride and Prejudice 16, 121–67
    editing 29, 135
    films 122, 126–7
    introductions in 151–8
    names in 140
    publication 196–7
    reviews 171
    as revolutionary novel 144–5, 166–7
    servants in 246–7
    setting 135–6
    television series 121–2
    war in 127–8
    see also First Impressions
primogeniture 79, 88–9, 98
'Providence' 298
publishers, prosecutions 22–3

R

Rackham, Oliver 227
Radcliffe, Ann 21, 55, 64, 65, 70, 100
radicalism 123, 140
refugees 83
religion, science and 264–6
Rennell, Thomas 317
Reynolds, Sir Joshua 193
Reynolds, Mrs 246–7
rhubarb 70–1
Richardson, Samuel 64, 114, 165, 303
robe à l'anglaise 135
Romanies *see* gipsies
Rumsfeld, Donald 32
Rushworth, Mr 187, 189, 193–4
Russell, Lady 284–5, 289, 294, 297

S

Sanditon 303–4
science, and religion 264–6
scissors 32, 93, 104–5, 116
Scott, Paul 126
Scott, Walter 23, 83, 123, 166, 173, 243, 319
Sense and Sensibility 17, 82–116
    as feminist novel 90–1
    film 105, 113
    introductions in 154
    and metal 91–4
    names in 92–4, 113–14
    reviews 171
    revision 83
    writing 83, 91
sensibility 89–90, 116
servants 246–8
Severus, Roman Emperor 191–2
sex 48–9, 67–9
Shakespeare, William 65–6, 160–1, 162,
    192, 307
Sheehan, Colleen 255
Sinclair, Sir John 226, 227
Sir Charles Grandison 64, 65
slavery 180–6, 187–8, 190–6, 198–202, 207,
    212–13
    Church of England and 198–202, 207,
    210, 318
Smith, Charlotte 21, 31, 83, 93, 148, 263–4
Smith, Harriet 93, 234, 236–8, 241, 243–5,
    249–53, 255
Smith, Mrs (*Persuasion*) 182, 293, 297
Smith, Mrs (*Sense and Sensibility*) 93, 95,
    99–100
social mobility 251–2
Society for the Promotion of Christian
    Knowledge (SPCK) 202, 204, 205,
    206–7
Society for the Propagation of the Gospel
    (SPG) 198–202, 204, 205, 207, 211,
    317–18
Somerset, James 181–2
Southampton, Castle Square 1–9, 14–15,
    84, 301
Southey, Robert 25, 227–8
Spence, Mr 169, 170
Steele, Lucy 85, 93, 98, 103–4, 106, 116
Sterne, Laurence 189–90
Steventon 14, 75–6, 80, 119–21, 198
Stewart, Charles 181
Stewart, Sir Walter 276

Stoneleigh Abbey 79
Strafford, Earl of 277–8
Stuart dynasty 276–8
succession 278–80
Susan 3, 7–8, 16–17, 38–9
Swithin, Saint 301, 306–7
symbolism 105

T

taboos 47–8
The Task 186, 187, 188–9, 243
Taylor, Jane 212
The Temple of Nature 264–5
Theobald, Lewis 66
Thompson, Emma 105, 113
Thorpe, Isabella 42, 56–8, 63
Thorpe, John 45, 57–8
Tilney, Eleanor 42, 58, 69
Tilney, General 61–2, 63, 65, 70, 71, 229
Tilney, Henry
    Catherine and 39, 41, 58–60, 62–3, 68,
        70
    on mother's death 71
    reading 57, 58
Tilney, Mrs 62, 70, 71
    room 48, 62–3, 66, 69–70
tithes 220–1, 225, 233
Tomalin, Claire 183
Tone, Wolfe 130
totalitarian state 22, 30
tourists 150
trade 146–8
treason 22
Turner, J.M.W. 304
Twain, Mark 121

U

Unicorn (HMS) 120, 129
United Irish Uprising 129–30
Uppercross 282–3, 287, 293, 296

V

Vancouver, Charles 231
visiting 152–3, 158

W

war 21–2, 126
    in Jane's novels 126
wastes 223–4, 227
The Watsons 16, 19, 129
Wentworth, Captain Frederick 126, 279,
        281–2, 284, 287–8, 291–3, 298
    and Anne 272, 281, 285, 288, 289, 293–7
West Indies 180–1, 182–3, 198–201
Westminster School 103, 179
Weston, Mr 127, 234, 239, 250, 251, 253
Weston, Mrs 53, 248, 249, 250, 251
Whateley, Richard 24–5, 66
Wickham, Mr 131–2, 133, 143–4, 146, 166–7
Wilberforce, William 193
William III, King 275, 278
Williams, Eliza 99–100, 107, 111–13
Williams, Raymond 245
Williams, Rowan 198–9
Willoughby, John 92, 93, 94–5, 99–101, 104,
        107, 112
    and Marianne 93, 99, 100, 104, 107, 115
Wimpole Street 194
Winchester 301–2, 305–7, 310–13, 317–19
Wollstonecraft, Mary 21, 31, 89–91, 116, 140, 164
women writers 21
Woodhouse, Emma 217, 232–3, 236–7, 241,
        249–50, 256
    and Knightley 234, 238, 240, 253–4
Woodhouse, Mr 217, 218, 234, 239–40, 247,
        250, 253–4
Woolf, Virginia 230
Wordsworth, Richard 23
Wordsworth, William 11–12, 23, 139, 227,
        231–2, 243
working people 246–8
Wright, Mrs 248

Y

Younge, Mrs 246

Z

Zapp, Morris 67
Zoonomia 264, 265